Published by Ockley Books Limited

First published November 2020

ISBN 978-1-910906-22-4

Layout & design by Michael Kinlan,
edited by David Hartrick and Roger Domeneghetti,
cover photo by Leon Gladwell.

Printed & bound by:

Biddles Printing, King's Lynn

WE LOSE EVERY WEEK

EVERY WEEK

THE HISTORY OF FOOTBALL CHANTING

ANDREW LAWN

OCKLEY BOOKS
.com

ABOUT THE AUTHOR

Andrew Lawn is a Norwich City and FC St Pauli fan, whose early love of football evolved from his fascination with the sights and sounds of watching the crowd, rather than the game. Andrew co-founded Norwich City fanzine and campaign group Along Come Norwich. He is also a youth football coach and now an author. This is his first book.

CONTENTS

FOREWORD *By George Caulkin*   8

1. CHANTING *What Is It And Why Does It Happen?*   10

2. VICTORIAN MUSIC HALLS *'On The Ball City'*   32

3. KARAOKE ON THE KOP *'Anyone Who Had A Heart'*   48

4. THE RISE OF HOOLIGANISM *'Those Were The Days, My Friend'*   64

5. AN ARMS RACE OF ABUSE *'Who's That Lying On The Runway?'*   78

6. RACISM *'There Ain't No Black In The Union Jack'*   102

7. HOMOPHOBIA *'Sol, Sol, Wherever You May Be'*   126

8. HUMOUR & OFFENCE *'Your Teeth Are Offside'*   144

9. THE ART OF SELF-DEPRECIATION *'We Lose Every Week'*   154

10. IT'S NOT ALL VOCAL 1 *'Claps, Clapping, Clappers And A Thunderclap'*   170

11. IT'S NOT ALL VOCAL 2 *'Silence'*   182

12. EUROPE *'Allez, Allez, Allez'*   202

13. FURTHER AFIELD *'Dale Boca'*   234

14. IT'S THE HOPE THAT GETS YOU *'I Had A Wheelbarrow'*   252

ACKNOWLEDGEMENTS *'Who Are Ya?'*   272

FOREWORD

BY GEORGE CAULKIN

We really are losing every week; every silent Saturday, every hushed Sunday, every muffled Monday. Game after game, played out to the sound of nothing. Or watching on television with canned applause, football transformed into the lamest of sitcoms rather than something elemental, raw and free. Rarely can a book title have captured so well the thing we have lost and miss most: you.

Coronavirus has changed the way we interact with the world and football has changed with it. In an era saturated with money, when ticket-buying supporters are marginalised, the first to pay but the last to know, we have been reminded just how fundamental human contact is, how important people are. Because from where I'm sitting (sanitising my hands in a press box in a deserted stadium, wearing a mask), this is no longer a recognisable sport.

It turns out that football on mute is no longer football. It becomes something else. Which is not to say we don't have appreciation for the skills of the game, for the art of attacking and defending or the strategy of tactics. We do. Those are the building blocks which make it the best game of all, but it's the mess around it – the noise, the spatter, the humour, the absolute cock-eyed certainty and fury – which give football life.

I spoke to a Premier League manager about it recently. "The whole thing is anaemic," he said. "There's just no adrenaline, no drama. I wish we weren't playing without fans and I can't wait to get them back again." It was reassuring to hear that, particularly from a figure who, on occasion, has been on the wrong end of supporter clamour and sometimes worse. Players may entertain and infuriate us, but we drive them on.

You would like to think this might be remembered when (or if), the whole thing is over and fans are allowed back, that there will be a recalibration in the way the paying public are regarded, although I wouldn't bank on it. You see some scorelines in this lockdown version of football and just know they wouldn't happen, wouldn't be tolerated, if supporters were there. The spikes of noise, the cheering of a tackle, encourage concentration.

It doesn't always come out right. A stadium's noise can shine a light on the very worst of us, but in the moments when it is right, that noise is an extension of who we are. It represents our towns and cities, our history and culture. It captures a second in time. It can be funny, it can be coarse, it can be scurrilous, supportive or foul. I'm not sure if I've ever laughed as hard as in a ground or ever felt more queasy. I've never felt so powerful, so part of something.

This fine book tells the story of noise, both good and bad, and it tells us why it matters. And it does. The great Sir Bobby Robson once asked a rhetorical question. "What is a club, in any case?" he wrote in his final book. The answer, he said, is, "the noise, the passion, the feeling of belonging, the pride in your city." He wasn't wrong. A club is people. Football is people. Life is people. We might lose every week, but we do it together and we sing regardless.

George Caulkin, Senior Writer at The Athletic

1. CHANTING

WHAT IS IT AND WHY DOES IT HAPPEN?

Illuminated by a row of floodlights burning with the light of a million candles, stands a football fan. Arms outstretched; they take a deep breath, filling their lungs and arching their back. Into the cold night air, they roar a single word stretched to the point of being all but unrecognisable to the untrained ear:

"Kiiiiiiiiiiiiiiiiiiiiiiiiiiiiiiiiicccccccccccccccccccccccccckkkkkkkkkkkkk..."

The word acts as a thread reaching back four, five maybe six generations, winding its way through two centuries of fellow supporters, before finally connecting with a man perched on a piano stool, illuminated by one single candle, tucked away in the corner of a Victorian music hall 130 years earlier.

Back in the present, that first roared word is picked up by three or four fans nearby and in unison the knot of people at the epicentre of this growing bubble of noise, add a second elongated word:

"iiiiiiiiiiiiiiiiiiiittttttttttttttttttt..."

Each new voice adds a thread of their own, reaching back into the past. The addition of more voices has amplified the call. By the third word the number of voices reaches comfortably into double figures:

"oooffffffffffffffffffffffffff"

The individual threads become a web, weaving the crowd together, as the cry is taken up by the 3,000 individuals crammed into the away end, a yellow-and-green corner of Norfolk 175 miles from home. Together the fans stand, defiant, arms aloft and continue to sing:

"Throw it in, Have a little scrimmage..."

These words connect each of them to that lone man, sat at a piano in 1890, and to the millions of fans of every club around the world who do what they're doing now: chanting at the football.

Anyone who has ever attended a football match, seen one on the television, picked up a newspaper or watched the news, knows that football fans around the world have a long and proud tradition of chanting at football matches. Their chants can be supportive or critical of their team, derogatory or mocking of the opposition, hostile, crude, humorous and on occasion, seemingly pointless. This is the story of how we got here, how football chanting went from bespoke piano compositions in Victorian music halls via Cilla Black and wheelbarrows, to the cultural phenomenon that is today reviled and revered in equal measure.

Chanting is a phenomenon born in the space where football and music have been pulled together with the disparate worlds of storytelling and joking, by the gravitational pull of tribal competitiveness, causing a collision that has, over the course of 130 years, spread chanting's influence far beyond the confines of the terraces, both shaping and being shaped by British society.

The two-way relationship between football and music has been long established. In *The People's Songs*, author Stuart Maconie tells the story of modern Britain through 50 songs and explains why the relationship between the two is so strong: "Both are essentially working class pursuits, that have gained a huge international audience, and both have offered social mobility to young people, mainly men, from industrial and post-industrial urban communities. Both depend on the passionate commitment and enthusiasm of a dedicated consumer who will spend money and time following their favourite artist, band or team".[1] The worlds of football and music are now forever intertwined, either through fans adopting tunes for chants, or bands adopting chants for their songs. For example, take the Tottenham Hotspur chant 'Nice one Cyril', which runs:

"Nice one Cyril,
Nice one son,
Nice one Cyril,
Let's have another one"

---

[1]   Maconie. S, 2013, 'The People's Songs', Ebony Press, London, p309

'Nice one Cyril' began life not as a chant or a pop song, but as a slogan in a bread advert for Wonderloaf.[2] From there it was picked up by Spurs fans, who turned it into a chant serenading their full-back Cyril Knowles. Within a year of the advert's debut, the Cockney Cockerels released a single titled 'Nice one Cyril', written by Harold Spiro and Helen Clarke and containing the lines from the chant, to celebrate Spurs reaching the League Cup Final. It reached number 14 in the UK charts and won an Ivor Novello Award for Best Novel or Unusual Song in 1974.[3] Through a combination of the advert, the chant, and the single, the phrase 'Nice one Cyril' cemented its place in wider-society and has even become cockney-rhyming slang for squirrel.[4]

From here came an increasing trend for football and music to mix as a raft of singles were released marking cup final appearances or World Cup finals qualification. It became *de rigueur* for clubs and national teams alike when they reached showpiece events throughout the 1970s, 1980s and 1990s. Those three decades saw 43 different single releases by various clubs[5] before the number slowed down considerably as the new millennium arrived. The 1970 England World Cup squad got everyone's hopes up, musically and otherwise, by reaching number one with 'Back Home' before jetting off to a quarter-final defeat to West Germany in Mexico.[6] Unfortunately, or fortunately depending on your viewpoint, it would be two decades before any football team matched their chart-topping feat.

It would take another World Cup to lift a football-inspired single to those dizzy heights, with what ended up being New Order's only UK number one: 'World in Motion'. The 1990 song opens with a nostalgic nod to another World Cup, Kenneth Wolstenhome's famous commentary from the 1966 final re-recorded especially for the single: "Well, some people are on the pitch. They think it's all over. It is now".

---

[2] *Parkinson. J, 2013, 'Catchphrase, Slogan and Cliche', Michael O'Mara Books Ltd, London, p119*

[3] *Billboard, 1974, 'Two in UK get writer Novellos', Billboard Magazine, 1 June 1974*

[4] *Smith. D, 2014, 'The Language of London; Cockney Rhyming Slang', Michael O'Mara Books Ltd, London, p261*

[5] *Roberts. D, 2005, 'British Hit Singles and Albums (18th Edition)', Guinness World Records Ltd*

[6] *Official Charts, 2018, 'England World Cup Squad; singles', Official Charts, Retrieved 17 October 2018*

It also featured numerous England squad members, as well as match footage from an earlier 1-0 friendly win against pre-World Cup favourites Brazil, clad in their blue away shirts, in the official video. Alongside the unlikely acoustic presence of Peter Beardsley, Chris Waddle and Paul Gascoigne, 'World in Motion' gave the world the first tactical masterclass rap, as John Barnes informed us: "You've got to hold or give, but do it at the right time, you can be slow or fast, but you must get to the line, they'll always hit you and hurt you, defend and attack, there's only one way to beat them, get round the back".[7] Proving the power of the football/music combination, the same World Cup saw an Italian operatic aria, Pavarotti's 'Nessun Dorma', reach number two in the UK singles charts after the BBC used it as the signature tune for their television coverage of the tournament.[8]

Six years later, David Baddiel, Frank Skinner and The Lightning Seeds released; 'Three Lions (Football's Coming Home)', described by music journalist Nick Hasted as an: "assertively passionate and patriotic if also movingly bittersweet anthem [which] actually thought about what it meant to be an England fan and perfectly captured a cultural moment".[9]

'Three Lions' completed the loop from football to charts and back, by making its way onto the terraces as a chant during the tournament and remaining a fan favourite all the way through to the 2018 World Cup, 22 years after it was originally released. The song was even blamed for inspiring England's semi-final opponents Croatia to their 2-1 win. As the song swept the nation, the Croatia squad felt its feel-good positivity belied an arrogant statement of English entitlement, with Croatian midfielder Ivan Rakitić noting: "We saw 'Football's Coming Home' and thought: yeah, but you still have to play us".[10]

Five months later, the song was centre stage as the sides met again. This time it was England who fought back from a goal down to win

[7]   Hasted. N, 2018, 'Why New Order's football song 'World in Motion' was a game-changer', The Independent, 13 June 2018

[8]   Hasted. N, 2018, 'Why New Order's football song 'World in Motion' was a game-changer', The Independent, 13 June 2018

[9]   Hasted. N, 2018, 'Why New Order's football song 'World in Motion' was a game-changer', The Independent, 13 June 2018

[10] Lowe, S, 2018, 'We saw Football's Coming Home', The Guardian, 16 November 2018

2-1, gaining a measure of revenge for their World Cup defeat and relegating Croatia, who were missing Rakitić, from Group A of the Nations League. As the full-time whistle echoed around Wembley, the PA system cranked up a celebratory 'Football's Coming Home', which was instantly augmented by a jubilant crowd.[11]

Partly thanks to the way fans borrow and re-purpose songs from the charts and elsewhere, academic studies on football chants often compare them to a modern version of folk music and storytelling. Influential folk musician Martin Carthy went as far as to label football chanting "the one surviving embodiment of an organic living folk tradition".[12] Carthy ascribes this role to chanting, because like folk music, football chants bear similar characteristics and are, as Carthy describes; "a network of songs which evolved out of existing songs, sung by the people, adapted to meet the specific needs of a geographical identity and seemingly created by spontaneous combustion, the unheralded originators remaining anonymous".[13]

Folk music being a form of expression by the people and for the people found a perfect match in football, a game that has had its roots deeply embedded in the working classes and working-class areas following its split from the social elites' own game rugby, during the Victorian era.[14] As comedian Russell Brand wrote in an article about his support of West Ham United: "Way down deep in our folk memory, deeper than the canal that bypassed Liverpool, deeper than the spilled blood between Millwall and West Ham or Celtic and Rangers, in a place we cannot name, in words that cannot be spoken, only sung, we know, we know that we are one. Great men leave, and lesser men fall but the game, the game belongs to us all".[15] The Social Issues Research Centre went even further than Brand and described football as a re-enactment of our development as a species: "When we watch

[11] McNulty. P, 2018, 'England 2-1 Croatia', BBC, 18 November 2018

[12] Irwin. C, 2006, 'Sing When You're Winning: Football Fans, Terrace Songs and a Search for the Soul of Soccer', Carlton, London, p13

[13] Irwin. C, 2006, 'Sing When You're Winning: Football Fans, Terrace Songs and a Search for the Soul of Soccer', Carlton, London, p13

[14] Jones. S, 'Sport, Politics and the Working Class', Manchester University Press, 1988; p4

[15] Brand. R, 2014, 'Theatre of Dreams is now the setting for a tragedy', The Guardian, 23 April 2014

a football match we do not simply observe a 'game'. We witness a replay of our evolutionary heritage, [which] embraces all those skills that were once essential for our survival as hunter-gatherers [and] which continues to shape much of our behaviour today".[16]

Just as the game belongs to the fans, so too does chanting. Journalist Christopher Morley picked up the idea of the game mimicking our evolutionary tribal hunter-gatherer survival instincts in his description of chanting: "Next time you take your seat, just listen, safe in the knowledge you're most definitely part of something, carrying on a tradition that may well be generations old [...] whichever language you speak there's no denying it's one of the best things about the build-up to kicking off on a match-day, growing louder, faster. A sort of extension of the caveman's 'battle trance' state which is considered by many the root of all human music, encouraging groups to stick together, pull through and stave off predators by sheer will".[17]

The popular image of a football crowd is one based on its working-class male roots; a macho male environment in which the "real fans are the vocal, aggressive lads".[18] Even the word given to describe a collective of football fans—'crowd'—evokes feelings of unruly or amorphous masses, while the same group at a cricket match are often referred to as 'spectators', suggesting dispassionate onlookers despite there often being a significant overlap between the people at each.[19] The nature of the sports themselves has an effect too. Football is a sport which celebrates and revels in schadenfreude more than any other, and this mix of joy and despair, coupled with the continuous rollercoaster nature of the action adds to the voracity with which the crowd involve themselves in the action. As early as 1968, author Arthur Hopcroft noted: "It is the continuous flow of football that excites this sustained crescendo [of chanting]. All other sports are episodic in action: rugby, cricket, tennis, boxing, are by their nature each a disjointed series of eruptions punctured by stoppages which

[16]   Social Issues Research Centre, 2008, 'Football Passions', Social Research Centre, London, p7

[17]   Morley. C, 2014, 'Singing in the Stands', FootyMag Magazine, 14 January 2014

[18]   Morris. D, 1981, 'The Soccer Tribe', Jonathon Cape Publishing, London, p153-168

[19]   Storry. M, 1997, 'British Cultural Identities', Routledge, London, p103

are unavoidable. In football the action is interrupted only by fouls, which add fiercely to the crowds' responses".[20]

With a history deeply rooted in a working class, male, environment, and a game that rarely pauses to catch its breath, football matches are a uniquely macho, competitive and tribal forum. Throughout the recorded history of the game in Britain, physicality and outright violence have been key features, both on and off the pitch. As early as the 12th century and long before the Football Association codified the game, formalising the split with rugby, William Fitzstephen wrote a description of a game in London during which "all the youth of the City" would go out onto the fields for "the famous game of ball" and which "aroused a stirring heat by viewing".[21]

Over time, those characteristics have been exacerbated and in turn created a setting in which identities are defined, celebrated and sustained through competition and one-upmanship, characterised by humour and abuse. Through our shared collective memories of football hooliganism of the 1970s and 1980s, a sensationalist media narrative and successive authoritative establishments that are hostile to football fans, we've conditioned ourselves to expect and in-turn exhibit different standards of behaviour at football, compared to in any other walk of life. All societies do this, establishing and maintaining particular conventions, which should be met, or rules to be followed, in order to function. These rules may not be written down but they evolve in the same way societies and tastes do, ultimately ensuring that, while they may differ across generations, or from place-to-place, each aspect of our day-to-day lives are informed by rules about what is and isn't deemed acceptable.

Take bikinis. Back in Victorian Britain a modern-day bikini would have been unthinkably inappropriate, but today it's socially acceptable, at least on the beach. It remains unacceptable however, to wear a bikini at, say, a funeral. These rules, which aren't written down, but are instinctively understood by all, ultimately boil down to expectation and choice. You expect to see bikinis on a beach, but not at a funeral.

---

[20] *Hopcroft, A, 1968, 'The Football Man', CPI Group, London, p178*

[21] *Quoted in Domeneghetti, R, 2017, 'From the Back Page to the Front Room', Ockley Books Ltd, Huddersfield, p6*

These pre-determined expectations define your reaction when confronted with a bikini. On a beach there is no flicker of emotion, at a funeral, you would be at the very least shocked and potentially offended. The same is true of unspoken behavioural rules at a football match and attendance at a game carries certain expectations. Principal among these is that when you attend a football match, it's likely that you will hear chants containing within them taboo themes and language. As such, attendees of games know what to expect, setting the stage for a prophecy which is likely, in part at least, to be self-fulfilling.

This process was described by a fan in an interview with the Social Issues Research Centre during their study on football fandom: "[Being a fan] is about being mentored—being told how to behave—what to do by your elders when you first start attending matches on your own".[22] Over time, we have arrived at a point where as a society we think it is acceptable to ridicule people and locations, as long as the ridicule is delivered dressed up as harmless rivalry or banter and as long as it is aired in the context of a football match. Journalist Daniel Hytner highlighted this difference by pointing out the differences between football and other sports, as well as everyday life: "It is always jarring when what is considered to be acceptable—however uneasily so—in football is transposed on to other sports or everyday society. Would a cricketer or tennis player be subjected to snarling insults? And, if they were, would the perpetrators not be ejected from the crowd? Imagine walking along Oxford Street and being threatened and abused by a passer-by. That person could be arrested".[23] In short, the rules that as a society we have created for the terrace are different to the rules of the office, or the rules of the street. That said, as Hytner adds: "Football supporting is all about passion and tribalism but there are lines, there are limits".[24]

Alongside this sense of playing a role and fulfilling an expectation, at the heart of modern football chanting is the idea that by singing and supporting your team you are playing a part in their success.

[22] *Social Issues Research Centre, 2008, 'Football Passions', Social Research Centre, London, p19*

[23] *Hytner. D, 2020, 'After Eric Dier snapped, let's turn the spotlight on the abusers too', The Guardian, 5 March 2020*

[24] *Hytner. D, 2020, 'After Eric Dier snapped, let's turn the spotlight on the abusers too', The Guardian, 5 March 2020*

The help you are providing can either be through encouraging them or by creating an intimidating atmosphere for their rivals. Often it is both. *New York Times* journalist Rory Smith described chanting as the reason "fans go to games and sing, and shout, and sometimes scream in the belief that it has some intangible effect on their team, and the opposition".[25] Or as one fan put it to the Social Issues Research Centre: "Support your team with your voice instead of [just sitting silently and] expecting to be entertained. You have a part to play as well".[26] While this aspect of chanting being about supporting and helping your team to win is certainly true, it is not chanting's *raison d'être*.

The reason that trying to influence the game is not the sole point of chanting is that football supporters aren't just mere enthusiasts of the game but a legion of people who share a common identity. In short, merely being part of a collective community, such as being the fan of a specific football club, is more important to most fans than their club's material success. It is for this reason that football fandom is often equated to a modern-day religion. The word 'fan' is itself a derivative of the Latin word 'fanaticus', meaning a "mad, enthusiastic [person], inspired by a god".[27] Furthermore, the word chant also has its roots in religion, beginning life in 14th century France as 'chanten', which was used to describe the simple, repetitive and thudding rhythms which provided the beat to accompany singing psalms.[28]

With this in mind, it is easy to see why in his study on football fan behaviour Sociology Professor Anthony King drew on work by French sociologist Émile Durkheim's experience of Aboriginal religious practices as an explanation for fan behaviour at football matches. Durkheim argued that Aboriginal clans would periodically come together and worship the totem. Within these ecstatic ritualistic celebrations, the Aborigines experienced the social existence of their clan viscerally. The Aborigines' emotions were focused on the totem of the clan and, since the totem represented the clan, the Aborigines were, in fact, worshipping their

[25] Smith. R, 2018, 'In a blur of smoke, jeers and then goals Liverpool humble Man City', New York Times, 4 April 2018

[26] Social Issues Research Centre, 2008, 'Football Passions', Social Research Centre, London, p7

[27] Etymology Dictionary, 2014, 'Origin of the word Fanatic', 27 April 2014

[28] Dictionary.com, 2018, 'Chant', Dictionary.com, Retrieved 3 October 2018

own society. Essayist Gideon Rachman used similar terms to describe why he followed an unsuccessful football team, writing; "My support is about who we are and where we are from".[29] As with Durkheim's assessment of Aborigines strengthening their bonds by worshipping the totem, King suggests that within football fandom such feelings of community and identity "are produced by the communal practice of singing and supporting the team".[30] The chants themselves draw this comparison between football and religion further by their frequent references to Biblical ideas, such as labelling a player who leaves for a rival a "Judas", or the frequent practice of commandeering hymns as the basis for their tunes, such as the amusingly incongruous: *"Shit support, my Lord, shit support"*[31] sung by the travelling Aston Villa fans during their 2019-20 Premier League game at Leicester City.

The atmosphere this communal support and the singing that embodies it creates is a crucial aspect of football chanting. Further academic studies, including one by world-leading social movement scientist Dr Cristina Fominaya, investigated how atmosphere can affect an individual's motivation within a group and what she found can be applied easily to football fandom: "Interviews with [supporters] revealed that the [atmosphere] created at [matches] was the key to their decision to stay with the [club] despite realising that the chances of [silverware] were very slim [...] the jokes and banter provided a welcome relief".[32] The fans Fominaya spoke to were far from unique in feeling this way.

Author and football fan Colin Irwin describes the same effect happening to him: "ask anyone what got them hooked, and they will tell you it was the atmosphere. By the atmosphere they mean the fans. By the fans they mean the singing. There is an extraordinary tribal spirit that binds fans together as one solid, fiercely united representation of a community and creates an almost irresistible intensity. At its worst it's violent and plain ugly, but at its very best, it creates its

[29] Rachman. G, 2012, 'Soccernomics', Harper Sport, London, p241

[30] King. A, 2002, 'The End of the Terraces', Continuum, London, p151

[31] Williams. T, 2020, '@tomwfootball', Twitter, 9 March 2020

[32] Fominaya. C, 2007, 'The Role of Humour in the Process of Collective Identity Formation', Cambridge University Press, Cambridge, p247

own swell of energy that permeates beyond the terraces. To be part of it is a deeply emotional, almost spiritual experience".[33]

The power of this atmosphere is such that in Egypt the chanting led by the different ultra groups at football matches was blamed, in part, for creating widespread political insecurity, and ultimately led to all fans being banned from domestic games in the country from 2012 until 2018. When they were finally allowed to return to the stadiums, the state insisted they provide their personal details to the Egyptian security services in order to gain admission. The idea being that by insisting that fans gave the government access to their data, the authorities had an additional method of control over them, because the fans knew that should they chant or behave in a way the state disliked, they could be easily identified and added to the long-list of Egyptian ultras behind bars. "The state is trying to teach [fans] how to cheer," Turki al-Sheikh, chairman of the Saudi Arabian General Sports Authority, told *The Guardian* "Look at the new club Pyramids FC, and their chants—they have pro-Sisi chants for example. It's not that the state has an issue with you chanting, it's that it has an issue with [what] you're chanting".[34]

The suspicion prevails that in an ideal world the Egyptian security services would prefer to keep the fans away entirely, but as Ziad Akl, an analyst with the Al-Ahram Centre for Political and Strategic Studies, explains, money talks: "You need to bring back the fans as this increases the economic value of the tournament and championships".[35] Writing several decades earlier, Desmond Morris outlined the problem the Egyptian security services and the bosses in an increasingly sterile English Premier League now have: "Without the atmosphere [the fans] create, without their fierce loyalties and their intense longings, the whole sport would collapse, not merely for financial reasons but because it would lose its spirit—its tribal agony and its tribal joy".[36]

[33] Irwin. C, 2006, 'Sing When You're Winning: Football Fans, Terrace Songs and a Search for the Soul of Soccer', Carlton, London, p13

[34] Michaelson. R, 2018, 'Six years after the Port Said riot, Egypt fans return to the stadiums', The Guardian, Wednesday 12 September

[35] Michaelson. R, 2018, 'Six years after the Port Said riot, Egypt fans return to the stadiums', The Guardian, Wednesday 12 September

[36] Morris. D, 1981, 'The Soccer Tribe', Jonathon Cape Publishing, London, p234

Such is the popularity of football and the role that chants play both within the sport and in the wider-popular culture, in 2004 a competition was launched by the former Poet Laureate Andrew Motion to crown a 'Barclays Premiership Chant Laureate'. "The search will seek out those fans who capture the humour and emotion of football, with the prize of a £10,000 bursary to watch Barclaycard Premiership fixtures throughout 2004/05, and compose chants observing key moments within the football season,"[37] ran the promotional blurb.

Motion wanted the competition to capture the working-class, folk-esque 'poetry' of football chants, later telling *The Guardian*: "Football chanting is a kind of animal, impulsive instinct, they can be bracingly vulgar, but they can often be very funny, and sometimes quite ingenious. Poetry is a simple, primitive thing and, although it's unusual to find football chants being elaborated to the point at which they'll make anything that resembles a poem as we ordinarily understand it, they are an aspect of poetry".[38]

The competition's winning entry was written by Jonny Hurst, a Birmingham City fan serenading striker Juan Pablo Angel, despite Angel playing for Birmingham's fierce cross-city rivals, Aston Villa.[39] As a chant, it never caught on and instead received a withering, disdainful response from fans.

The negative reception the winning entry received, revealed the complex set of rules that make football chanting unique as a form of identity expression. Author Colin Irwin drew on football chanting's community and folk roots to explain why. "A song written by a Birmingham City fan, hailing the star striker of their bitterest rivals? Sorry, it doesn't matter how much the [prize] is worth, it's just not right," Irwin argued, adding: "There's one thing this [competition] proves; terrace anthems can't be artificially inseminated, they evolve naturally from genuine fans drawing on the passion, identity, adrenalin, comradeship, excitement and atmosphere of the moment".[40]

[37] *4the Game Website; 2003, 'Andrew Motion to Appoint Chant Laureate'*

[38] *Lamont. T, 2009, 'The chant-makers of English football', The Guardian, 3 May 2009*

[39] *4the Game Website; 2003, 'Andrew Motion to Appoint Chant Laureate'*

[40] *Irwin; 2006, 'Sing When You're Winning: Football Fans, Terrace Songs and a Search for the Soul of Soccer', Carlton, London, p131-2*

Irwin was not alone in his condemnation of the appointment of one person to represent and conceive of football chants for the nation. The idea of having a chant laureate was never repeated and quickly faded into obscurity.

A large part of the reason Motion's competition was doomed to fail from the moment of its conception is that many of the folk-esque, poetic chants Motion had in mind, are products of a unique moment-in-time and highly reliant on the specific context of that moment. Furthermore, the driving force of football chanting is the creation of collective identities, both positive for the 'us' and negative for the 'other', or 'them'.

As with the chants that express them, the identities exhibited within football fan culture are constructed from a vast and varied number of sources, which are constantly developing and changing as the political and social landscape alters around them. Within the broad topic of collective identity there are many inter-related and concurrent themes and concepts that help to create and sustain the collective identities that are explicitly and implicitly expressed within chants. For example, an individual locality's particular cultural history will play a part in shaping its sense of identity, as will external stereotypes and perceptions of that area. As Sociology Professors and authors Richard Giulanotti and Gerry Finn concluded: "because social identity is so complex, involving many dimensions, different facets come to the fore in different situations resulting in different behaviour. Crowds of people behave in a fashion constructed out of all the facets of all participants, with the situation exacerbating various tendencies and dominant themes".[41]

The main theme within collective identity expression is the way communities create an 'us'—a positive version of themselves from which they draw pride and, when the going gets tough, find solace. Giulanotti and Finn suggest that: "collective identity is built up [when] similarities are accentuated, and differences set aside".[42] Professor of Social Sciences at Loughbrough University Michael Billig agrees,

[41] Finn. G and Giulanotti. R, 1998, 'Scottish Fans not English Hooligans', Routledge, London, p189

[42] Finn. G and Giulanotti. R, 1998, 'Scottish Fans not English Hooligans', Routledge, London, p190

suggesting that the creation of an 'us' and 'them' is essential in the creation of communities within which the participants feel valued,[43] which is an essential aspect in sustaining an individual's desire to spend large amounts of time and money following a football team. Colin Irwin recognises this sense of community within the football fans of Stockport County: "[The club] may be on its haunches, but it's astonishing fans illuminate the spirit of football as the public expression of a community".[44] This is also why at international matches, club colours are largely avoided in favour of national colours, as wearing national colours accentuates the group's collective 'us' identity and avoiding club colours downplays any differences fans may have at domestic club level.

Within football chanting, this can be primarily seen with the frequent use of personal pronouns, particularly 'we'. Take Liverpool's adaptation of 'L'Estate Sta Finendo' (translated as 'The Summer Is Ending'), a 1985 hit for Italian disco duo Righeira, which 23 years later became the sound of their run to the 2018 Champions League final as 'Allez, Allez, Allez';[45]

> *"We've conquered all of Europe,*
> *We're never gonna stop,*
> *From Paris down to Turkey,*
> *We've won the fucking lot,*
> *Bob Paisley and Bill Shankly,*
> *The fields of Anfield Road,*
> *We are loyal supporters,*
> *And we come from Liverpool,*
> *Allez, Allez, Allez,*
> *Allez, Allez, Allez"*

'Allez, Allez, Allez' is peppered with references to the collective identity of Liverpool fans and overt in its establishment of an 'us'

[43] Billig. M, 1995, 'Banal Nationalism ', Sage Publications Ltd, London, p83

[44] Irwin. C, 2006, 'Sing When You're Winning: Football Fans, Terrace Songs and a Search for the Soul of Soccer', Carlton, London, p147

[45] Smith. R, 2018, 'How an Italian Disco Hit Became Liverpool's Champions League Anthem', New York Times, 23 May 2018

identity. Right from the opening line, the song details the club's proud European record, detailing famous European Cup nights in Paris and Istanbul. Then the chant moves on to name check two of the club's most successful managers, adding a layer of nostalgia by picking two from almost three decades earlier, a period before the younger fans would have been born, but which by being a Liverpool fan they share, rather than are excluded from. Finally, the chant moves on to reference another Liverpool fan chant, 'The Fields of Anfield Road', before hammering home the 'us' point: *"We are loyal supporters, and we come from Liverpool"*.

Within football, that tribal 'us' vs 'them' is a key component of fan culture and for there to be an 'us', there often needs to be something to compare and contrast the 'us' with, which in-turn requires the creation of a 'them'. For example, Giulanotti and Finn in their discussion on Scottish identity, suggest that the starting point for Scottish identity is primarily that they're not English.[46] Sociologist Jon Garland agrees with this premise and suggests that: "identity [is] defined more by what it is not, rather than what it is".[47] Fominaya, like Billig, also concluded: "collective identity is always formed in tension with other actors in the field [...] the definition of what the group [is] not, fosters a common bond among them and a common barrier against the 'other'".[48] Frequently in football chanting, this is achieved by stigmatising a characteristic, real or stereotyped, displayed by a rival. This can be seen in the way Scottish fans might stigmatise England fans as hooligans and then express their own contempt for this behaviour by being positively and exuberantly friendly towards the opposition. This creates a negative 'other' in the form of 'English hooligans', around which Scotland fans can then build an opposite, and thus positive, identity. The constructed positive 'us' identity in turn strengthens the shared characteristic of what it is to be a Scotland fan. Success on the field is not an important factor within the collective

---

[46] Finn. G and Giulanotti. R, 1998, 'Scottish Fans not English Hooligans', Routledge, London, p192

[47] Garland. J, 2004, 'The Same Old Story? Englishness, the Tabloid Press and the 2002 FIFA World Cup' from 'Leisure Studies' Vol. 23, Routledge, London, p89

[48] Fominaya. C, 2007, 'The Role of Humour in the Process of Collective Identity Formation', Cambridge University Press, Cambridge, p244-252

identity of Scottish football fans, instead their creation of a positive Scottish identity, is based primarily as being in opposition to a negative English identity. The importance of this positive identity expression is also seen as an achievement in its own right and more important than any on-field success. As the *Scotland on Sunday* newspaper remarked: "it's far better to lose a football match than to gain a reputation on the continent for thuggery and xenophobia. Ask England".[49]

A similar process of creating and expressing differing identities through chanting occurs at a domestic level too. For example, take an exchange between Newcastle United and Chelsea fans noted by broadcaster and author Tim Marshall for taking inspiration in regional and national stereotypes, rooted in their industrial pasts and cultural heritage: "Should Newcastle even hint that Chelsea fans are *'soft southern bastards'*, the Londoners are likely to respond with a rendition of *'Speak fucking English, why don't you speak fucking English?'*".[50]

The effect is even stronger at a hyper-local level, and if you were to ask any fan about the differences between their club and other clubs in their local area, they will be able to provide a comprehensive list. However, should you put the same question to an outsider, even if they are a football fan themselves, while they can see that clubs come in different sizes and have varying success, they would be at a loss to see any particular differences beyond shirt colour.

Football writer Paul Hyland considered this from a psychoanalytical point of view and concluded that often the fiercest rivalries are derived not from huge differences, but where rivals' identities are most similar:

"Home is important in football. The feeling of going to a stadium to cheer on your team is almost always of a pilgrimage to some Edenic space of safety, comfortably surrounded by thousands unified by their common emotional connection to the place. But the boundaries between home and away are diffuse. Anfield and Goodison Park are separated only by a public park; Dens Park and Tannadice Park in Dundee are practically next door to each other; in Italy major rivals in Rome and Milan are both tenants of the same home. Roma and Lazio, Liverpool

[49] *Finn. G and Giulanotti. R, 1998, 'Scottish Fans not English Hooligans', Routledge, London, p191-193*

[50] *Marshall. T, 2014, 'Where do chants come from', The Telegraph, 1 August 2014*

—

and Everton, Dundee and Dundee United are similar yet different, opposite yet equal. This is a specific reason as to why rivalry forms.

A deep sense of resentment and rejection develops because the rival threatens the other's claim to their home space. Beating one's local rival is to overcome another version of oneself, a team similar to us but just not quite similar enough. When a team threatens our sense of safety at home, a sense of hatred brews. That hatred is channelled into trying to wrest our home back from our rival, to undermine the other team's claim to represent the community they're in.

Clubs' identities are bound up together. We are us, and we are also not them. Being you also means not being someone else. Club identity is strengthened by taking rivals. Setting yourself in opposition to a rival gives a club a better sense of who they are. And, for a rivalry to work, there has to be some shared feature. So, on some level, a rival is always a kind of double of your own team. Doubles are always rivals and rivals are always doubles.

Common to practically all human literature that [considers] doubles and doppelgängers is the theme of enmity. In Dostoyevsky's novel *The Double*, Golyadkin is chased out of St Petersburg and drowns. He's made obsolete by the physical double of himself. The double became automatically his enemy. Poe's William Wilson is thwarted in his every life's endeavour by a double of himself bearing the same name. Dickens' *A Tale of Two Cities* and José Saramago's *The Double* both tell the story of men with an uncanny resemblance to another, and both are rivals for the love of the same woman. These narratives are common to practically every human culture. We're drawn to them because they tell us something about ourselves. Our identity must be our own. When our identity is shared, it is threatened, and it becomes the object of a battle with an "other" in order to wrest it from their grasp. That duality is common to footballing rivalries.

Clubs need rivals because it satisfies that narcissistic need for an identity of our own. Our rivals strengthen us just as much as they threaten us. Look at how often clubs affirm their own identity not by telling you who they are, but who they are not. Local rivals are the ones with whom we have most in common. We often live in the same cities, attend the same schools, drink in the same pubs and speak with the same accents. The smaller the difference between rivals, the greater the hatred. Those rivals take us out of our home space and bring us into a place where we have to face ourselves, see ourselves for who we are. It is the narcissism of small differences that makes our closest neighbours our fiercest enemies. A derby is only a derby when a team is within an arbitrary geographical proximity to us. But common to all rivalries, whether local or not, is that they spring up because they threaten the myths we tell ourselves about ourselves and the football clubs that represent us".[51]

To illustrate how granular such differences can be when expressed, author Colin Irwin provides the example of Stockport County, who currently reside outside the Football League and who are based on the doorstep of two of English football's biggest clubs, Manchester's behemoths United and City. "[Stockport's] unfortunate geographical location right on the edge of Manchester squeezes its fan base to a point where bunker mentality prevails. Despite its proximity to Manchester, Stockport clings to its own identity with regular chants of *"Cheshire, Cheshire"* leaving no doubts there's a cultural as well as geographical barrier between the town and the big bad city on its doorstep. The passionate singing evoked by the football club is indicative of a community that steadfastly believes in itself".[52] Irwin shows how Stockport's fans retain a sense of hyper-local differentiation even though to an outsider, they would likely be considered merely be a suburb of Manchester.

The same thing is remarked upon in countless rivalries across the UK. "Teams without a direct local rival are determined to find one. Ipswich v Norwich is not truly a local derby, but one based on being the best East Anglia has to offer—to demonstrate Suffolk's superiority over Norfolk or vice versa, and to be recognised on a national level as the best in the region," explains Hyland.[53] The East Anglian derby is a good example of two clubs considered by many to have similar rural fan-bases, and as such developing a fierce rivalry. As one Norwich fan remarked: "Ipswich are public enemy number one both because

[51] Hyland. P, 2020, 'The psychology of football rivalries', The Guardian, 23 January 2020

[52] Irwin. C, 2006, 'Sing When You're Winning: Football Fans, Terrace Songs and a Search for the Soul of Soccer', Carlton, London, p147

[53] Hyland. P, 2020, 'The psychology of football rivalries', The Guardian, 23 January 2020

it's local, but also because there is a massive cultural divide. Norwich fans see Ipswich as representing the encroachment of London into East Anglia, whereas Ipswich sees Norwich as a stubborn backwater".[54] These identities are illustrated in chants sung by the clubs. Norwich fans celebrate their rural-ness with:

"I can't read and I can't write,
But that don't really matter,
'cos I'm a Norwich City fan and I can drive a tractor"

While Ipswich fans have taken the tune of the Adams Family theme to turn that rural pride into a negative with their retort:

"Your sister is your mother,
Your father is your brother,
You all fuck one another,
The Norwich family"

Likewise, Portsmouth and Southampton are to the outsider, both ports in Hampshire. However, the presence of the sea has had distinctly opposite effects on the mentality of the local communities. When Eli Mengem visited both in 2019 for the *Copa 90* 'Derby Days' series to investigate the rivalry, one Southampton fan told him "the two towns are inherently different. [Portsmouth] will say that they are the working-class city, but they are the city with a Conservative MP. We are the gateway to the world because we took passengers and freight all over, with our arms open because we wanted things to come in, whereas Portsmouth had their arms up to say 'stop'. They are an island, with an insular island mentality. [The rivalry] is not about football, it is about life itself. It's about two cities who live close by, but there is a wall between us and whatever side of that wall you're in influences your view on life. Other derbies are two cities divided by football teams, we're two cities divided by culture, divided by everything. This is hatred facilitated by football".[55]

54 *Williams. J and Johnson. M, 1995, 'Football Fan's Guide', Harper Collins, London, p172*

55 *Mengem. E, 2019, 'My city could beat up your city', Copa 90, 17 November 2019*

This rivalry is underpinned, in part at least, by Portsmouth fans' belief that a dock strike in the city in the 1930s was undermined by dockers from Southampton crossing the picket line.[56] As Portsmouth fans told Mengem; "They're scummers. They only way they could beat the dock strike in Portsmouth was by bringing busloads of scummers in, so everyone in this town lost their jobs. Scum stands for 'Southampton Company Union Men'".[57] Although this is disputed in Southampton as a "Ports-myth", where a Saints fan retorts; "They make up stories about 'South Coast Union Men'. No such union exists, Portsmouth have made this up. It never happened. Portsmouth is a naval dock, you're not allowed to strike in a naval dock".[58]

One thing that fans across the rivalries agrees on however, is that they're a key part of the fan experience. When fans of both were asked if there was a chance they could reconcile and put their differences behind them, the Southampton fans replied, "I hope not", while his Portsmouth equivalent concurred "We don't want to get along".[59]

Another surreal and telling example of this hyper-local differentiation, comes from East London where Millwall fans hate West Ham, not because they are Cockneys, but because they are not Cockney enough, something they paradoxically achieve by trying to be too Cockney. Garry Robson, editor of Millwall fanzine 'No-one Likes Us', which takes its name from the club's famed chant, sums it up: "the rivalry with West Ham is played out entirely in terms of toughness, virility and cultural authenticity within London-ness".[60]

This phenomenon of familiarity and similarity breeding contempt is not confined to the UK, as Copa 90's 'Derby Days' trip to Lombardy for the Italian derby between Atalanta from Bergamo and their neighbours Brescia illustrates. As Brescia fan Dario notes, "from an anthropological point of view there is no other group of people so similar, with both positive and negative qualities than the Bresciani

[56] Williams. J and Johnson. M, 1995, 'Football Fan's Guide', Harper Collins, London, p207

[57] Mengem. E, 2019, 'My city could beat up your city', Copa 90, 17 November 2019

[58] Mengem. E, 2019, 'My city could beat up your city', Copa 90, 17 November 2019

[59] Mengem. E, 2019, 'My city could beat up your city', Copa 90, 17 November 2019

[60] Mitten. A, 2008, 'Mad For It – From Blackpool to Barcelona, Football's Great Rivalries', Harper Sport, London

and the Bergamaschi".[61] Or as Italian football journalist Martino Simcik puts it: "In a lot of ways, this is a derby based on similarities. It is what makes them so twinned. If racism is a fear of someone being different from you, a fear of something you don't understand, here the rivalry comes from a fear of being too the same".[62]

In a game packed full of deeply nuanced local rivalries and tribal identities it is impossible to unpick chanting from football or from wider society and conclusively say whether one leads the other or is merely a reflection.

The interlinked nature of football chanting, the game and society is such that a description of the English media's relationship with football written by Roger Domeneghetti could just as easily apply to football chanting: "[It] has played a crucial role in shaping key aspects of English culture, including notions of patriotism and the stereotyping of other nationalities. It has reinforced class divisions as well as the definition of masculinity and the related marginalisation of women and tacit homophobia".[63]

Precisely because of these powerful linkages, chanting is a vital component and key driving force governing the experience of going to a football match and sharing in these feelings of identity and community, similar to the religious experiences and totem worship described by Durkheim. The link is strong enough that according to academics Giovanna Del Negro and Harris M. Berger, chants are the primary medium through which ideas about class, race, gender or other forms of identity are inculcated, debated and resisted[64] in exactly the same way folk songs were before them. It is these complex and contextual ingredients which create within football a unique forum for public individual and collective identity expression.

61 Mengem. E, 2020, '900 years of hate', Copa 90, 26 January 2020

62 Mengem. E, 2020, '900 years of hate', Copa 90, 26 January 2020

63 Domeneghetti, R, 2017, 'From the back page to the front room', Ockley Books Ltd, Huddersfield, pXVI

64 Del Negro. G and Berger. H, 2004, 'Identity and Everyday Life: Essays in the Study of Folklore, Music and Popular Culture', Wesleyan University Press, Connecticut, p3

2. VICTORIAN MUSIC HALLS

'ON THE BALL CITY'

Despite football's formative years being deeply rooted in Britain's industrial working classes and the modern perception of football chants as the preserve of thuggish louts, chanting has remarkably classical origins. Unlike modern-day chanting, which often seems spontaneous and arises from individuals or small groups on the terraces, early chants were effectively bespoke compositions. However, like their present-day equivalents these chants were often still rooted in the folk tradition of borrowing and adapting tunes and melodies.

The earliest recorded example of a football chant provides another link between football and music, as it was penned by classical composer Sir Edward Elgar. Less well known today than 'Land and Hope of Glory', Elgar's football chant was titled 'He Banged the Leather for Goal' and written in honour of popular Wolverhampton Wanderers right half, Billy Malpass.

Elgar developed his affection for football, and in particular for Wolves, in early 1895 when he accompanied the local rector's daughter, Dora Penny to Molineux. When Dora later wrote about the time she spent with Elgar, she recalled: "I quickly found out that music was the last thing he wanted to talk about. We talked about football. He wanted to know if I ever saw Wolverhampton Wanderers play and when he heard that our house was a stone's throw from their ground he was quite excited." She added that the composer loved the crowds, the fluctuating sounds of the terraces and the roar that followed a goal. Four years after their first Molineux visit, Elgar would immortalise Dora with the tune 'Dorabella', which is included in his 'Enigma Variations'.[1]

By 1898, Elgar had become besotted with the game and is said to have regularly cycled from Worcester to Wolverhampton for matches; a 60-mile round trip. In February that year, Elgar watched from a freezing Molineux terrace as Wolves ended an uncharacteristic five-game winless run with a comprehensive 4-2 win against Stoke City. The 1897-98 season was to prove a successful one for Wolves, who finished an impressive third, making Elgar's frequent long cycle ride more welcome. Stoke would go on to finish bottom of the 16-team

[1]   Ball. T, 2007, 'Elgar the Wolves Fan, Express and Star, 28 June 2007

division. The day after the Stoke game, knowing her friend would be delighted with the success of the previous afternoon, Dora sent Elgar a newspaper cutting that waxed lyrical on the importance of Malpass to Wolves' success. One sentence, deep in the match report, stated that Malpass had "banged the leather for goal". The phrase captured the composer's imagination. Flushed with inspiration and the joy of the victory, Elgar added a 'he' and set the sentence to a piece of his piano music. The football chant was born.

Elgar's chant was widely shared but an editorial in *The Times* doubted it would catch on noting "the melody may be too complex for the grandstand". Unfortunately, *The Times'* assessment of Elgar's work ultimately proved accurate, even if their reasoning that crowds would be unable to carry, or remember, complex melodies was wrong, and 'He Banged the Leather for Goal' fell out of use.[2] It wasn't forgotten however and was aired again in 2010 as part of a charity concert in Wolverhampton organised by Rachel Heyhoe-Flint, the former England women's cricket captain and Wolverhampton Wanderers director, to raise money for the church's organ restoration fund. Flint arranged for the chant to be performed by the choirs of St Peter's Collegiate Church, under the baton of Peter Morris, the conductor of the Wolverhampton Symphony Orchestra. In an additional nod to nostalgia the opera singer Rita Cullis, niece of Stan Cullis, the club's most successful manager, was chosen as the featured soloist.[3]

Elgar's chant may not have caught on, but *The Times* was wrong that the grandstand was not ready for complex melodies and another chant composed to piano accompaniment was about to take hold.

Credited to Albert T Smith, Norwich City's 'On the Ball City' composed in the 1890s is the oldest chant on record, sung regularly from its composition through to the present day. As with 'He banged the Leather for the Goal', it was composed and originally sung with full piano accompaniment. 'On the Ball City' actually predates the football club it is now synonymous with and was originally written for the collection of local works teams based in Norwich at the time,

[2]   *Alleyne. R, 2010, 'Sir Edward Elgar wrote football chant', The Telegraph, 26 September 2010*

[3]   *BirminghamLive, 2010, 'Wolves fan Elgar penned first ever chant', BirminghamLive, 26 September 2010*

including: the local chocolate factory's Caley's FC, Norwich Teachers, Swifians and the church-run team Norwich CEYMS.

In June 1902, a group led by two schoolmasters, Robert Webster and Joseph Cowper-Nutchey, came together with the idea of forming a single club that would represent the entire city, stating that a city with a population of 110,000 "should at least trouble the football world".[4] On the 17 June 1902, papers were signed and Norwich City was born. With the formation of a united club to represent the city, fans of the smaller works teams began gravitating to the new team drawing crowds of around 1,000. The team, initially known as 'The Citizens', were first based at a school field, but as interest in them increased they moved to a bespoke home constructed in the excavated bowl of a former chalk pit, evocatively known as 'The Nest' to match their recently adopted yellow and green colours and 'Canaries' nickname.

The Nest held an impressive 25,000 people and began to regularly draw five-figure crowds. As spectator numbers grew so did the noise levels, and in the same way as modern fans take tunes and inspiration from popular culture, the fans who had gravitated from their local works teams to the new 'City club' did the same and with its origins incorporating those disparate teams, 'On the Ball City' united a city. When the Canaries flew The Nest to their new Carrow Road home in 1935, attendances had grown to around 30,000 and the fans took the song with them. Some 120 years later it continues to ring out before, during and after every game.

Unsurprisingly, given its 19th century conception and lack of any major revisions since, 'On the Ball City' sounds like no other chant heard on terraces elsewhere. Featuring two verses and a chorus, the song features none of the tub-thumping one-upmanship which characterises many modern chants and instead focuses fully on the club and the sense of hope, joy and community fostered by the collective playing of sport:

"On the days to call, which we have left behind,
Our boyhood's glorious game,
And our youthful vigour has declined

4   Glory Magazine, 2019, 'Norwich City Special Edition, 2019, Glory Magazine

With its mirth and its lonesome end;
You will think of the time, the happy time,
Its memories fond recall,
When in the bloom of your youthful prime,
We've kept upon the ball

Kick off, throw it in, have a little scrimmage,
Keep it low, a splendid rush, bravo, win or die;
On the ball, City, never mind the danger,
Steady on, now's your chance,
Hurrah, we've scored a goal

Let all tonight then drink with me,
To the football game we love,
And wish it may successful be,
Join player, game and song,
And fondly pledge your pride and toast,
Success to the City club

Kick it off, throw it in, have a little scrimmage,
Keep it low, a splendid rush, bravo, win or die;
On the ball, City, never mind the danger,
Steady on, now's your chance,
Hurrah, we've scored a goal,
City, City, City"

More than a century later it is the chorus beginning *"Kick it off..."* which remains a staple chant for Norwich fans, home and away. Lyrically unaltered, 'On the Ball City' belies its early 19th century composition through its use of arcane language and old-fashioned turn of phrase, such as "splendid rush" which showcases how the game was being played at the time it was written. Jonathan Wilson, in his history of tactics, *Inverting the Pyramid*, describes the style of play during the late 19th century in terms which resonate with the lyrics of 'On the Ball City'. For example, Wilson wrote: "Interplay among forwards, if it happened at all, was rudimentary. The game was all about dribbling; passing, co-operation and defending were perceived as somehow inferior. Head down charging, certainly was preferred to thinking".[5]

To this day, the term 'rush' retains a place in the heart of American football, which evolved from both association football and rugby, to describe an offensive run with the ball, lacking in any attempts to pass. Interestingly, in American football, 'rush' is frequently used to describe runs coming from behind the 'scrimmage', which also features early in the chorus here, where the 'splendid rush' comes one-line after the 'scrimmage'. Smith's likely deliberate use of the word 'scrimmage' has multiple potential meanings in this context. However, like 'rush' the term survives in American football where it is used to describe a running back receiving a hand-off from the quarterback, possessing the ball and charging towards the opposition's end zone, picking up as many yards as possible in the process. Given its placement in the song after the *"kick off and throw-in"* and marking the passage of play ultimately finishing in a goal, this is likely to be Smith's intended meaning here.

From the throw-in to the goal, 'On the Ball City' is evocative in its description of the game, more akin to a modern-day commentary than a chant: *"keep it low, splendid rush... steady on, now's your chance, hurrah, we've scored a goal"*. The described neat, attacking passage of play is briefly interrupted by what sounds like defensive actions of the unnamed opponents, as the *"splendid rush, bravo"* becomes *"win or die, On the Ball City, never mind the danger"*; presumably describing the team being briefly dispossessed and counter-attacked upon. Possession of the ball is then quickly regained, and the attack recovers momentum, resulting in a scoring chance presenting itself and being calmly taken: *"steady on, now's your chance, Hurrah, we've scored a goal"*.

The only noticeable change from 1902 to today is one of tempo with a recent increase in the speed with which the song is sung, leading to campaigns seeking a return to the original more-pronounced slower tempo making national news in 2017.[6]

Speed and elocution aside, very little has changed since the chorus was written, and were Smith to return to Carrow Road today he would undoubtedly recognise his work. He would also likely be proud

[5]   Wilson. J, 2010, 'Inverting the Pyramid', 2010, Hachette, London, p62

[6]   BBC, 2016, 'Should Norwich City fans slow down?'

to see how intertwined his song has become with both the club and the wider city with 'On the Ball City' retaining a unique place in Norwich culture akin to that of Colman's Mustard or the insurance company Aviva (which was formerly Norwich Union and still features the city's cathedral in its logo). The football club's badge, which from 1907 when the club adopted their Canaries nickname featured a bird perched on a branch, was updated in the 1960s to have the bird posed literally, on the ball. City's matchday programme is named 'OTBC' and the same abbreviation is sewn into the collar of the players' shirts. This shortening has also become a staple sign-off of communication between fans such as text messages, work emails and Twitter hashtags. Meanwhile 'The Scrimmage' is the name of BBC Radio Norfolk's Norwich City weekly talk show and podcast.

As 'On the Ball City' started to be heard around Britain it was joined by other similar, jovial, location-specific chants, which had begun to spring up around the nation. Vying with 'On the Ball City' for the title of earliest chant, Portsmouth's 'Play up Pompey' can also be dated to the turn of the 20th century and as with 'On the Ball City', it began life associated to a different club, but over time was adapted to fit its new club and new home at Fratton Park. It differs from its older relative however in its instrumental accompaniment, with 'Play up Pompey' accompanied not by a piano, but by the chiming bells of Portsmouth Town Hall clock:

> *"Play up Pompey,*
> *Pompey play up,*
> *Play up Pompey,*
> *Pompey play up"*

This chant's evolution began when Portsmouth's Royal Artillery FC, were disqualified from the 1898-99 FA Amateurs Cup, a forerunner to the FA Cup, for the contemporary crime of 'professionalism'. As well as throwing them out of the cup, the FA also forced Royal Artillery to field only their strictly amateur reserve players for the remainder of the 1898-99 Southern Football League season. The additional punishment saw the club's form collapse and they finished bottom of the league. Relegated and disgraced, Royal Artillery FC disbanded. Deprived of their club, a number of fans and players alike looked elsewhere for their football fix, handily finding a newly formed, ready-made football club on their doorstep: Portsmouth FC.

Just as Norwich-based football fans took 'On the Ball City' to the unified city club, Royal Artillery's supporters would eventually take their chant, then known as 'The Town Hall Chimes', with them, along with their nickname, Pompey.

According to David Francis the earliest written reference to Portsmouth as 'Pompey' refers to the football team, although it's believed by many that the town was associated with the term from much earlier. Among a litany of other possible explanations for the nickname, there is a claim that a lady named Aggie Weston who ran *The Sailors' Rest* hostel in the early 1900s is responsible for the nickname. Aggie, so the story goes, would frequently regale her clientele with historical tales. One night in 1904 Aggie passionately described the assassination of Roman Consul Gnaeus Pompeius Magnus, known in English as 'Pompey'. As Aggie reached the dramatic scene of Pompey's murder one of the sailors shouted "Poor old Pompey" to much amusement. A few days later the same group of sailors took in a football match at Fratton Park where they witnessed a below-par performance from the home team. When the opposition took the lead late into the second-half the same sailor is said to have again shouted "Poor old Pompey",[7] a line which, in the same way modern chants spread, was taken up enthusiastically by those around him. The new words scanned perfectly with the old 'Town Hall Chimes' tune and after a brief hiatus, the chant made its comeback. The lyrics were updated over time to their now-familiar "Play up" call-to-arms, which like 'On the Ball City', continues to be sung by Portsmouth fans, week-in and week-out.

Another club with a surviving chant rooted in the Music Halls of Victorian England is Newcastle United whose anthem 'Blaydon Races' was originally written by the Victorian-era, Gateshead-born music hall performer George 'Geordie' Ridley. Like 'On the Ball City', it is the chorus of a much longer song which survives on the Gallowgate to this day. The original features a number of verses, which, written in a thick North East dialect, tell the story of an eventful coach journey

[7] Francis. D, 2018, 'Origins of Pompey', University of Portsmouth Library

from Newcastle to a horse race held in the small town of Blaydon on the other side of the River Tyne on 9 June 1862:

"Aa went to Blaydon Races, 'twas on the ninth of Joon,
Eiteen hundred an' sixty-two, on a summer's efternoon;
Aa tyuk the 'bus frae Balmbra's, an' she wis heavy laden,
Away we went 'lang Collin'wood Street, that's on the road to Blaydon.

*Chorus
Ah me lads, ye shudda seen us gannin',
We pass'd the foaks alang the road just as they wor stannin';
Thor wis lots o' lads an' lassies there, aal wi' smiling faces,
Gannin' alang the Scotswood Road, to see the Blaydon Races.

We flew past Airmstrang's factory, and up to the "Robin Adair",
Just gannin' doon te the railway bridge, the 'bus wheel flew off there.
The lassies lost their crinolines off, an' the veils that hide their faces,
An' aw got two black eyes an' a broken nose
gannin' te Blaydon Races.

*Chorus

When we gat the wheel put on away we went agyen,
But them that had their noses broke they cam back ower hyem;
Sum went to the Dispensary an' uthers to Doctor Gibbs,
An' sum sought out the Infirmary to mend their broken ribs.

*Chorus

Noo when we gat to Paradise thor wes bonny gam begun;
Thor was fower-an-twenty on the 'bus, man,
hoo they danced an' sung;
They called on me to sing a sang, aa sung them "Paddy Fagan",
Aa danced a jig an' swung my twig that day aa went to Blaydon.

*Chorus

We flew across the Chain Bridge reet into Blaydon toon,
The bellman he was callin' there, they call him Jackie Broon;
Aa saw him talkin' to sum cheps, an' them he was pursuadin'
To gan an' see Geordy Ridley's concert in the
Mechanics' Hall at Blaydon.

*Chorus

The rain it poor'd aall the day an' mayed the groons quite muddy,
Coffy Johnny had a white hat on – they war shootin'
'Whe stole the cuddy'
There wis spice stalls an' munkey shows an' aud wives selling ciders,
An' a chep wiv a hapenny roond aboot, shootin'
'Noo, me lads, for riders'"

Ridley didn't live to see the chant capture the imagination of his local football team having died at the age of 30 in 1864 just two years after the race he commemorated.[8] As well as being another example of a chant emerging from Victorian Music Halls, 'Blaydon Races' is also the earliest example of a chant being adapted for use by other clubs, who have taken the tune but adapted the geographical references and regional words like *"gannin"* to suit their own clubs. For example, Queens Park Rangers fans sing;

"Oh me lads you should have seen us coming,
Running down the Uxbridge Road,
You should have seen us coming,
All the lads and lasses smiles, upon their faces,
Running down the Uxbridge Road,
To see the Queens Park Rangers..."

'Blaydon Races' may be the first example, but by the time the football calendar resumed after World War Two, chanting's folk tradition of borrowing from elsewhere had become firmly established. As fans

---

8   *This is Gateshead, 2020, '19th Century Gateshead', ThisIsGateshead.com, Retrieved 7 March 2020*

began to look further afield for inspiration, they found a rich source of material in religion and, with it fresh in the collective memory, war. The first example of this came from a Scottish comedian and singer, Hector Nicol, who in the late 1950s took his inspiration from 'Glory, Glory, Hallelujah', changing *"Hallelujah"* to *"the Hibees"*:[9]

"There is a bonny fitba team at Easter Road they play,
I go along to cheer them every other Saturday,
In colours green and white the finest in the land today,
The Hibs go marching on

*Chorus
Glory, glory to the Hibees,
Glory, glory to the Hibees,
Glory, glory to the Hibees,
We are the Hibee Boys

Against the Continentals we have always stood the test,
Against the famous English clubs we're better than the rest,
We've beat the champs of Europe and we are by far the best,
As we go marching on,

And when I dream of bygone days, as I do now and then,
I dream about the forward line who were our greatest men,
Smith, Johnstone, Reilly, Turnbull, Ormond we won't see again,
But their memory marches on, gie the ba' tae Reilly

And now we've got a younger team I dinnae want to brag,
I only want to say the Scottish Cup is in the bag,
We're going to top the league next year and win the Scottish flag,
As we go marching on"

Despite his loving ode to Hibernian's 'Famous Five'—Gordon Smith, Bobby Johnstone, Lawrie Reilly, Eddie Turnbull and Willie

[9]   McLean. D, 2017, 'The origins of Scotland's most popular football chants', The Scotsman, 26 January 2017

Ormond—Nicol was not wholly devoted to Hibs. He had however developed a taste for writing chants. In one prolific spell, Nicol went on to pen one for Hibs' Edinburgh rivals Hearts, simply titled 'The Hearts Song', before uniting another pair of city rivals by gifting Dundee United's 'The Terrors of Tannadice' and 'Dark Blue of Dundee' for next door neighbours Dundee.[10]

As Nicol found with Hibernian, the tune and structure of 'Glory, Glory' made it popular for a number of football clubs, particularly suiting those with a four-syllable name, most famously Tottenham Hotspur.

The history of the 'Glory, Glory' tune is a long and complex one. It began life as a call-and-response song titled 'Say, Brothers, Will You Meet Us', sung around campfires across the United States as early as the 18th century. In true folk music tradition the song was adapted to the local areas it was sung in before being adopted as an American Civil War marching song titled 'John Brown's Body' about the abolitionist John Brown.

Ironically, given that the tune ended up as a staple in an environment known for its deliberate offensive repertoire, the words to 'John Brown's Body' were initially changed because the "flavour of coarseness, possibly of irreverence"[11] led many of the era to feel uncomfortable with the original lyrics. This in turn led to the creation of many variant versions of the text that aspired to a higher literary quality, most famously by American author and poet Julia Ward Howe who took the tune but adapted the words creating 'The Battle Hymn of the Republic', sometimes also known as 'Mine Eyes Have Seen the Glory'. Howe was allegedly inspired to rework the song after a friend suggested she "write some good words for that stirring tune".[12] Howe's version, helped by its publication on the front page of *The Atlantic* in February 1862, caught the public's imagination and became a staple of concert performances, remaining in the public consciousness and frequently being covered by the biggest musical acts of the early to mid-20th century including Bing

---

[10] Roberts. D, 2018, 'British Hit Singles and Albums; 19th Edition', Guiness World Records Ltd, London, p394

[11] Kimball. G, 1890, 'Origin of the John Brown song', New England Magazine, Series 1, 1890, Cornell University

[12] Kimball. G, 1890, 'Origin of the John Brown song', New England Magazine, Series 1, 1890, Cornell University

Crosby, Judy Garland, Andy Williams, Johnny Cash and Elvis Presley.

Whereas 'On the Ball City' and 'Play up Pompey' gradually became popular as crowd numbers grew, the date 'Glory, Glory' first become synonymous with Spurs can be pinpointed exactly to 20 September 1961, when it emerged during a European Cup second-leg qualifier against Polish side Górnik Zabrze in an early example of fans not taking kindly to outside criticism of their team. In the first leg Zabrze won 4-2 in front of 55,000. After the game, the Polish media described Spurs as "no angels" following their physical approach and aggressive tackling. In response, some Spurs fans dressed as angels, while others took banners proclaiming: *'Glory be to shining White Hart Lane'* and *'Rejoice! This is a night of vengeance'*. The later proved prophetic and Spurs, aided by a Cliff Jones first-half hat-trick, ended up with a convincing 8-1 win sealing a goal-laden 10-5 aggregate victory.

With the game as good as won by half-time, a carnivalesque atmosphere enveloped White Hart Lane. Refrains of *"Glory, Glory Tottenham Hotspur"* started to be heard among the crowd of almost 60,000, and a tradition was born.[13] Spurs went on to beat Feyenoord and Dukla Prague, before losing the semi-final to eventual champions Benfica.

Just as Hibernian had to learn to share Nicol with the rest of Scottish football, they soon also had to share 'Glory, Glory' with English football as Leeds United and Manchester United followed Spurs' lead and developed their own versions. The chant's popularity didn't stop there though and has since crossed both continents and sporting disciplines, with Australian rugby league club South Sydney Rabbitohs frequently belting out their own version.

However, the chant was synonymous with Spurs and became so intertwined with the club's identity that two decades after it was first adopted, the squad were joined by London pop-duo Chas and Dave to record a version, ultimately releasing it as the B side to the single 'Ossie's Dream (Spurs Are on Their Way to Wembley)' ahead of the 1981 FA Cup Final in the aforementioned obligatory fashion of the times. 'Glory, Glory' went on to survive Chas and Dave's cover and the club's temporary move to Wembley and is still played ahead of every

---

[13] *Cloake. M, 2012, 'The Glory, Glory Nights', The New Statesmen, 12 December 2012*

home game, while also being regularly heard among Spurs' travelling away support.

By the time Chas and Dave subjected the pop world to 'Glory, Glory', Leeds United had found their own unique anthem, 'Marching on Together'. It was written by Barry Mason and Les Reed, not the former Southampton and Charlton Athletic manager but the prolific song writer responsible for, among others, Elvis' 'Sylvia' and Tom Jones' 'Delilah', which was itself adopted by Stoke City fans in the late 1980s.[14] Ironically 'Marching on Together' appeared on the B-side of Leeds' 1972 FA Cup Final single, accompanying the imaginatively named single 'Leeds United'. Like 'On the Ball City', 'Marching on Together' features a number of verses, alongside the chorus:

"Here we go with Leeds United,
We're gonna give the boys a hand,
Stand up and sing for Leeds United,
They are the greatest in the land

Na, na, na,

Everyday we're all gonna say
We love you,
Leeds, Leeds, Leeds,
Everywhere we're gonna be there,
We love you,
Leeds, Leeds, Leeds

Marching on together,
We're gonna see you win,
Na na na na na na,
We are so proud,
We shout it out loud,
We love you,
Leeds, Leeds, Leeds

---

[14] *Brown. P, 2016, 'Why Stoke fans sing Delilah', Four Four Two, 25 March 2016*

We've been through it all together,
And we've had our ups and downs (ups and downs),
We're gonna stay with you forever,
At least until the world stops going round

Na, na, na

Everyday we're all gonna say
We love you,
Leeds, Leeds, Leeds,
Everywhere we're gonna be there,
We love you,
Leeds, Leeds, Leeds

Marching on together,
We're gonna see you win,
Na na na na na na,
We are so proud,
We shout it out loud,
We love you,
Leeds, Leeds, Leeds"

Leeds fans were at the heart of 'Marching on Together' from the outset and a few had their voices featured alongside the club's 1972 squad in the original recording, which spent almost three months in the UK Top 40, peaking as high as number ten. The song's popularity saw Leeds' support adopt it, belting out renditions before, during and after games in the same way 'On the Ball City', 'Play Up Pompey', 'Blaydon Races' and 'Glory, Glory' all were.

As with those other anthems, 'Marching on Together' has remained popular and continues to be sung four decades on, also providing a sign-off for fans' emails and text messages as well as the '#MOT' hashtag. As football writers Paul Doyle and Barry Glendenning explain: "['Marching on Together' is] a rousing, almost arousing, paean to Leeds United. Its blend of jauntiness and faux militaristic bombast melodically capturing the power of a crowd mobilised in the name of fun and communal pride".[15] After Leeds' promotion back to the Championship in May 2010, 'Marching on Together' was digitally re-mastered and re-released in an effort to get the song into the UK Singles Chart. Just like the original, the remastered version scraped into the top 10 in a result not too dissimilar to the Elland Road side's performances in the Championship over the next decade before Marcelo Bielsa finally led them back to the Premier League in 2020.

What all of these early football chants have in common is that, unlike the majority of their modern-day counterparts, they were non-threatening and cheerfully parochial. It would be Cilla Black and The Beatles who would spark a change.

[15] *Doyle, P, and Glendenning. B, 2016, 'The Joy of Six: Football Chants', The Guardian*

3. KARAOKE ON THE KOP

'ANYONE WHO HAD A HEART'

The parochial joviality of the pre-war football chant began to shift towards the more antagonistic ditties we know today at the same time as pop music became prolific in the UK. Nowhere were these shifts more pronounced than in Liverpool. With an estimated 350 bands in the city at the beginning of the 1960s, the banks of the Mersey were fertile grounds from which two phenomena that would dominate English popular culture for the next 50 years would flourish: pop music and football chanting.

The 1960s were a golden age for the Liverpool music scene, seeing the development of the city's own brand of music, Merseybeat, which in turn led to the invasion of British pop music into the US charts. Beat culture saw creativity in the city explode and exported around the world, causing American poet Allen Ginsberg to describe Liverpool as "the centre of consciousness of the human universe".[1] The city boasted an incredible 33 UK number one singles through the decade, with over half of those coming in 1963 and 1964, including seven from The Beatles, three from Gerry and the Pacemakers and two from Cilla Black.[2] Such is the ongoing connection between music and Liverpool, coupled with the unprecedented volume of number one singles to have emerged from the city, in 2001 the *Guinness Book of Records* declared it their "City of Pop".[3]

During this period, it wasn't just the city's bands that were finding success, as their two biggest clubs, Liverpool and Everton, were slugging it out at the top of the First Division, claiming a pair of League titles each in the decade. The two clubs' on-field success, coming just as Cilla Black and The Beatles were finding international stardom, ensured it was no coincidence that the city's pop music success and football success would come together.

Prior to the early 1960s fans of both Liverpool and Everton were undoubtedly loud, and while Anfield and Goodison Park were both

[1] *The Tate, 2018, 'Room 2; Beat City', Retrieved 28 October 2018*

[2] *Liverpool Museums, 2018, 'The Beat Goes On', Retrieved 26 September 2018*

[3] *Leonard. M, 2009, 'The Beat Goes On; Liverpool, Popular Music and the Changing City', Liverpool University Press, 2009, p8*

inspiring and intimidating places to watch or play football, neither set of fans had yet adopted an anthem of their own. For Liverpool, this was about to change.

The focus of Anfield's noise, both then and now, was the 'Spion Kop' located in the south-west corner of the ground behind the goal to the right of the players' tunnel. The Spion Kop, takes its name from a hill between Johannesburg and Durban in South Africa, which was the scene of a bloody defeat for the British Army Fusiliers in the Boer War in January 1900. Six years after that defeat Liverpool constructed an ash and cinder bank for supporters on the Walton Breck Road, which *Liverpool Echo* sports editor Ernest Edwards nicknamed 'The Kop'.

Edwards' comments echoed an earlier description of Woolwich Arsenal's Manor Ground from 1904, in which an unnamed local newsman had likened the silhouette of fans standing on a newly raised bank of earth to soldiers standing atop the hill during the battle.[4] Edwards liked the description and applied it to Liverpool's new mound in homage to the fact that many Liverpudlians had been in the Fusiliers.[5] The visual metaphor was a powerful one and soon Kops were springing up across English football.

Over a century later, the Kop, as it's now frequently referred to, remains the home end not just at Anfield but also at Birmingham City's St Andrews, Leeds United's Elland Road, Notts County's Meadow Lane and both major grounds in Sheffield: Wednesday's Hillsborough and United's Bramall Lane. Chesterfield left their Kop behind when they deserted Saltergate for the less evocatively named Proact Stadium. Clubs in Europe were inspired too, and Windsor Park in Northern Ireland, En Avant Guingamp's Stade du Roudourou and Paris St Germain's Parc de Princes in France, as well as NAC Breda's old Aan de Beatrixstraat in the Netherlands all featured a stand known as the Kop.

The fans who stood on the Kop also tended to be the vocal ones. "The Kop was always a noisy place, people shouted and roared, and there was banter and bad language. In the early Sixties however, the noise changed. The Kop began to sing and [the] singing made

---

[4]   *The Globe and Mail, 2010, 'Showdown in Durban',*

[5]   *The Daily Mail, 2010, 'The Liverpool link: How the Kop rose up from agony of war'*

the fans feel good" note sports historians Andrew Ward and John Williams[6] in words that echo the "ecstatic ritualistic celebrations" Durkheim discovered in the Aborigines experiencing and celebrating the quasi-religious, physical and social existence of their clan.[7] The ideas expressed by Ward, Williams and Durkheim that communal singing could have a powerful and positive effect on human emotions had long been suspected and led to a number of scientific studies. One such study, led by the Sidney De Haan Research Centre for Arts and Health in Kent, confirmed the link, finding that the act of singing in a large group had significant psychological benefits from the release of endorphins, as well as physiological ones including stimulating circulation and improving lung function. Professor Don Stewart, Head of Public Health at Griffith University in Queensland noted the importance the study attributed to singing within a group environment in order to fully realise the benefits, commenting: "If the benefits were physical alone anyone could get them from singing in the shower, and that is not the case. It's very much about the act of togetherness, the importance of being involved with others gives people this strong sense of connectedness and wellbeing. It seems to be quite a powerful effect".[8]

As the Kop began to sing, its inhabitants didn't have to look far for inspiration. Local acts such as Cilla Black, Gerry and the Pacemakers and, of course, The Beatles leapt to the top of the UK music charts. Almost immediately the Kop picked up their nationally known tunes as a transferable and nationally recognisable vehicle for expressing local pride.

Examples of this fierce identification with local sources of pride can be found across world football. Writer Pete Miles, who has travelled the world watching football from different clubs' versions of the Kop, wrote an essay on fan culture in which he describes a number of examples of this in Europe, including Rott-Weis Essen and Athletic Bilboa. The former, who baring a couple of seasons in Bundesliga 2, have bounced around the German Regional Leagues, repeatedly

[6] Ward. A and Williams. J, 2010, 'Football Nation', Bloomsbury Publishing, London, p113

[7] King. A, 2002, 'The End of the Terraces', Continuum, London, p151

[8] McLean. T, 2008, 'Choral singing makes you happy', Sydney Morning Herald

showcase their city's pride in the mining industry that shaped both Essen and the wider Ruhr Valley. The latter have adopted a Basque players-only rule that has strengthened the links between the club, its city, its region and its people.[9] As local journalist Jorge Cerrato notes: "It is a self-imposed limitation that ultimately gives you much more strength because you know you are competing from an inferior position against big clubs who can sign players from anywhere, but you have a motivational pride [...] because of a tradition, a custom that gives you the strength to keep trying to better yourself as a club".[10]

Initially though this shift from parochial chants to chants inspired by a location's industrial or cultural output took place on Liverpool's Kop. Arthur Hopcraft's classic book, *The Football Man* captured the moment chanting changed, noting; "rehearsed chants and verses, created in Liverpool, where the city character with its pervading harshness of waterfront life, and bitterly combative Irish exile content was given a sudden flowering of arrogant expression with the simultaneous rise of its pop musicians and of both its leading football teams".[11]

Author and broadcaster Tim Marshall felt that Liverpool's unique cultural heritage of welcoming immigrants, drawn from two prodigiously talented musical nations played its part in ensuring the banks of the Mersey fostered and nourished this growing, spiked, melodiousness: "Perhaps it's the Irish and Welsh influence on Liverpool that has helped create both the famous Scouse wit and penchant for singing. Whatever it is, Liverpool's supporters put some other top clubs to shame when it comes to chants".[12]

Unlike modern chanting where lines, tunes, or short riffs are repurposed and altered, the Kop's first venture into chanting took the songs of their city, singing them in their entirety. When BBC's *Panorama* rocked up to document the finale of the 1964 season, visiting Anfield to see Liverpool take on Arsenal and clinch the First Division title, their cameras captured the Kop in full voice. The Kop's set list that

[9] *Miles. P, 2016, 'Beyond the Turnstiles', Ockley Book, Huddersfield, Yorkshire, p22*

[10] *Copa 90, 2016, 'This Is Athletic Club Bilbao - Basque Identity vs Modern Football', Copa 90, 10 January 2016*

[11] *Hopcroft. A, 1968, 'The Football Man', CPI Group, London, p194*

[12] *Marshall. T, 2014, 'Where do football chants come from', The Telegraph, 1 August 2014*

afternoon included an almost four-minute long complete rendition of Cilla Black's cover of 'Anyone Who Had a Heart', released a few months earlier in January 1964. The song was the first UK number one for a solo female artist for almost three years[13] and a proud Kop broadcast her musical success to the footballing world.

> *"Knowing I love you so,*
> *Anyone who had a heart,*
> *Would take me in his arms and love me, too,*
> *You couldn't really have a heart and hurt me,*
> *Like you hurt me and be so untrue,*
> *What am I to do"*

While 'Anyone Who Had a Heart' was obviously not about football, the song's message of undying love and frequently broken hearts chimed with the experience of supporting a football club and proved a hit in both record shops and on the terraces. The Kop's message was clear: Cilla is Liverpool and we are Cilla.

As Cilla's name went global, her fellow Cavern Club graduates The Beatles were also well on their way to superstardom. As with Cilla, the Kop was quick to latch on to their popular and distinctive sound, covering a succession of Beatles songs soon after they appeared. Only a few weeks after Cilla was knocked off the top of the charts, on a sunny May afternoon described by *Panorama's* Pathe News-style narrator as "a fine Scouse occasion", the BBC cameras and microphones captured the Kop follow up 'Anyone Who Had a Heart' with an a surprisingly tuneful encore of The Beatles' hit 'She Loves You'. *Panorama's* man on the mic, John Morgan, described the scene in front of him as "unlike any other football crowd [in which] the music the crowd sings is the music that Liverpool has sent echoing around the world. They seem, mysteriously, to be in touch with one another, with the spirit of scouse".[14]

Along with Cilla and The Beatles, the Sixties also saw Anfield

---

[13] Lawson, M, 'Ta-ra to Cilla Black; it had to be in Liverpool, it had to be on TV', *The Guardian*. 20 August 2015

[14] BBC Panorama. 1964, 'The Anfield Kop'

adopt an anthem that remains synonymous with the club to this day: 'You'll Never Walk Alone'. The song was written in 1945 by Rodgers and Hammerstein as the grand finale of their new musical *Carousel*. It is sung by the character Nettie Fowler in a bid to comfort her cousin Julie, after her lover Billy Bigelow had killed himself in order to avoid capture after a failed robbery.

Like Norwich's 'On the Ball City' before it, the full version of 'You'll Never Walk Alone' is much longer than the now famous chorus, although the full lyrics continue to be sung prior to Liverpool home matches.

"When you walk through a storm,
Hold your head up high,
And don't be afraid of the dark,

At the end of a storm,
There's a golden sky,
And the sweet silver song of a lark,

Walk on through the wind,
Walk on through the rain,
Though your dreams be tossed and blown,

Walk on, walk on,
With hope in your heart,
And you'll never walk alone,

You'll never walk alone,

Walk on, walk on,
With hope in your heart,
And you'll never walk alone,

You'll never walk alone."

The first recorded mentions of 'You'll Never Walk Alone' being sung at Anfield coincide with the cover of the song released by local band Gerry and the Pacemakers, which reached number one in the UK charts in October 1963 and remained there for four weeks.[15] However, it has been claimed that the song was being sung at Anfield as early as 1958. Jane Hardwick, a grandmother from Staffordshire recalls starting a rendition of it during an evening match shortly after the Munich air disaster. The then teenage schoolgirl had performed in *Carousel*, with her local operatic society, and in 2015 she told *The Independent* that given the emotions swirling around the football community at the time "it just seemed an appropriate song and I started singing it and it just caught on".[16] Whoever introduced it first, 'You'll Never Walk Alone' caught the imagination of the Kop.

Just as Rogers and Hammerstein wrote it, 'You'll Never Walk Alone' was designed to provide comfort in dark times and in that regard, over time it has come to be more than just a football chant in Liverpool. As former Liverpool player and manager Kenny Dalglish told a 2014 BT Sport documentary on the chant: "As well as being a footballing song, it also filled a huge void for people who lost somebody at Hillsborough. It was emotive for many reasons, football was one of them, but not the most important one. It covers adversity and sadness and it covers the success [...] It covers everything that it needs to cover."[17]

With its message of solidarity, support and loyalty, the chant not only caught on with fans at Liverpool, but has also been adopted by Celtic in Scotland (there are competing claims that Celtic sang it first, but given *Panorama* recorded Liverpool fans singing it almost immediately after Gerry and the Pacemakers' single came out, it is unlikely) and has a large following around the world with fans of Borussia Dortmund, Mainz, Hoffenheim, FC St Pauli and Kaiserslautern in Germany, Feyenoord, Twente and Cambuur in the Netherlands and FC Tokyo in Japan all routinely belting out their own renditions.

However, it is Liverpool with whom 'You'll Never Walk Alone' is most closely associated and such is the affinity between the club and the song, its title featured on the club's crest and is cast in iron atop the famed Shankly Gates at Anfield. Tommy Smith, who played

[15] *The Independent, 2014, 'The story of You'll Never Walk Alone'*

[16] *The Independent, 2015, 'Was Liverpool the home of the singing sixties'*

[17] *BT Sport, 2014, 'Walk on'*

for Liverpool under Shankly wrote that Gerry Marsden, the Gerry of Gerry and the Pacemakers, had presented Bill Shankly with a tape recording of the song and recalled that hearing it for the first time on the team bus during a pre-season tour was akin to a religious experience for him.[18] It certainly seemed to live in his memory and Shankly would go on to pick the song as his final selection for BBC Radio's *Desert Island Discs* broadcast on the eve of the 1965 FA Cup Final win over Leeds. Shankly later chose to have his ashes interred at Anfield, specifically behind the goal, in front of the Kop.[19]

While it began with Cilla, Liverpool were not the only club to sing pop songs verbatim. Premier League rivals Crystal Palace and their fans adopted The Dave Clarke Five's only number one single 'Glad All Over' (which was the song to knock The Beatles' 'I Want to Hold Your Hand' off the top of the UK pop charts in 1964[20]) as their anthem after the band played a concert at Selhurst Park in 1968.[21] Immediately after the concert, the song became a permanent fixture of matchdays at the ground and ultimately led to the Palace squad recording a cover version ahead of the 1990 FA Cup Final, which scraped into the UK top 50.[22]

The chant version takes just the chorus of the single, retaining the original lyrics, and is sung in a call-and-response style, in which one group of Palace fans will sing the first line, before a second group repeat it back to them, before coming together for the finale.

"You say that you love me,
(Say that you love me),
All of the time,
(All of the time),
You say that you need me,
(Say that you need me),
You'll always be mine,

[18] *Doyle, P, and Glendenning. B, 2016, 'The Joy of Six: Football Chants', 6 May 2016*

[19] *Kelly, S, 1997, 'Bill Shankly; It's much more important than that', p312*

[20] *Official Charts, 2018, 'Glad All Over, OfficialCharts.com, Retrieved 24 October 2018*

[21] *Booker. J, 2016, 'Crystal Palace are Glad All Over', Croydon Advertiser, 20 May 2016*

[22] *Official Charts, 2018, 'Glad All Over', OfficialCharts.com, Retrieved 24 October 2018*

(Always be mine),
And I'm feeling,
Glad all over,
I'm feeling,
Glad all over."

'Glad All Over' is another pop song, which, while not about football, speaks to the experience of being a football fan in which you know your team will be your team for life regardless of what happens on the pitch. Plus, just occasionally, they can make you glad all over. Palace's version has inspired additional versions to crop up across Britain, with Blackpool, Rotherham United, Port Vale, Swindon Town and Yeovil Town all adopting it in England, and Partick Thistle and Dunfermline Athletic in Scotland.

Another chant which avoids reference to football but takes a pop song and, with a couple of tweaks, speaks instead about the experience of being a fan is Sheffield United's 'Greasy Chip Butty Song'. Originally written in 1974 by American singer-songwriter John Denver as 'Annie's Song', Sheffield United's version uses Denver's tune and structure, but tweaks the experiences to make it their own;

"You fill up my senses,
Like a gallon of Magnet,
Like a packet of Woodbine,
Like a good pinch of snuff,
Like a night out in Sheffield,
Like a greasy chip butty,
Oh Sheffield United,
Come thrill me again,
Nah nah nah nah nah nah oooh,
Nah nah nah nah nah nah oooh oooh"

The hyper-local identity of the 'Greasy Chip Butty Song', with its romanticised view of life in the Steel City, is said to have originated during United's opening match of the 1985-86 season when Blades fans were heard singing it during their 3-1 away win over Stoke City. Unfortunately, the reason it was re-discovered a decade after Denver released it is unknown. Incidentally 'Annie's Song' would be Denver's only UK number one,[23] just as 'Glad All Over' was The Dave Clarke Five's only chart-topper. One theory that lurks on internet forums is that it reappeared after an away win over Bournemouth at the end of the previous season, featuring "Like a night out in Bournemouth" as an alternative opening line. Meanwhile, fans of Rotherham United claim they were singing their version long before United.[24]

In 2010 there was concern the 'Greasy Chip Butty Song' might be made obsolete after brewery John Smith's ceased production of their Magnet brew,[25] referenced in the second line. So far, those fears have proven unfounded and if anything, the demise of Magnet added additional layers of reminiscing and heritage to the proud Sheffield identity expressed in the song.

Back on the banks of the Mersey, as well as being a vehicle for local pride, and the subsequent positive identity it helped create and sustain among the Liverpool faithful, the appearance of 'You'll Never Walk Alone' on the terraces was mirrored by a level of on-field success that prompted another key moment in the evolution of football fandom in Britain.

As Liverpool acts dominated the 1964 UK pop charts, the team won the First Division title in front of record crowds as attendances started to be boosted by away fans able to travel in greater numbers thanks to cheaper transport provided by the introduction of British Rail's Football Special trains[26] . The Kop growing in volume coincided with two League Championships for Liverpool in 1964 and again in 1966, and with Panorama on hand to imply cause and effect between vocal backing and on-field success, the Kop's reputation spread across British football and around the world.

The BBC's John Morgan invoked the Duke of Wellington's description of his troops to describe the crowd's affect on the game, quoting the military leader's remarks about his troops: "I don't know what

[23] *Official Charts, 2018, 'Annie's Song', OfficialCharts.com, Retrieved 24 October 2018*

[24] *Official Charts, 2018, 'Annie's Song', OfficialCharts.com, Retrieved 24 October 2018*

[25] *Sheffield Star, 2010, 'Last orders for Sheffield United's Greasy Chip Butty song', Sheffield Star, 3 February 2010*

[26] *BBC Panorama, 1964, 'The Anfield Kop', Television Programme*

they do to the opposition, but my God they frighten me," adding that the affect on Liverpool's opponents was "surely the same when faced with this wall of noise and massed, swaying bodies".[27]

Ian Callaghan, a member of the first Liverpool team to win at Wembley, in the 1965 FA Cup final, echoed those thoughts when he spoke in 2015 about the huge affect the crowd had on the side: "The Beatles, Gerry and the Pacemakers, all that Liverpool sound was there, plus the football was coming up so the combination of the two was just fantastic." Callaghan went on to recall how the crowd had the power to intimidate the opposition through humour, giving the example of the Kop singing the recent Des O'Connor cover of 'Careless Hands' to Leeds goalkeeper Gary Sprake after he threw the ball into his own goal.[28] Half a decade later non-league Dulwich Hamlet fans have taken advantage of the more intimate surrounds of their Champion Hill home to put a new twist on distracting the opposition goalkeeper. Rather than chanting at him, their most passionate fans, known as 'The Rabble', will loudly read his old Facebook posts back to him.[29]

Callaghan is not the only one to specifically mention how the Kop and their vocal backing has helped Liverpool sides. Former captain Steven Gerrard told BT Sport: "When you walk out with a Liverpool kit on, you shouldn't need a song to motivate you but when 'You'll Never Walk Alone' is in full flow on that terrace, there's no better place to be. You're 3-0 down [against AC Milan in a Champions League final and] you think your dream is in tatters, you're waiting for the half-time whistle, waiting for a chorus of boos. You've let them down, you've let yourself down. You've been totally played off the park for 45 minutes, and then you hear the chorus of 'You'll Never Walk Alone' probably the loudest and most emotional rendition I've ever heard as a player...".[30] Inspired, Liverpool famously recovered after half-time in Istanbul, hauling themselves level at 3-3, before going on to win on penalties.

In reaching that final, Liverpool had earlier overcome recently

[27] BBC Panorama, 1964, 'The Anfield Kop', Television Programme

[28] The Independent, 2015, 'Was Liverpool the home of the singing sixties'

[29] Lamont. T, 2018, 'Dulwich Hamlet; the improbable tale', The Guardian, 26 October 2018

[30] BT Sport, 2014, 'Walk on', Television Documentary

crowned Premier League Champions Chelsea in front of an Anfield crowd that was so ferociously vocal that Chelsea captain John Terry left the field in tears and later described the atmosphere that evening as the best he'd ever played in.[31] Liverpool midfielder Alex Oxlade-Chamberlain went out of his way to praise the effect of the Kop after an impressive 3-0 win over Manchester City in the quarter-finals of the 2018 Champions League, saying: "It was an amazing atmosphere, the best I've ever played in. You have to give credit to the fans because it is never nice coming to Anfield and hearing that crowd—I've been on the other end of it and it is not easy. The fans play a massive part. I've never witnessed anything like that. Coming into the stadium for a game which was not a final it almost set it up to be like a final. It definitely got us going and you could see that. If you are the away team and the crowd gets going like that it is horrible. City are an amazing football team, but they are only human and you put anyone in a pressure environment in an atmosphere like that maybe it can disturb them. I wouldn't say to the extent it did that because they still played some good stuff and dominated the ball, but it definitely played a part in the first half. It got us going and it would probably shake anyone up, so you have to give the fans credit for that".[32]

Liverpool fan and *Guardian* writer Sachin Nakrani echoed Oxlade-Chamberlain's thoughts; "Liverpool supporters should, in the main, feel chuffed with their team and themselves. This was a collective triumph—one spurred on by the other. Anfield at its best".[33] Kenny Dalglish also expressed the sentiment that winning football matches is a collective effort: "It's all about helping each other. It helps when you go on to a pitch to know they're right behind you. It helps when you're struggling on a pitch, it helps when you're winning".[34] One unnamed coach who has managed opposition teams in the Champions League at Anfield reported a similar effect, in an interview with

[31] Nakrani. S, 2018, 'Wild, furious, almost feral: from the Kop this felt like a collective triumph', 5 April 2018

[32] Hunter, A, 2018, 'Alex Oxlade-Chamberlain praises fans for horrible Anfield atmosphere', 5 April 2018

[33] Nakrani. S, 2018, 'Wild, furious, almost feral: from the Kop this felt like a collective triumph', 5 April 2018

[34] BT Sport, 2014, 'Walk on', Television Documentary

The Athletic explaining: "I don't think top players are intimidated by a stadium. But the thing about Anfield is that the momentum of games seemed to swing with greater intensity than other places. When the energy is positive, those fans play such a big part in affecting their own players. Perhaps it is something in the character of the people from Liverpool and how Jurgen Klopp has harnessed a bond with his players and supporters. We always found that you could be very in control of a game at Anfield but then one, seemingly little thing could just ignite the whole stadium and swing a game. All you can do as a coach to protect you is design a clear style of play, develop resilience and hope your players cope with tough and external pressure".[35]

Stats back up this anecdotal evidence. For example, in the 27 Premier League seasons between 1992 and 2019, there were 10,725 Premier League fixtures. A massive 46% of those games featured home wins, compared to just 28% away victories.[36] Within games themselves, a similar effect can be seen with the award of penalty kicks with numerous studies recording statistically relevant discrepancies in the number of home and away penalties awarded. This is not just noticeable in the number of spot kicks awarded to home and away teams, but at an even more granular level, away teams are awarded fewer penalties in the area located closest to a home team's most vocally supportive end, compared to the other end of the same stadium.[37]

The Kop is equally important to the fans that stood on it as it is to the players it helped inspire. The experience of standing and singing was summed up by one Liverpool fan interviewed by Ward and Williams, as somewhere "you lose all your worries, for two hours it's all that matters. Everything outside is irrelevant. But what you do in that two hours lives with you for the rest of the week. You don't leave the Kop behind. That comes with you".[38]

[35] Crafton. A, 2020, 'Lower testosterone, long journeys or overheated dressing rooms? Why is it harder to win away from home?', The Athletic, 20 January 2020

[36] Crafton. A, 2020, 'Lower testosterone, long journeys or overheated dressing rooms? Why is it harder to win away from home?', The Athletic, 20 January 2020

[37] Social Issues Research Centre, 2008, 'Football Passions', Social Issues Research Centre, London, p21

[38] Ward. A and Williams. J, 2010, 'Football Nation', Bloomsbury Publishing, London, p113

As the terraces became more lyrical, and Liverpool's Kop began to gain a reputation for being boisterous, fun and, crucially, credited with being a key part of Liverpool's on-field success, it was naturally enough, mimicked by clubs across Britain. Fans who wanted to get together, vocally support their club and help them win began to gather on the terraces of clubs across Britain, in their own versions of the Kop. Each club's vocal area became known as the "home end" and it was the appearance as these 'ends' around the country that would go on to shape both future chants and the game itself.

4. THE RISE OF HOOLIGANISM

'THOSE WERE THE DAYS, MY FRIEND'

By the time 1970 arrived the average length of the British working week had fallen from around 60 hours to 42 and was continuing to drop.[1] This reduction in working hours allowed more people, and crucially in this context, more men, the freedom and time to travel around Britain following their club when Saturday came. As football and railway enthusiast John Simpkin explains: "men [previously] had the problem of having to work on a Saturday. Although some trades granted their workers a half-day holiday, it did not give them much time to travel very far to see a game [and] even a local game [could] cause considerable problems".[2] A study in 1972, at the very beginning of the explosion in away support found that every time the distance required to travel to an away game doubled, there was a 29% reduction in the numbers of away fans.[3]

Just as people were getting more free time, travel became easier and more affordable too, meaning distances became less onerous and in-turn encouraging more fans to travel around the country for their weekend football fix.[4] An increasingly mobile fanbase had three implications. First it increased the proportion of away fans at matches; second it weakened the traditionally local identities expressed in the parochial or hyper-local chants that had gone before, and; third it increased the frequency and variety of chanting.

Rising levels of disposable income, combined with improvements in both public and private transport, particularly the explosion in levels of individual car ownership and the construction of the motorway network, led to important changes in the geographical composition of where football clubs drew their support from and studies on the location fans of particular clubs lived began to show that the proportion of home supporters drawn from each club's immediate vicinity was

[1] Roser, M, 2018, 'Working hours', Our world in data, OurWorldInData.org, Retrieved 7 March 2020

[2] Simpkin, J, 1997, 'Railways and football', Spartacus Education

[3] Hart. RA, Hutton. J and Sharot. T, 1975, 'A Statistical Analysis of Association Football Attendances', Royal Statistical Society, p23

[4] Hart. RA, Hutton. J and Sharot. T, 1975, 'A Statistical Analysis of Association Football Attendances', Royal Statistical Society, p23

for the first time, falling dramatically. With long-distance travel now practical both financially and logistically, the top clubs began to drain support from their smaller counterparts. For example, Manchester United's hooligan firm 'Men in Black' drew a distinctive and vociferous group of fans based 200 miles away in London. As home fans came from further and further afield, hyper-local identities faded, and fans began to proactively choose the club they supported more than ever before. Just as some fans began gravitating towards the bigger clubs, the spectators who remained loyal to their local sides appeared to become increasingly hostile towards the supporters of neighbouring teams and in-turn the tribal "us" and "them" identities on display grew ever fiercer, adding fuel to the growing flames of hooliganism.[5]

By the turn of the decade, and only four years after Gerry and the Pacemakers released 'You'll Never Walk Alone', weakening hyper-local identities and the heightening of tribal identities coupled with the creation of dedicated ends for the most vocal home fans, which away fans saw as a 'prize' to be taken with violence, led to a new wave of hooliganism sweeping the nation. Hooligan firms began to take hold and new identities were forged to fill the vacuum left by the collapse of the hyper-local geographical bonds.

With many football grounds conveniently located by railway stations and British Rail keen to maximise passenger numbers by offering bespoke football trains, including one train known as the 'League Liner' which was kitted out with music, VCRs showing football and even a 'disco carriage' featuring DJs and coloured disco lights,[6] Britain's railways played a key role in ferrying thousands of people cross-country. Clubs, and initially the authorities, were keen on the arrangement, partly because as Simpkin explains "it [was suggested] that 10,000 spectators could be easily handled by trains arriving every five minutes",[7] all in one easily policed location, in the build-up to kick-off.

However, as 'us' and 'them' identities hardened, British Rail's Football Special trains, that had run almost without incident throughout

[5]   Dobson. S, and Goddard. J, 2014, 'The Economics of Football', Edward Elgar Publishing, p68

[6]   Turner. G, 2013, 'All aboard the League Liner', The Guardian

[7]   Simpkin, J, 1997, 'Railways and football', Spartacus Education

the 1960s, were now increasingly a hotbed of violence. Such was the connection between hooliganism and the railway, that West Ham United's hooligan firm gave themselves the moniker 'The Inter City Firm', closely matched by Manchester United's 'Inter-City Jibbers', both named after the InterCity trains they travelled to away games on. Portsmouth's firm the '6.57 Crew' was named after the time the Portsmouth to London Waterloo train left Portsmouth.[8] While, Leeds United's 'Leeds United Service Crew' acquired their name after the firm took the decision to move away from the now heavily policed Football Specials onto regular service lines.[9]

The aforementioned 'League Liner' was initially conceived as a potential way to try and stem the trouble with the now laughable plan to simply dilute the majority male clientele, and subsequent testosterone levels, with females. The people behind the plan seemed to wilfully ignore any possible pitfalls of adding an additional source of machismo posturing to an already tinderbox environment. Burnley commercial manager Jack Butterfield, who was involved in setting the scheme up in 1973, stated his cheerfully naïve, and to modern eyes ridiculously stereotyped, view ahead of Burnley fans using it for a game in the nation's capital. "I feel that much of the trouble on football specials, the hooliganism and the vandalism, is caused because the youngsters have nothing to interest them," said Butterfield. "We hope that wives and girlfriends of the fans will take the chance for this cheap excursion to London". British Rail's Alan Hardaker suggested: "The added touch of luxury provided by the League Liner, together with its unusual and novel facilities, will encourage supporters to bring their wives and families, and girlfriends, with them". Essentially as Georgina Turner eloquently sums up: "the plan was that the chicks side-step alluringly to David Cassidy and distract their men for long enough to stop too much damage being done to the light fittings and then they could go up west and get themselves something pretty".[10] Sadly, the 'League Liner' didn't prove as successful in practice as

8   The Portsmouth News, 2002, 'Book glorifies hooligans say Pompey bosses', The Portsmouth News

9   Milmo, D, 2007, 'Bring back football specials, says rail police boss', The Guardian

10 Turner. G, 2013, 'All aboard the League Liner', The Guardian

Butterfield and Hardaker had thought and after suffering repeated damage the 'League Liner' was finally withdrawn in 1976, a mere three years after it began.

Continuing the folkloric tradition of documenting history through song, Millwall fans were known to chant;

> **"If we lose,**
> **If we fail,**
> **We take it out on British Rail,**
> **Wreck the train,**
> **Wreck the train,**
> **Wreck the train"** [11]

Trashed disco carriages notwithstanding, to this day the train remains a popular way to travel to away games, with an estimated 3.5 million rail journeys made solely for the purpose of attending football matches around Great Britain each season.[12] Such is their popularity that following a PA announcement of major train disruption in London during a comfortable Premier League home win at Arsenal's Emirates in January 2015, the home fans mocked their visitors from Stoke City with;

> **"3-0 and you can't get home,**
> **3-0 and you can't get home"**

The vast majority of train trips made by football fans are, of course, trouble-free but the link between football fan and violence remains strong in the minds of the authorities. In 2007, in response to a question from a local authority official about whether British Transport Police could "herd match day 'animals' into special trains" British Transport Police deputy chief constable Andy Trotter told a transport security conference: "I would much prefer if there is something done

---

[11] Campbell, P, 2015, 'What are the wittiest chants you have heard at a football match', The Guardian

[12] Railway Safety and Standards Board, 2018, 'Management of football fans on the railway'

not to have [football fans] coming on the [railway] system at all".[13] As late as 2018 the Railway Safety and Standards board continued to maintain a page on their website that stated: "Apart from the operating challenge of conveying large groups of football fans, train operators are regularly faced with the difficulties of managing the violence and abusive behaviour associated with a small but important minority of those attending football matches, much of it fuelled by alcohol".[14]

Thus, by the end of the 1970s violence and football fans were becoming so intrinsically linked that half a century later the link remains. In this environment the point of chanting in support of your team or expressing local pride had changed. Now, rather than local civic pride, the principal identity being expressed through chanting was masculinity and according to political scientist Anthony King, specifically the masculine quest for status and social recognition.[15] With hooligan firms taking root, the quest to take the opponent's home end by process of violent invasion became as important as on-field success and in-turn the main inspiration for chants. As a result, chants, which still drew on pop classics for their tunes began to draw on memories of violent skirmishes in faraway places.

As 'You'll Never Walk Alone' was firmly establishing itself at Anfield, across Stanley Park Everton fans were borrowing the tune from 1968 number one 'Those Were the Days', sung by folk musician Mary Hopkin and produced by Paul McCartney. The Everton hooligan firm 'The Street', named after their version of the Kop the Gwladys Street End, changed the words from the original:

"Those were the days my friend
We thought they'd never end,
We'd sing and dance forever and a day,
We'd live the life we choose,
We'd fight and never lose,
For we were young and sure to have our way,
La, la, la, la, lala, la la la, la, lala..."

[13] Milmo, D, 2007, 'Bring back football specials, says rail police boss', The Guardian

[14] Railway Safety and Standards Board, 2018, 'Management of football fans on the railway'

[15] King. A, 2002, 'The End of the Terraces', Continuum, London, p15

...to suit their new aggressive posturing:

"Those were the days my friend,
We took the Stretford End,
We took the Shed,
The North Bank Highbury,
We took the Geordies too,
We fight for Everton,
We are The Street of Everton FC,
La, la, la, la, lala, la la la, la, lala..."

Whereas 'You'll Never Walk Alone' referenced the positive success of a local band from their city and spoke of loyalty through dark times, 'Those Were the Days' fondly recalls away games, not for on-field success, but for the violent skirmishes that preceded the firm taking the home ends of Manchester United (the Stretford End), Chelsea (the Shed), Arsenal (the North Bank) and Newcastle United (the unmentioned Gallowgate).

'Those Were the Days' is also notable in that alongside masculinity and strength, the main identity expressed is not wholly of Everton. While the earlier parochial chants of 'On the Ball City', 'Glory, Glory Tottenham Hotspur' or 'Play up, Pompey' had been about, or at least were concerned with Norwich City, Tottenham Hotspur and Portsmouth respectively, 'Those Were the Days' is principally about Everton's hooligan firm The Street, not the football club.

Other examples from Everton's firm include this violence-laden chant to the tune of the children's nursery rhyme 'The Grand Old Duke of York':

"We don't carry bottles,
We don't carry lead,
We only carry hatchets,
To bury in your head,
We are loyal supporters,
Fanatics every one,
In case you do not know our name,
Our name is Everton"

The 'Loyal Supporters' chant is interesting in that it distinguishes between types of weapon, although it's unclear if the suggestion is that by not carrying bottles and lead in favour of hatchets the firm are trying to portray themselves as more threatening, or conforming to an unwritten code of what it is and isn't acceptable to fight your fellow fans with. Note also the fluid identities being expressed, with 'Loyal Supporters' reverting back to being that of Everton as a whole, rather than just the firm.

Another example of violence-heavy Everton chanting, with an identity broader than that of the firm, came in the form of 'Run, Run', set to the remarkably popular chanting tune of the 1963 Sydney Carter hymn 'Lord of the Dance':

"Run, Run wherever you may be,
We are the famous EFC,
We'll fuck you up,
Wherever you may be,
We are the famous EFC"

Finally, there's the 'Street End Boys' chant that is back to expressing the identity of the firm, rather than the club as a whole and which expresses a different, violence-free type of masculinity:

"Street End Boys we are here,
Woah, Woah,
Street End Boys we are here,
Woah, Woah,
Street End Boys we are here,
Shag your women,
And drink your beer,
Woooaaah"

The version of masculinity expressed in 'Street End Boys' is one rooted in their heterosexual sexual prowess and their ability to consume large quantities of beer. The role of women in 'Street End Boys' is reduced to being objects, owned by the opposition's male fans and there only to be sexually conquered. This suggestion of conquering or invading an area in the same manner of taking, or threatening to take, 'the home end', made 'Street End Boys' a favourite at away games.

Alongside sexual proclivity and the ability to drink, outright abuse and needless cruelty had become staple ingredients of football chanting. Now the height of wit was to rip off old chants with violent equivalents, highlighted in the conversion of 'You'll Never Walk Alone' into the rather more ominous 'You'll Never Walk Again'. This amplification of aggression took place during games as well, with fans of clubs from rural areas such as East Anglia or the West Country beginning a game by being mocked with a harmless *"You're going home in a combine harvester"*, transformed into *"You're going home in a fucking ambulance"*, or *"You're going home in a foreign ambulance"* for European ties, all of which ignored the obvious error, that very rarely do ambulances take the victims of a severe beating home. Suggesting aggression rather than accuracy was now the order of the day as the mood darkened, and violence flared.

Interestingly, such was the cultural reach of chanting at this point that roles were being reversed and pop groups began to take chants to use in their songs, rather than vice-versa as had happened before. For example, *"You're going home in a fucking ambulance"* is the opening line of the Specials' song 'Concrete Jungle', released in 1979. One year later the Ramones then used the same tub-thumping hand-clap tune to open 'Do You Remember Rock 'n' Roll Radio?'. Two decades on, Supergrass released 'You'll Never Walk Again' with their single 'Pumping on Your Stereo' which combines a number of hooligan staple chants into a two-minute acoustic track:

> *"Come and have a go if you think you're hard enough,*
> *'Cos you're going to get your fucking heads kicked in,*
> *So come and have a go if you think you're hard enough,*
> *'Cos you're going home in a foreign ambulance"*

It wasn't just pop music that provided a backing track for this new breed of aggressive chants, but hymns and even Christmas carols were being repurposed. One such example comes from Ipswich Town, among other clubs, whose fans repurposed 18th century hymn-come-carol 'Hark! The Herald Angels Sing', one of roughly 6,500 hymns composed by prolific hymn-machine Reverend Charles Wesley:[16]

"Hark now hear,
The Ipswich sing,
The Norwich run away,
And we will fight forever more,
Because of Boxing Day"

'Hark! The Herald Angels Sing' plays on the ideas of numerous psychological studies on masculinity which have found that acts of aggression and violence are a key concept of masculinity,[17] with those who perform, or threaten to perform them being seen as more masculine than those who avoid them.[18] Masculinity in this context, according to Rachel Adams and David Savran involves "values such as courage, certain forms of aggression, technological skill, group solidarity, and a considerable amount of toughness".[19] Professor Kath Woodward also cites ideas of masculine social status as the key factor within her study of sporting masculinity.[20]

These definitions of masculinity tie into the creation of 'us' vs. 'them' identities discussed previously, which perfectly suited the new tribal nature of football and football support. Through their chants those singing fans were attempting to promote themselves as exhibiting more masculine qualities than the opposition. As Anthony King suggests: "[the] notion of pride is an important one in the lads' everyday lives, for it is football that substantially defines their masculinity, by the demonstration of loyal support; regular attendance and singing, even when losing [...] the songs the lads sing, and the conviction and frequency with which they sing them, demonstrate their status, and almost every song refers to their superiority and

16 Watson. J, 1997, 'The English Hymn; A Critical and Historical Study', Clarendon Press, Oxford, p205-229

17 Woodward. K, 2004, 'Rumbles in the Jungle: Boxing, Racialization and the Performance of Masculinity' from 'Leisure Studies' Vol. 23, Routledge, London

18 King. A, 2002, 'The End of the Terraces', Continuum, London

19 Adams. R and Savran. D, 2002, 'The Masculinity Studies Reader', Blackwell Publishing, London, p104

20 Woodward. K, 2004, 'Rumbles in the Jungle: Boxing, Racialization and the Performance of Masculinity' from 'Leisure Studies' Vol. 23, Routledge, London, p6

the opposition's inferiority".[21] 'The lads' King refers to here are the group of fans who chant most frequently, a group Desmond Morris describes as the "true fans" on the basis that "to be a member of the fan-clusters in [the vocal section] is a tribal privilege and it requires the observance of certain customs and rules. These fans must all join in the ritual chants, hurling abuse at their opponents and offering praise to tribal heroes".[22]

These concepts are clearly visible within both 'Street End Boys', in which Everton fans are suggesting they have invaded their rivals' territory (*"We are here"*) and marked it as their own by having sex with local women and consuming all the local beer, and 'Hark! The Herald Angels Sing' in which Ipswich fans are attempting to promote themselves—the 'us'—as masculine, both through their singing and their fighting, while ridiculing, and possibly threatening the 'them'— local rivals Norwich fans—who by nature of their running away from a violent encounter are deemed not as masculine as their Ipswich counterparts. Like 'Those Were the Days' the chant also references specific incidents of violence within it, in this case previous derby matches between the two clubs, which had traditionally taken place over the Christmas period and in which Ipswich had been victorious away at Norwich in both 1960 and 1973.

Extreme violence was also the inspiration for a particularly aggressive Millwall chant during the 1970s and 1980s, which celebrated the 1966 murder of three policeman in Shepherd's Bush instigated by a London career-criminal named Harry Roberts:

> **"Harry Roberts is our friend,**
> **Is our friend,**
> **Is our friend,**
> **Harry Roberts is our friend,**
> **He kills coppers,**
>
> **Let him out to kill some more,**
> **Kill some more,**

---

[21] King. A, 2002, 'The End of the Terraces', Continuum, London, p153-168

[22] Morris. D, 1981, 'The Soccer Tribe', Jonathon Cape Publishing, London, p237-238

Kill some more,
Let him out to kill some more,
He kills coppers

He shot three down in Shepherd's Bush,
Shepherd's Bush,
Shepherd's Bush,
He shot three down in Shepherd's Bush,
Our mate Harry"

The chant came at a time when tensions between Millwall fans and the police were high and the 'Millwall Bushwackers' firm were developing a reputation for being among the most violent in Britain. It was also one of the first chants to emigrate from the terraces into wider society, where it began to be used to taunt and attempt to provoke police, being sung outside police stations.

By now, aggression was commonplace in chanting. Furthermore, it was not purely the domain of top-flight clubs, or reserved for local rivalries as Desmond Morris found when he studied the chants sung by Oxford United fans during a non-descript Division Two game with Cardiff City in 1981, which featured:

"Hello, Hello,
We are the Oxford boys,
Hello, Hello,
We are the Oxford boys,
And if you are a Cardiff fan,
Surrender or you'll die,
We all follow United"

And the just as ominous:

"You'll never make the coaches,
You'll never make the coaches"[23]

---

[23] Morris. D, 1981, 'The Soccer Tribe', Jonathon Cape Publishing, London, p313

While the masculine identities of aggression, mastery, group solidarity and toughness as suggested by Adams and Savran are evident within chanting, it must be pointed out that football chanting is not enjoyed entirely by a male audience, and neither does it communicate one type of masculinity. As such it has been argued by psychologists that, within the crowd, women who join in are performing a version of masculine identity.[24] In England alone, the FA reported that participation amongst women was up from 10,400 in 1993 to 2.5m in 2019[25] and it will be interesting to see how the increase in the popularity of football among women, and the women's game, affects this aspect of chanting in years to come.

Supporters groups themselves are reflective of this growing change within football. German liberal, left-wing, flag-bearers FC St Pauli are leading the way, with more female supporters attending games at the famously loud and atmospheric Millerntor-Stadion than any other club or stadium in Europe.[26] Traditional masculine attitudes are also being confronted at the club with adverts for the men's magazine *Maxim* withdrawn from the Millerntor after the club's own fans complained they were sexist.[27] St Pauli's fans were also forced to protest back in 2012 when they felt "the tentacles of commercialisation starting to get a stranglehold on the club". The 'Bring Back St Pauli to me' campaign sought to address a number of issues, including the sale of a corporate box in the new Haupttribune (Main Stand) to a local strip club who promptly installed a pole and had scantily clad women dancing during the game. This was described by author Nick Davidson as a "kick in the teeth" for fans of a club who "had for many years fought sexism in football as hard as they fought racist, fascist and homophobic attitudes".[28] The campaign came to a head during their Bundesliga game against SC Freiburg during which fans repeatedly chanted the campaign slogan to the tune of traditional Scottish folk song 'My Bonnie Lies Over the Ocean':

[24] Negus. K, 1998, 'Popular Music in Theory', Wesleyan University Press, New England, p126

[25] The FA, 2019, 'About Women's and Girls Football', The FA website, 2 July 2019

[26] Smith. M, 2011, 'Pirates of the Bundesliga', Socialist Review, 31 March 2014

[27] Dans. C, 2013, 'FC Sankt Pauli, the counter-culture of European football', A World of Football

[28] Davidson. N, 2014, 'Pirates, Punks and Politics, Randall Sports Books, York, p176

"Bring back St Pauli,
Bring back St Pauli to me"

Back in Britain, as the 1980s dawned, the shift was complete. Fans had discarded traditional location specific 'us' identities and now saw themselves as a group in their own right. This shift forever altered the pattern of chanting and by the end of the decade it had adopted the back-and-forth tribal nature of modern-day chanting. Desmond Morris recorded the shift and conducted a study to highlight the fans' newly varied songbook. After recording audio from a number of games across the Football League during the 1979-80 season Morris reported each club's "choir" was belting out an average of 147 individual chants per match, comfortably more than one a minute. Gone too were the days of repetition and anthems, with Morris noting each choir averaged an incredibly diverse repertoire of 67 different chants per game, 57 of which were highly contextual to what was happening on the pitch.[29]

After half a century of stability, in the space of two decades chanting had changed, almost beyond recognition, and was now considered one of the tools in a new tribal armoury with which to hurt people. Chants were therefore no longer just about celebrating the identity of a place, but a masculine quest for status and social recognition. In effect, chants had become weaponised, and an arms race of abuse had begun.

---

[29] *Morris. D, 1981, 'The Soccer Tribe', Jonathon Cape Publishing, London, p306*

5. AN ARMS RACE OF ABUSE

'WHO'S THAT LYING ON THE RUNWAY?'

As intimidation, viciousness and overt displays of masculinity replaced *Top of the Pops* as the main motivation for chanting, the chants themselves became darker, inspired now by violence, death and disaster, rather than civic pride in a location, or on-field success. And, just as the best of chanting began on Liverpool's Kop, the worst of it originated there too, born in a burgeoning rivalry with Manchester United.

The two most successful English clubs, domestically and in Europe, share a rivalry which runs deeper than football and takes in two fiercely proud cities. Since the beginning of the industrial revolution, the two cities have fought for economic supremacy in the north west. Manchester's mills, which dominated the textile industry, made the early running. Before Liverpool's port, a gateway to the lucrative North American markets and a key link in the trading of slaves and sugar, helped the city fight back. Over time, Manchester merchants, lacking a port of their own, became disenchanted with the level of dues they had to pay to export and import their goods through Liverpool. Consequently, they decided to construct their own ship canal, linking them directly to the sea, a move that raised fierce opposition from Liverpudlian politicians which the Manchester merchants duly ignored.

The Manchester Ship Canal was the largest in the world when it opened in January 1894, highlighting just how far the merchants had been prepared to go to avoid paying those dues and having ignored the opposition from Merseyside, the opening of the ship canal is generally agreed to have ignited the rivalry between the cities.[1] However, even by the time the canal opened *The Guardian* was reporting earlier "lamentable incidents" clouding relations between the cities, including one at the opening of the first Manchester-Liverpool railway which took place 64 years earlier in September 1830.[2] The same report described the opening of the canal as an "epoch making event in the history of Manchester [and] evidence of the magnitude of the producing and consuming populations which will be brought into more direct

---

[1] Roher. F, 2007, 'Scouse v Manc', BBC News, 21 August 2007

[2] Encyclopaedia Britannica, 2018, 'George Stephenson', Encyclopaedia Britannica

friendly commerce".[3] Such was the impact of the canal on the city the badges of both Manchester City and Manchester United continue to feature a golden ship facing west, past Liverpool and out into the Irish Sea beyond.

There is rivalry too on the music scene with Liverpool boasting The Beatles, Cilla and Gerry and the Pacemakers while Manchester can lay claim to New Order, Oasis, Joy Division and The Stone Roses, whose 1989 hit 'This is The One' remains the song United walk out to at Old Trafford three decades on. However, the rivalry in terms of economics or music is at its worst the stuff of heated pub conversations and contains no vitriol. The venomous hatred is only found in football.

As with the local rivalries of Norwich-Ipswich and Southampton-Portsmouth the Manchester-Liverpool rivalry is also sustained by the creation of local 'us' and 'them' identities, which overlook the many similarities between the two Northern powerhouses and focus on their subtle differences. The difference with this rivalry is the viciousness with which those identities are sometimes expressed. A BBC investigation into the Manchester-Liverpool rivalry, inspired by the two clubs competing for the signature of Argentina defender Gabriel Heinze in 2007, illustrated the hyper-local differentiation at play between the cities, reporting: "One might assume that Manchester and Liverpool would find common ground in being cities that have coped with periods of decline and unemployment. Both have areas— Toxteth and Moss Side come to mind—that are national bywords for deprivation. [And yet] Mancunians are happy to mock their Liverpudlian cousins in stereotypical terms. [While] Liverpudlians regard Manchester as the more dangerous city to live in, associating it with guns and gang violence. It is often suggested that Liverpool looked down its nose at Manchester, feeling itself to be grounded in the loftier areas of insurance, finance and shipping, while its opposite number at the end of the East Lancs Road made its money from the altogether grubbier business of cotton mills. There was a saying [in Liverpool]: 'the Liverpool gentleman and the Manchester man'. But whatever the mythology, the tables have been turned in recent years.

....

3   The Guardian Archives, 2011, 'Opening of the Manchester Ship Canal', The Guardian, 1
    January 1894

Manchester has adapted more confidently and more completely to the post-manufacturing, post-heavy industry British economy. It would take a particularly blinkered, rose-spectacled Liverpudlian not to admit that, despite Liverpool's furious last decade of redevelopment, their regional rivals have the drop on them economically".[4]

Those economic differences can be seen being played out on the terraces and used to accentuate the 'us' of Manchester and the 'them' of Liverpool, through chants such as this from United fans, which honoured their South Korean midfielder Park Ji-Sung and which, like Everton's 'Run Run' chant, took the tune of hymn 'Lord of the Dance':

> **"Park, Park,**
> **Wherever you may be,**
> **You eat dogs in your own country,**
> **It could be worse,**
> **You could be Scouse,**
> **Eating rats in your council house"**

Ignoring for a moment the abhorrent racist generalisation that South Koreans routinely eat dogs, the Park Ji-Sung chant is layered with cultural symbolism of what it means to be poor in the UK including the perceived shame of living in local authority housing, something which the chant implies is rife in Liverpool and would never happen in the economically superior Manchester.

Alongside the historical rivalry between the two cities, the red footballing halves of both were competing for supremacy at the top of English football, leading to a rivalry which surpassed the two clubs' own inter-city rivalries with their blue halves, Manchester City and Everton, primarily because United and Liverpool are the most successful English teams in both domestic and European competitions.

From their very first meeting there was needle. Liverpool were formed in 1892 and they won the Second Division in 1893-94, going undefeated all season. Thus, they earned the right to play a one-off test match, an early forerunner for the play-offs, against Newton Heath, the bottom side of the First Division, for a place in the top-flight. Liverpool

4   Roher. F, 2007, 'Scouse v Manc', BBC News, 21 August 2007

won 2-0 relegating their rivals. By the time Newton Heath, renamed Manchester United, returned to the top-flight in 1906, Liverpool had clinched their first couple of League titles.

Two global conflicts then disrupted English football, but when it resumed after World War Two, both clubs found era-defining managers, who would between them cement their clubs at the pinnacle of English football: Bill Shankly and Matt Busby. With Liverpool backed by a Kop that had found its singing voice and back in the First Division after almost a decade in the Second Division, the two clubs found themselves in direct competition with each other for major honours and went on to share four league titles between 1964 and 1967. When Busby resigned his post in 1969, it marked the start of a United slump which helped pave the way for two decades of Liverpool dominance, including a further 11 First Division titles, a host of domestic cups and their first European trophies including their first four European Cup triumphs. Finally, under Alex Ferguson in 1992, United ended their 26-year top-flight title drought. Almost immediately the roles were reversed and United would go on to snaffle a further 13 titles, along with their own haul of domestic cups and three European trophies under Ferguson, allowing the now knighted Sir Alex to claim success in his famously stated objective to "knock them off their fucking perch".[5]

As the clubs fought for supremacy on the pitch, the off-field rivalry bubbled along, with its effect spilling from the terraces and galvanising the players which in turn heightened the off-field rivalry. In the immediate aftermath of the 1996 FA Cup Final, a Liverpool fan spat at Eric Cantona and threw a punch at Alex Ferguson as the victorious Manchester United side climbed the famous Wembley steps to collect the trophy.[6] A 2006 FA Cup tie between the sides at Anfield featured a variety of objects thrown at United fans by Liverpool supporters, including human excrement.[7] United full-back Gary Neville would later state: "I can't stand Liverpool, I can't stand the people, I can't

[5] Taylor. D, 2011, 'The greatest challenge of Sir Alex Ferguson's career is almost over', The Guardian

[6] Taylor. D, 2006, 'He hates scousers, scousers hate him, The Guardian

[7] ESPN, 2006, 'Anfield admits excrement thrown at United fans'

stand anything to do with them,"[8] shortly before earning himself a two-match ban for celebrating Rio Ferdinand's late Old Trafford winner by running towards the Liverpool fans enthusiastically kissing the United badge. United fans rewarded Neville with his own chant:

> **"Gary Neville is a red,**
> **Is a red,**
> **Is a red,**
> **Gary Neville is a red,**
> **He hates scousers"**

Journalist Brian Reade summed up how unfriendly things had become when the two sides met for an FA Cup semi-final in 1985 saying: "There were re-enactments of medieval pitched battles in the streets, a Stanley knife exhibition in Stanley Park and, on the terraces, the kind of tribal exchanges you see in Gaza on a bad day".[9] The exchanges described by Reade, included the emergence of one of the most infamous chants in English football, which marked the escalating levels of vitriol between fans.

The new chant mocked the victims of the Munich air disaster which happened almost three decades earlier when Flight 609, which was carrying the Manchester United squad back from a European Cup tie in Belgrade, crashed on an icy runway in Germany, claiming the lives of 23 people, including eight players, three staff, two crew, a travel agent, a fan and eight journalists. Having cut-short the lives of some of English football's brightest talents, the Munich crash was national headline news and the country united in sympathy around United. Footballing rivalries were forgotten and clubs, including Liverpool, offered to loan United players to help them rebuild.[10] When Liverpool hosted Charlton at Anfield shortly after the crash, the *Liverpool Daily Post* reported: "Men's minds were very much still on the Munich tragedy and the hush which descended on this so boisterous ground

[8]   Taylor. D, 2011, 'The greatest challenge of Sir Alex Ferguson's career is almost over', The Guardian

[9]   Reade. B, 1985, 'Manchester United 2-2 Liverpool match report', The Mirror

[10] Graves. S, 2016, 'Liverpool and Man United; the times the teams and fans put rivalry aside', Liverpool Echo

when the black arm-banded players lined up for two minutes' silence was almost uncanny".[11]

However, almost 30 years later this sympathy had evaporated in the minds of some on Merseyside and as fans gathered in Stanley Park, ahead of the semi-final being held at Liverpool's city neighbours Goodison Park home, among the "medieval pitched battles" described by Reade, Liverpool's fans had stopped singing Beatles hits and had a new song:

> *"Who's that lying on the runway?*
> *Who's that dying in the snow?*
> *It's Matt Busby and his boys,*
> *Making all the fucking noise,*
> *'Cos they couldn't get the plane to go"*

Which was often followed up with the simpler:

> *"Munich – 58,*
> *Munich, Munich – 58"*

Both chants celebrated the tragic deaths of a United team, wiped out as it approached its prime and were often accompanied with those singing stretching their arms out to their sides and rocking from side-to-side in a childlike playground game of mimicking aeroplanes. The 'Munich 58' chant was also the inspiration for a number of banners and graffitied slogans which began to appear at Liverpool games and around the city. The crash's relevance to Liverpool, the club or the city, was negligible beyond the club's initial offer to loan players and all those years later was all-but non-existent, meaning the only purpose of the chants was to cause distress to the opposition in what Liverpool fan Gareth Roberts termed "a form of currency in the competition to aggravate, upset and taunt".[12]

Liverpool fans were far from alone in weaponising chants and using death as the ammunition. While a section of Liverpool fans

---

[11] *Roberts. G, 2016, 'Hate, Heysel, Hillsborough and Munich', The Anfield Wrap*

[12] *Roberts. G, 2016, 'Hate, Heysel, Hillsborough and Munich', The Anfield Wrap, 9 March 2016*

sung about Munich, United fans had a chant of their own;

"Shankly – 81,
Shankly, Shankly – 81"

Which took the tune of Liverpool's 'Munich 58' chant, and instead celebrated the death of Liverpool's iconic manager four years earlier.[13]

On 29 May 1985, just over a month after the FA Cup semi-final featuring songs about Munich and Shankly, and with football hooliganism now rife, Liverpool themselves were involved in a tragedy when they met Juventus in the European Cup Final. The showpiece event was held at Heysel Stadium, in the Belgian city of Brussels. As a neutral venue, the plan was to segregate fans, with opposing supporters located at either end of the ground, separated by neutral areas and UEFA dignitaries. However, while Juventus fans were allocated three blocks at one end, Liverpool's allocation was only two blocks, with the third block at the Liverpool end being designated neutral and named 'Block Z'. Separating the Liverpool fans from those in the neutral Block Z was an inadequate wire fence patrolled by a threadbare police force that had already worked overtime that week supervising a state visit from the Pope. Surrounding it all was a crumbling cinder block wall, that ticketless fans were able to literally kick holes in, in order to gain access to the ground.[14] Journalist Ed Vulliamy who was at the game for Granada TV described security as "non-existent", adding: "UEFA's choice of a crumbling stadium was woeful, as was its releasing a third of the tickets at the Liverpool end for "neutral" football fans to buy in Belgium. They were snapped up by tour operators who then sold them to Juventus fans, mostly families, across central and southern Italy; the club's Ultras were at the other, far, end and played no part in the horror".[15]

Around an hour before kick-off, a steady barrage of missiles readily available from the lumps of concrete which were scattered across the crumbling terrace were exchanged between the adjacent blocks. This

[13] Roberts. G, 2016, 'Hate, Heysel, Hillsborough and Munich', The Anfield Wrap, 9 March 2016

[14] Digby. A, 2015, 'Juventus', Ockley Books, Huddersfield, p56

[15] Vulliamy. E, 2015, 'Heysel stadium disaster', The Guardian, 27 May 2015

became a riotous charge as Liverpool hooligans steamed into the groups of Juventus fans gathered next to them in Block Z. Photos show a "Munich – 58" banner among Liverpool's fans that evening. As fans fled the violence many were crushed to death against one of the cinder block perimeter walls, which ultimately collapsed under the pressure. Among the 39-people killed were 32 Italians, four Belgians, two French fans and one from Northern Ireland. A further 600 were injured.[16]

Liverpool fans were widely blamed for the tragedy and 14 went on to be found guilty of manslaughter and jailed for three years. While an investigation did concede that some culpability lay with the authorities—Captain Johan Mahieu, the police officer who was responsible for Block Z and Albert Roosens, the former general sec-retary of the Belgian Football Association, were both given suspended sentences[17] and there was heavy criticism of the crumbling state of the stadium—the hooligan-led violence resulted in all English football clubs being banned from playing in Europe for five years.[18] Back home the press saw the opportunity to continue their over-blown, exaggerated coverage of hooliganism in line with the right-wing ideology of the day, which painted all football fans as thugs. In the immediate after-math, David Miller felt it appropriate to write in *The Times*: "The facts are as yet imprecise, but there is grounding for belief that the quite clearly organised assault by alleged Liverpool supporters in the Heysel Stadium had financial and ideological backing from left-wing agencies outside Britain".[19]

While the press saw Heysel as a chance to sensationalise, United fans saw it as a chance for revenge for Liverpool's Munich chant and immediately began to mock what happened with chants of their own including;

[16] Mullen. T, 2015, 'Heysel disaster: English football's forgotten tragedy?', BBC, 29 May 2015

[17] Shennan. P, 2015, 'Heysel 30 years on', Liverpool Echo, 23 May 2015

[18] Mullen. T, 2015, 'Heysel disaster: English football's forgotten tragedy?', BBC, 29 May 2015

[19] Edwards. R, 2015, 'The worst five months in English football', FourFourTwo, 14 January 2015

"1, 2, 3, 4, 5, 6, 7, 8, 9, 10, 11, 12, 13, 14, 15, 16, 17, 18, 19, 20, 21,
22, 23, 24, 25, 26, 27, 28, 29, 30, 31, 32, 33, 34, 35, 36, 37, 38, 39,
Singing 39 Italians can't be wrong (Murderers),
Singing 39 Italians can't be wrong (Murderers),
Singing 39 Italians,
39 Italians,
39 Italians can't be wrong (Murderers)."

And simply:

"Murderers,
Murderers."

Four years later, on 15 April 1989 Liverpool would again experience tragedy at Sheffield Wednesday's Hillsborough stadium. Whereas violence had played a part at Heysel, it was not a factor in Sheffield. However, the undeniable backdrop of hooliganism coupled with the authorities' dim view of football fans were undoubtedly contributing factors.

As with Heysel, the authority's choice of venue was also to play a key role. Hillsborough was chosen despite it being the scene of a number of near-disastrous crushes, including one in 1981 in a game between Tottenham Hotspur and Wolves which led to several fans incurring broken arms and legs[20] and another just 12 months earlier, also between Liverpool and Nottingham Forest in the 1988 semi-final. Despite these incidents, and as emerged afterwards the fact that Hillsborough no longer held a valid safety certificate[21] it was again chosen to host the FA Cup semi-final. If that was the first mistake to be made, a number of others were soon to follow.

As they were at Heysel, Liverpool were allocated the smaller end of the stadium, on Leppings Lane. Due to the size of their following, the Football Association requested that the ends be swapped so that Liverpool fans would be housed in the larger Spion Kop which could

----

[20] *Lord Justice Taylor, 1990, 'The Hillsborough Stadium Disaster', Home Office, London, p21*

[21] *Ross. S, 2012, 'David Bernstein makes unreserved apology for Hillsborough disaster', Metro, 13 September 2012*

hold 21,000, over double the number in Leppings Lane. However, this was rejected by Chief Supt Brian Mole, who wanted the same arrangements from the year previously to be made as this allowed for easier segregation of fans outside the ground, due to the respective transport links between Nottingham in the south, Liverpool in the north and Sheffield in the middle. The key consideration for the authorities' decision-making was to keep the fans as far apart as possible and thus prevent any violent disorder.

Then, 19 days before the semi-final South Yorkshire police underwent a personnel reshuffle in response to a prank played on a fellow South Yorkshire police officer who colleagues felt was making too many radio distress calls. To teach the officer a lesson, those colleagues staged a fake kidnapping. On learning of the incident and after conducting an inquiry Chief Constable Peter Wright sacked four officers and disciplined four others. Shortly afterwards, Wright also removed the experienced Chief Supt Mole from his position overseeing the semi-final, but claimed this wasn't linked to the earlier prank, rather it was for "career development reasons". Officers in Mole's 'F' Division were unconvinced, and no explanation was offered for why the move was so sudden. In Mole's place, Wright appointed David Duckenfield, who had never commanded any fixture at Hillsborough and hadn't even been on-duty at the ground in over a decade.

Due to the haste of the operational reshuffle, and despite Mole having been responsible for arranging distribution of police personnel during the semi-final, he gave no handover to Duckenfield. Mole simply cleared his desk and left. Duckenfield has since admitted he arrived at the game with no knowledge of the crushes that had developed in 1981 or 1988. He also admitted to no knowledge of the geographical bottle-neck of the Leppings Lane end, nor the way his predecessor had managed the fans' approach to the turnstiles to mitigate it. Furthermore, he has admitted to having had no idea that the 10,100 Liverpool fans with tickets for that end would all need to enter through just seven turnstiles. Nor did Duckenfield know that all seven turnstiles opened into a small, walled enclosure, which, as well as two, less-obvious routes into the ground, included a tunnel through which the pitch could be glimpsed and led into two small fenced-in "pens", numbered 3 and 4, directly behind the goal. Finally, he did not even know that it was the police who were responsible for monitoring when those pens were approaching their safe operating capacity, nor that the police had developed a tactic in response to this known issue, by closing off the most obvious tunnel once the pens were full, known as the 'Freeman tactic' after the police officer who had first implemented it.[22]

Duckenfield assigned Supt Roger Marshall, another officer new to his role, to police fans arriving at Leppings Lane. Marshall told the 2016 inquests he had no plan to filter fans through the natural bottleneck and limited his activities to some random ticket checks and watching out for drunkenness. Marshall has since said that with hindsight he now feels there was a problem as early as 2:15pm and within 20 minutes the police had completely lost control of the situation. At 2:48pm, Marshall reported there was a dangerous crush outside the Leppings Lane turnstiles and requested Exit Gate C be opened to help alleviate it. Four minutes later Duckenfield assented, despite telling the inquests he'd given "no thought" to where the people escaping the crush outside would go. About 2,000 people entered Gate C and the majority, naturally, headed straight down the tunnel towards the pitch. 96 people were killed in the crush. Of those, 30, were still outside the ground at 14:52, entered Gate C and were crushed to death within 15 minutes. Survivors of the resultant crush recounted the horror of an increasing vice-like grip that compacted them to the point that arms and legs fractured, ribs cracked, mouths filled with vomit, bladders and bowels involuntarily emptied and chests no longer had the room to expand to enable people to take a breath in.[23]

Within minutes of the gate being opened and with people still being crushed to death in the pens below them, the FA Secretary Graham Kelly went to the police control room which overlooked the Leppings Lane terraces to find out from Duckenfield what was happening. Duckenfield told Kelly a lie that would endure: Liverpool

[22]   Conn. D, 2016, 'Hillsborough disaster; deadly mistake and lies that lasted decades', The Guardian, 26 April 2016

[23]   Conn. D, 2016, 'Hillsborough disaster; deadly mistake and lies that lasted decades', The Guardian, 26 April 2016

fans had forced the gate.[24] The lie made it to the BBC's commentary team covering the game who reported both on television and radio "unconfirmed reports of a broken-down door", by 4:30pm Alan Green told BBC Radio 2 listeners that police had said a gate was forced.[25]

A narrative was being put together which shifted the blame for the disaster from the police onto the fans. Just before 6pm, police inspector Gordon Sykes sent an official force photographer outside to take photos of the rubbish left on Leppings Lane, to show whether or not Liverpool fans had been drunk. Photographs showed the bins outside the Leppings Lane end, which 24,000 Liverpool supporters had passed, about a third full mostly of soft drinks cans including Vimto, Sprite and Coke, with a few beer bottles or cans.[26] Nonetheless the coroner Dr Stefan Popper ordered blood samples to be taken from all the victims, including the youngest victim ten-year-old Jon-Paul Gilhooley and tested for alcohol.[27]

Chief Constable Wright opened his fact-finding meeting in their Niagara Sports and Social Club at 9am the day after the disaster and, immediately exonerating his force, with the minutes recording him saying; "I'm not in the business of questioning decisions. You did a good job". He moved on to discuss how the story of "drunken, marauding fans" would be got out, saying the force could not do it too publicly because it had to respond "professionally". But, he said, the "animalistic" behaviour of fans would emerge. The minutes from that meeting also record a conversation with a group including Duckenfield and all senior officers responsible for the match, who told Wright stories which apportioned blame to the fans, including that they were not inside the ground by 2.30pm because there were "hordes of people drinking" and that Liverpool's fans were "not normal". Nobody mentioned the lack of measures to control fans moving into the Leppings Lane bottleneck or the

[24] *Conn. D, 2015, 'Hillsborough officer admits he lied about crucial order to open exit gate', The Guardian, 11 March 2015*

[25] *Conn. D, 2016, 'Hillsborough disaster; deadly mistake and lies that lasted decades', The Guardian, 26 April 2016*

[26] *Conn. D, 2016, 'Hillsborough disaster; deadly mistake and lies that lasted decades', The Guardian, 26 April 2016*

[27] *Conn. D, 2016, 'Hillsborough disaster; deadly mistake and lies that lasted decades', The Guardian, 26 April 2016*

police's failure to close the tunnel prior to Gate C being ordered open. Nobody, Duckenfield included, accepted any responsibility for what had happened. Later that same day, Margaret Thatcher and her press secretary, Bernard Ingham, visited Hillsborough, where they were met by Wright who briefed them and took them on a tour of the stadium. In a letter in 1996 Ingham said of Hillsborough that he "learned on the day" the disaster was caused by a "tanked-up mob",[28] something for which he has subsequently refused to apologise.

The press, primed by Heysel four years earlier, were ready to lap up the lie and four days later *The Sun* published their infamous front page "The Truth" which alleged that Liverpool fans had pickpocketed the dead, urinated on police officers and beat them up as they gave people CPR. It quoted one "furious policeman" claiming: "As we struggled in appalling conditions to save lives, fans standing further up the terrace were openly urinating on us and the bodies of the dead". It also quoted Sheffield's Conservative MP Irvine Patrick as revealing the blouse of one young female victim had risen above her breasts and that as an officer tried to revive her, a "mob" had shouted; "Throw her up here and we will fuck her".[29] None of it was true and it would emerge at the inquests 27 years later that not only had fans not pickpocketed the dead, the police had always had evidence that it was untrue, having made routine logs of all the cash and other property found on each person.[30]

When he published his final report in January 1990, Lord Justice Taylor attempted to dispel the myths that had been spread, concluding that the main cause of the tragedy was "a failure of police control".[31] The damage was done however and a public perception of violent, out-of-control Liverpool fans, killing their

---

[28] Conn. D, 2016, 'Hillsborough disaster; deadly mistake and lies that lasted decades', The Guardian, 26 April 2016

[29] Gibson. O, 2004, 'What the Sun said 15 years ago', The Guardian, 7 July 2004

[30] Conn. D, 2016, 'Hillsborough disaster; deadly mistake and lies that lasted decades', The Guardian, 26 April 2016

[31] Press Association, 2012, 'David Cameron's Hillsborough statement in full', The Independent, 12 September 2012

own was established. Tellingly, neither *The Sun* or *The Times* covered the inquest which finally exonerated the fans in 2016.[32]

Not long after the disaster, Manchester United fans picked up the narrative the press had set and adapted Liverpool's Munich chant, to mock Hillsborough;

> *"Who's that choking on their vomit?*
> *Who's that turning blue?*
> *It's a Scouser and his mates,*
> *Crushed by the Hillsborough gates,*
> *Well, they won't be singing Munich anymore"*

Alongside the "choking" chant, United fans were frequently seen making choking gestures or mimicking crushed faces.[33] Then to cement the point, that in United's view the Liverpool fans deserved Hillsborough chants to be directed at them, was frequently followed with;

> *"Where's your famous Munich song,*
> *Where's your famous,*
> *Where's your famous Munich song?"*

United's Hillsborough chant in turn helped some Liverpool fans legitimise their own continued referencing of the Munich Air Crash, as the flow of chants took on what Liverpool fan Gareth Roberts termed "tragedy tennis"[34] illustrated by Liverpool fans' chanting;

> *"Justice, for the 96,*
> *Justice, for the 96"*

Which United fans follow with;

> *"Justice, for the 39,*
> *Justice, for the 39"*

---

[32] *BBC, 2016, 'Hillsborough; Times admits front page mistake', BBC, 27 April 2016*

[33] *Walsh. K, 2012, 'Mindless few must not shift focus for justice', ESPN, 22 September 2012*

[34] *Roberts. G, 2017, 'To Manchester From Liverpool With Love', The Anfield Wrap, 24 May 2017*

Or this from a 2016 Europa League tie that saw one match report of the game including references to two chants, with Liverpool fans singing:

> **"Fergie's right,**
> **Your fans are shite"**

To which the United section responded:

> **"The Sun was right,**
> **You're murderers".**[35]

Then, after United clinched their third European Cup in 2008 their fans adopted a chant of:

> **"We've won it three times,**
> **We've won it three times,**
> **Without killing anyone,**
> **We've won it three times"**

Which is interesting in its conflicting moral standpoint of both celebrating on-field success and the deaths of 39 people, by implying Liverpool's then-five European titles were worth less than United's three by virtue of what happened at Heysel.

The furious, and justifiable response to *The Sun's* 'The Truth' article and ongoing campaign for justice, created an additional subject for opposition chants which remains controversial and open to different interpretations. The tune is The Beach Boys' 1966 cover of Caribbean folk song, 'Sloop John B', which despite only reaching number two in the UK charts, provides the riff for countless chants, which can still be heard not just Old Trafford but at grounds across England, three decades on:

---

[35] *Goal.com, 2016, 'Man United fans sing 'murderers' chants at Anfield', Goal.com, 10 March 2016*

"It's never your fault,
It's never your fault,
Always the victims,
It's never your fault"

'Always the victims' remained a staple sound at Liverpool games throughout the 1990s and 2000s, but hit the headlines again in 2012 when, in the week a report came out stating Liverpool fans were absolutely not to blame for the deaths at Hillsborough, United fans were heard chanting *'Always the victims'* during their game against Wigan Athletic. The chant was picked up by a number of media outlets including the BBC[36] and *The Daily Express*,[37] with both linking it to Hillsborough.

The media furore quickly led to the official Manchester United Supporters Trust releasing a statement claiming the chant did not refer to Hillsborough, stating; "Following this week's developments and release of revelatory information on the Hillsborough tragedy, the Manchester United Supporters Trust wishes to make it absolutely clear that just as we condemn chants mocking the Munich air disaster we also condemn any chants relating to Hillsborough or indeed any other human tragedy. We did hear the usual anti-Liverpool chants at the match today, but we're pleased to say, despite some reports to the contrary, there was nothing that was specifically referencing Hillsborough. Any attempt to suggest otherwise is irresponsible given the forthcoming fixture between the clubs".[38] The claim from United fans was that, on this occasion, the chant was not about Hillsborough, but was instead about Liverpool's striker Luis Suarez, who had recently been banned for racially abusing Manchester United player Patrice Evra. Liverpool had first appealed the ban and then players had controversially worn t-shirts in support of their star player.

A United fanzine ran a piece which clarified what they believed the chant was about, which followed the same line as the official

---

[36] Smith. B, 2012, 'Man United deplore fans' anti-Liverpool chanting', BBC, 15 September 2012

[37] Dennis. M, 2012, 'Manchester United fans mock Hillsborough tragedy on day of shame', The Express, 17 September 2012

[38] Smith. B, 2012, 'Man United deplore fans' anti-Liverpool chanting', BBC, 15 September 2012

Supporters Trust and listed Luis Suarez; Michael Shields, a Liverpool fan arrested for the attempted murder of a Bulgarian man in 2005 while celebrating Liverpool's Champions League victory and who the club very publicly backed; Heysel, and; the stereotypical perception of the Liverpudlian character. The article argued that "While it was Liverpool's reaction to Suarez's guilt that lead to the creation of the song, there are deeper meanings behind it. It's likely that some people singing it are purely referring to Suarez but I'd guess the vast majority are referring to the nature of Scousers in general. The stereotype being that they are a whining, grief-hungry bunch of victims, who revel in self-pity and aren't prepared to take responsibility for their own actions." The piece went on to admit that while that may have been their reason for singing it, other interpretations were not hard to fathom:

"However, there seem to be some fans and sections of the press that want the chant to be about Hillsborough. Rival fans want a stick to beat United with and the papers want to have a tasty story to write about. They have pointed to the words 'always' and 'never' which certainly suggest that the chant, while first sung because of Suarez, isn't just about him.

"Of course, we have some idiots who chant about Hillsborough and they bring shame on the club, but to suggest that 1,000s of us are chanting about Hillsborough every game, and have been doing for almost a year, is beyond ridiculous. All clubs have an idiotic minority but this song is sung *en masse* by people who wouldn't ever consider using Hillsborough as a tool to wind up a rival. Yes, we hate Scousers, but Hillsborough was about sons, daughters, mothers and fathers, it was about people, not Liverpool FC, and if you can't differentiate between the deaths of human beings and the deaths of Liverpool fans, thinking one is worthy of ridicule and mocking, there is something very wrong with you. The press have told us the song is about Hillsborough, not even attempting to provide a rational argument concerning what else it could be about. I am now being told by the papers that when I've sung that song for months, what I have actually been singing about is Hillsborough. How on earth can out-of-touch journalists, who have no clue about the ill-feeling between rival fans, determine what I am singing about, what you are singing about? They know us better than we know ourselves, apparently.

"Likewise, I'm not going to make the same mistake of saying that every single United fan who sings that song is coming from the same state of mind as me. I can't categorically say there aren't some United fans, that idiotic minority, that may sing the song with thoughts of Hillsborough in mind. For that reason, it was stupid for fans to sing it on Saturday, as even though your intention might not be to mock Hillsborough, it is easy to draw conclusions that singing *it's never your fault* is in direct reference to what Liverpool fans have been saying about what happened in Sheffield for the past 23 years. The fans who may sing the song with Hillsborough in mind would argue that Liverpool fans had been singing about Munich for years before Hillsborough happened".[39]

This explanation highlights how, in the competitively tribal nature of football, particularly when it comes to fierce rivalries, justifications can be sought and reasons can be given that excuse certain types of behaviour, even when the chant itself is recognised as potentially problematic and easy to misconstrue. Sportswriter Joel Rabinowitz eloquently sums up the issue with the fanzine's position saying; "Let's be clear on this. The connotations of this chant are quite obviously linked to Hillsborough. If not Hillsborough, then what? Heysel? Another tragedy. The words clearly state *always* the *victims* and *never* your fault. Always; i.e. every single time. Anyone claiming otherwise is either naive, or just making excuses".[40]

For their part, Liverpool, led by former captain Jamie Carragher ultimately apologised for the way they handled the Suarez affair. In his role as a pundit for Sky Sports, Carragher was paired on screen with the victim of Suarez's remarks Patrice Evra for the Premier League game between Sheffield United and Arsenal and took the opportunity to publicly apologise to the Frenchman saying: "There is no doubt we made a massive mistake. I don't think everyone within Liverpool Football Club thought what we were doing was

[39] A United fanzine, 2012, 'It's never their fault', A United fanzine, 19 September 2012

[40] Rabinowitz. J, 2017, 'Always the victims; the real implications behind the chant', Medium.com, 9 September 2017

right but I do think as a football club, or you as a family, your first reaction is to support them even if you know that they are wrong, and that is wrong. I am not condoning it, but that is the first reaction. Apologies. We got it massively wrong".[41] Shortly afterwards Damien Comolli, Liverpool's Director of Football at the time of the incident, added his apology in an interview with *The Athletic* adding: "I regret pretty much everything, I regret our attitude, I regret the way we approached it. It was probably the worst moment of my career. The fact it was a player from Manchester United almost made things for us a thousand times worse than it should have been. We reacted in the worst way because it was Manchester United and the rivalry between the two clubs. I feel that we didn't look after Luis as we should have. We didn't give him the defence or the advice he should have got. Usually, I see the players as my children. It was the first time I felt I had really let a player down. We let the club down, we let football down probably as well because we acted in the wrong way".[42]

To this day, 'Always the victims' is still frequently aired at games involving Liverpool and as late as September 2018 *New York Times* journalist Rory Smith, while covering a Premier League game noted Chelsea fans singing it, seemingly in response to Liverpool fans appealing for a corner and then remonstrating with the officials that it wasn't given.[43] A month later an FA Vase game between non-league sides Hebburn Town and City of Liverpool FC ended in the police being called after Hebburn fans chanted about Hillsborough.[44]

It is not just Munich, Heysel and Hillsborough which provide an excuse to celebrate tragedy or wish death on their rivals however. For example, take this United chant, to the to the tune of 'Oh My Darling (Clementine)', which also lumps in their rivalry with Manchester City:

[41] BBC, 2019, 'Patrice Evra: Jamie Carragher apologises for Luis Suarez t-shirts',BBC, 22 October 2019

[42] Ornstein. D and Pearce. J, 2017, 'Damien Comolli: I was wrong on Suarez case but right about Henderson and Edwards', The Athletic, 27 February 2020

[43] Smith. R, 2018, '@RorySmith', Twitter, 29 September 2018

[44] Traynor. L, 2018, 'Hillsborough chants and bottles thrown as Liverpool football fans caught in brawl after match', Liverpool Echo, 14 October 2018

"Build a bonfire,
Build a bonfire,
Put the Scousers on the top,
Put City in the middle,
And burn the fucking lot"

A chant that United fans re-purposed in 2020 to protest against the ownership of the Glazer family and Chief Executive Ed Woodward, substituting "Scousers" for "Glazers" and "City" for Woodward.[45]

Tribalism through accentuated difference is, as we have seen, key to sustaining football fandom and identity, offering what journalist Tom Lamont calls "a good old-fashioned excuse to hate people", but noting that "for most people, [that hate is] contextual".[46] On the terraces, separated by a segregating line of stewards and police officers, our differences are accentuated, both physically and through chanting, verbally. Outside the stadium and away from the game, those differences are less pronounced. Although there is a sense that social media is changing this. The suggestion is that as fans' relationships with their clubs become more geographically distant, their expression of tribal identities is becoming increasingly pronounced away from matches, with journalist Daniel Storey going as far as to label some fans "the militant PR arms of their football clubs".[47] Storey argues, that:

"When such a low percentage of your support is able to attend matches in person regularly, they seek out other strategies to prove that they are a 'proper' fan (itself an entirely meaningless term). Becoming a crusader whose divine mission is to defend the good name of the club is their best option. They are not supporters of the club; they are the club and it is them. These supporters have become the militant PR arms of their football clubs. If it is criticised or accused of foul play, they cry that it—and so therefore they—are the subject of a witch hunt or agenda. If those accusations are proven, on comes a rush of

[45] Mitten. E, 2020, 'There's anger (rightly), there's singing for the Glazers to go and then there's asking for Woodward to die. It's not OK', The Athletic, 24 January 2020

[46] Lamont. T, 2009, 'The chant-makers of English football', The Guardian, 3 May 2009

[47] Storey. D, 2020, 'Somewhere along the line, tribalism warped fan behaviour and 'fandamentalism' became the norm', The I, 21 February 2020

angry whataboutery. Football support has changed; fandementalism has been established.

This is unique to football, at least amongst the list of things that simultaneously matter much and nothing at all. People don't rush out to defend their soap brand of choice, and there is not a group of Toffee Crisp Ultras who wage online war against those who prefer a Double Decker. Coffee and alcohol brands do not enjoy a fraction of the same loyalty, despite their addictive characteristics. If your favourite band was accused of deeply immoral acts, would you defend it to the hilt? The loyalty that football provokes extends far beyond any other cultural or commercial competitor.

The great irony here is that this rush by fans to defend their football clubs comes at a time when have never been treated worse by them or mattered less. It would be easier to understand if this extreme loyalty was a two-way street, clubs welcoming supporters inside their bubble, but this is not a tale of requited love. Elite clubs care about fans as consumers, not through some moral duty or honour, whatever the PR spiel might claim. Never have supporters been treated more emphatically as customers, yet never have they reacted more emphatically as if this is a relationship based on mutual respect. The more the game ties itself to hyper-capitalism, the more clubs will attract criticism. The more clubs attract criticism, the more these supporters feel that their belief system is being attacked. The more they feel their belief system is being attacked, the angrier they will get".[48]

Journalist Joe Humphreys adds another dimension on the prevalence of football fan tribalism and the hate it can engender, particularly when expressed through chanting arguing that: "it would be wrong to dismiss hatred in sport as relatively unimportant, let alone to dismiss it as the 'bit of fun' that many sports fans regard it to be. First, even if you never raise a fist in anger at a rival fan, your hatred may well encourage others to do so. There is such a crime as hate-speak, and football fans are profoundly guilty of it".[49]

The experience of the late columnist AA Gill at a match between

[48] Storey. D, 2020, 'Somewhere along the line, tribalism warped fan behaviour and 'fandamentalism' became the norm', The I, 21 February 2020

[49] Humphreys. J, 2008, 'Foul Play', Icon Books, Cambridge, p128

Tottenham and London rivals Chelsea, shows just how ugly tribal football chanting can be. The journalist wrote: "I sat in the terraces at Chelsea and heard the crowd make a hissing sound as the two teams ran onto the pitch. 'Yids,' my neighbour said helpfully, 'they're North London, Jewish, and, well, it's the noise of the gas going into the ovens isn't it?' It was so shocking, so astonishingly surreally nothing to do with football, that I laughed".[50]

Gill's experience, coupled with Humphrey's argument that football fans are guilty of the crime of "hate-speak" prompts an additional layer of complexity, which is whether 'hate' is a necessary ingredient because some clubs create and maintain identities that are deeply rooted and defined by the things they hate and even how they hate those things. In the case of Liverpool and Manchester United and most local derbies, without some needle the spectacle would be much poorer. Liverpool fan Gareth Roberts sums up the cause-effect relationship at play: "All of [the hate] is played out in the context of a football match. None of it plays out on a visit to the Trafford Centre. Or a walk around the Albert Dock. Fans will travel both ways every day to go to work; back to life, back to reality. The tribal nature of the fixtures is a joy when it doesn't venture into behaviour that prompts a wince. It's why we get a faster pace, a louder crowd and a better spectacle. There's more riding on it. It matters. It's no ordinary game. The rivalry can be enjoyed without the terrace tragedy tennis played across an expanse of grass in Liverpool or Manchester. Alex Ferguson is hated by Liverpool fans for wanting to knock us off our 'fucking perch'. As tough as it is to take, he did it. And he did it fuelled by anger. Fuelled by hate but the right kind of hate".[51]

Germany provides a potential example of the 'right kind of hate' through Hamburg-based FC St Pauli, the club mentioned previously that boasts the largest percentage of female fans and whose identity is constructed around their, sometimes forceful and occasionally violent, opposition to fascism and right-wing politics. As fan Sven Brux told *The Guardian* "We are football fans with [socialist] political thinking, who don't forget our politics when we go into the football ground.

[50]   *Gill. AA, 2005, 'The Angry Island', 2005, Orion Books, London, p113*

[51]   *Roberts. G, 2016, 'Hate, Heysel, Hillsborough and Munich', The Anfield Wrap, 9 March 2016*

Even in the football ground we are against racists, commercialism and those sort of things".[52] Official club merchandise includes t-shirts bearing the slogan "Love St Pauli – Hate fascism", while their Millerntor-Stadion home is decorated with murals painted by the fans themselves, including one which spells out that the Millerntor is: "No place for – homophobia, fascism, sexism, racism", in five-foot-high letters, sentiments that paradoxically express a hatred of hate itself. In the same vein St Pauli were the first club in Europe to officially ban racist chants and Nazi banners[53] and in 2014 the club made official complaints to the German Football Association after a mural reading "No football for fascists" at their Millerntor home was covered up during a national team training session at the ground.[54]

This culture comes from the club's fans, whose chants range from the simple:

"Anti-fascism,
Anti-fascism"

to the more complex and on-field success-linked;

"Never again fascism,
Never again war,
Never again the Third Division"[55]

The FC St Pauli example aside, hate had colonised the terraces, laying down roots that would nurture the fruits of discontent: fear, blame and fascism.

[52] Theroux. M and Fernando.S, 2011, 'St Pauli: a socialist football club in Hamburg's red light district', The Guardian, 16 March 2011

[53] Davidson. N, 2014, 'Pirates, Punks and Politics', SportsBooks, York, p103

[54] Uersfeld. S, 2014, 'DFB under fire for censoring stadium', ESPN Website, 13 May 2014

[55] Davidson. N, 2014, 'Pirates, Punks and Politics', SportsBooks, York, p8-103

6. RACISM

'THERE AIN'T NO BLACK IN THE UNION JACK'

As hate was thrusting its roots deep into English football's crumbling terraces, the country was suffering from economic turmoil and the disintegration of traditional ideas about community. So, English football grounds became a window through which society's ills were broadcast to the world.

When Margaret Thatcher won the Conservative party a majority in May 1979 her political mandate was to end a decade of economic decline. Inflation rates had been high since the mid-1970s on the back of nine million days lost to strike action in 1974 and the oil crisis which had led to the three-day week a year earlier.[1] On entering office Thatcher made it clear where she thought the problem lay, and set about dismantling the state, cutting benefits and squeezing public services. The first line of her first public spending White Paper declared: "Public expenditure is at the heart of Britain's present economic difficulties".

Malcolm Dean, a journalist and former special adviser to the Secretary of State for Health and Social Security, described the situation: "From the very beginning of the 18 years of Conservative rule the poor were under the cosh. No developed state, with the exception of New Zealand, suffered such a brutal widening of inequality. In 1979 the post-tax income of the top 10% of the population was five times that of the bottom 10%; by 1997 it had doubled to ten times as much. [...] Child poverty more than doubled".[2]

As the rich got richer, the poor got poorer, or as political journalist Andrew Marr explains: "Two Britains emerged in the 1980s. The rich got richer but the bottom 10% saw their incomes fall by about 17%. A lot of people fell through the cracks. Once Britain had prided itself on not seeing people sleeping on the streets or begging. Not anymore".[3]

Into this economic tinderbox, Thatcher tossed a lit match. As leader of the Conservative party Thatcher took to the television to point the finger of blame for the suffering of the nation: "If we [go] on as we

[1] Sofat. A, 2012, '1970s Britain', The Telegraph, 10 July 2012

[2] Dean. M 2013, 'Margaret Thatcher's policies hit the poor hardest', The Guardian, 9 April 2013

[3] Marr. A 2009, 'A History of Modern Britain, Pan Macmillan, London, p207

are then by the end of the century there would be four million people of the new Commonwealth or Pakistan here. Now, that is an awful lot and I think it means that people are really rather afraid that this country might be rather swamped by people with a different culture. The British character has done so much for democracy, for law and done so much throughout the world that if there is any fear that it might be swamped, people are going to react and be rather hostile to those coming in".[4]

After taking office, her government had the support of the traditionally right-leaning newspapers. In a barrage of fictional stories the same tactics used to obfuscate after both Heysel and Hillsborough were unleashed, designed to stir up racial tensions. In an early example of fake news, the media began reporting fictional accounts of people no longer being able to ask for a 'black coffee' or sing 'Baa Baa Black sheep' and railed against the removal of Tufty the squirrel from a Lambeth road safety campaign.[5] All of which made for titillating copy, sold newspapers, and served to stoke the fires of division still further.

Faced with economic hardship and a negative perception of the rise in multiculturalism, sections of young British men felt powerless. Football terraces offered an unlikely source of solace in which their voice was amplified, and with it a new sense of power and strength was discovered. Writer Pete Miles describes the terraces as: "a magnet of diaspora often marginalised, by political belief, appearance and lifestyle. From often discordant solitary everyday lives, joining an ultras group can bring lasting friendship, camaraderie and a sense of purpose [including but not limited to] large ursine males who use the match to vent their anger or aggression".[6] Or as one Portsmouth fan told *Copa 90*: "You have to put football violence against the backdrop of society at that time. Depravation. 1979. Thatcher's Britain. People had no jobs. There was nothing for youth culture. You could suddenly be a part of something [and] go away to towns you'd never been to".[7]

4   *Bourne. J 2013, 'May we bring harmony', Institute of Race Relations, 11 April 2013*

5   *Bourne. J 2013, 'May we bring harmony', Institute of Race Relations, 11 April 2013*

6   *Miles. P, 2016, 'Beyond the Turnstiles', Ockley Books, Huddersfield, Yorkshire, p23*

7   *Mengem. E, 2019, 'My City could beat up your city', Copa 90,*

In football, in which there is an increasing feeling of disloyalty as clubs change hands with growing frequency and star players kiss the badge one week then demand a transfer the next, the identity these groups can provide, the friendships and a yearning for loyalty, create an environment in which ultra groups are the one constant. As the fanzine *The Gentleman Ultra* notes: "In a rootless world, [the ultras] offer a sense of belonging".[8]

As early as 1976 studies were being conducted into how individuals behave differently within the safety of an amorphous mass of bodies because of the anonymity afforded. Sociologist Richard Sennett observed: "crowds are the mode in which the most venal passions of man are most spontaneously expressed—the crowd is man the animal let off the leash".[9]

Anonymity, group dynamics, and surrounding oneself with one's footballing tribe, was, and remains, infectious. In the increasingly fractured world of Thatcher's Britain, the terraces could sweep up even the most passive of its members. The inherent power of crowds and the atmosphere within them, to affect and influence individuals within them led University of St. Andrews Psychology professor Stephen Reicher to describe crowds as: "the elephant man of the social sciences". Introducing his study of crowd dynamics, he went on: "They are viewed as something strange, something pathological, something monstrous." Reicher adds that the effect of crowds makes us more aware of some aspects of our individual identity, such as race, and this can exacerbate their appeal to the far-right: "Once individual identity, and the capability to control behaviour disappears, crowd members become subject to contagion. That is, they are unable to resist any passing idea or, more particularly and because the intellect is all but obliterated, any passing emotion. Contagion, however, is but an effect of suggestibility. The ideas and emotions which sweep unhindered through the crowd derive primarily from the 'racial unconscious', which underlies our conscious personality and which is revealed when the conscious personality is swept way. Hence the

[8]   Hodges-Ramon. L, Girard. W and Morris. N, 2018, 'A culture of violence; How political and social turmoil gave rise to Rome's radical ultras', The Gentleman Ultra, 1 May 2018

[9]   Sennett. R, 1976, 'The Fall of Public Man', Penguin Books, London, p299

primitivism of that unconscious is reflected in the character of crowd behaviour".[10]

Football crowds are by their nature tribal, competitive and anonymous and thus are the perfect environment for this primal unleashing of the repressed urges within members of society. By 1981 the idea that football grounds and their crowded terraces were a place people could go to release the pent-up aggression accrued during the course of a working week, was being recognised subconsciously by attendees and academically by anthropologists.

Desmond Morris highlights the specific role that attending a match can have for those in attendance: "the match is a special kind of therapy, rather like visiting a public 'rage room'".[11] As one German fan told a 2008 survey on passion in football: "A football match is a sort of moment of giving vent to one's feelings, as in sport where one releases one's aggressiveness, bitterness or frustration of the previous week, being an active supporter allows one to 'empty oneself' by singing, clapping or waving a flag".[12] As author Nick Hornby found, this venting of pent-up emotion is liberating: "Who wants to be stuck with who they are the whole time? I for one wanted time out from being a jug-eared, bespectacled, suburban twerp once in a while".[13] The same thing was described by author AA Gill: "the whole ghastly secret, vile, dark laundry basket of young Englishmen's fears, prejudices and braggadocio is tipped out under the floodlights and bellowed at the top of their voices. It's hideous and invigorating and group therapy,"[14] while the Social Issues Research Centre echoed the same virus-like language of Reicher to describe crowded stadiums: "The passions and emotions associated with the game itself spread like a kind of irresistible contagion through the stands and terraces".[15]

As fans began to use tragedies as the lyrical content of abusive

[10] *Reicher. S, 2018, 'The Psychology of Crowd Dynamics', University of St Andrews, Fife, Retrieved 12 October 2018*

[11] *Morris. D, 1981, 'The Soccer Tribe', Jonathan Cape Publishing, London, p236*

[12] *Social Issues Research Centre, 2008, 'Football Passions', Social Research Centre, London, p7*

[13] *Hornby. N, 1996, 'Fever Pitch', Indigo, London, p54*

[14] *Gill. A.A, 2005, 'The Angry Island', Orion Books, London, p113*

[15] *Social Issues Research Centre, 2008, 'Football Passions', Social Research Centre, London, p12*

chants aimed at rival fans, the expressions of hate for players, both rival and otherwise, became increasingly personal. Fuelled by a surge of extreme right-wing supporter groups, including the BNP and National Front, who used the easy access to large groups of young men as recruitment areas, racism and homophobia become commonplace on 1980s terraces, more than a decade on from the 1965 Race Relations Act set-up to counteract racism across UK society.

The links between football and fascism became so intertwined that legendary manager Brian Clough was moved to join forces with the Sex Pistols front man John Lydon in an anti-fascist campaign, including a banner reading "NF = No Future".[16] By 1993 the scale of this far-right infiltration of football terraces began to be laid bare. That year a report by *The Independent's* Tim Kelsey spoke about how British neo-Nazi organisations were continuing to form ever-closer links with gangs of football hooligans. By this point these links were so well established that American far-right groups, who used images of black and Jewish people as shooting range targets, invited some hooligan groups to join them on bespoke weapons training courses.[17]

Kelsey's report was based on a book released at the time by Tim Hepple, a former BNP activist turned informant. Hepple's story was not an uncommon one. It began when he joined his local club's hooligan firm the 'Berkshire Boot Boys', who followed Reading in the early 1980s. In 1984 Hepple was recruited into the National Front, before his musical talent as a pianist and conductor won him a scholarship to the Royal College of Music in Glasgow in 1986. Having moved to Scotland, and finding himself a long way from Reading's Elm Park home, Hepple switched his footballing allegiance to Ibrox and joined Glasgow Rangers' Inter-City Firm, shortly afterwards being recruited through the firm into the BNP. Hepple described his state of mind at the time, saying: "I just wanted to smash the state, to show my anger, to hate somebody. Like many others I was scared for the future and had little respect for myself. The BNP provided me with a sense of identity".[18]

[16] Gilroy. P, 1987, 'There Ain't No Black in the Union Jack', Routledge Classics, p173

[17] Kelsey. T, 1993, 'Informer exposes neo-Nazi football gangs', The Independent, 7 August 1993

[18] Kelsey. T, 1993, 'Informer exposes neo-Nazi football gangs', The Independent, 7 August 1993

Many other disenchanted people followed a similar path. Former Chelsea player and prominent anti-racism campaigner Paul Elliott explained what the situation had been like when he addressed the Commons Culture, Media and Sport Committee in 2012: "Extremists tried to launch their own recruitment drives and used football clubs as a catalyst to do that".[19] The effect was most telling on the minority of black footballers, estimated to number around 50, who plied their trade in the Football League during that time.[20] Elliot, who was one of them, described what was happening: "Black players became the scourge of that [hate]. It was a difficult challenge for us. Fundamentally for us there was no legislation in place. Myself and others had to put up with it, focus on our game, to the best of our ability". He added that the terraces he was performing in front of contained the "ugliness of society" due to the influence of extremist groups.[21]

Thatcher claimed that the football crowds themselves were the cause of that ugliness, hastening societal breakdown, rather than a symptom of a wider problem. In 1985, following a mass brawl during an FA Cup quarter-final between Luton Town and Millwall, she set-up a 'war cabinet' to try and eradicate what she felt were the innate violent tendencies of the young working classes. In response *The Times* published an editorial calling football: "a slum sport, played in slum stadiums, by slum people".[22] Sports journalist Henry Winter notes: "The Iron Lady seemed to have come to the opinion that all fans were feral and she was not for turning on that blinkered outlook. She saw criminals where there were simply civilians, many tragically victims".[23]

Thatcher's Home Secretary Douglas Hurd summed up the attitude of the government at the time, writing to the Prime Minister

[19] *Bennet. A, 2012, 'National Front Used Football Grounds as Recruitment Grounds', The Guardian 15 May 2012*

[20] *Rees. P, 2014, 'We got off the coach and the National Front was there', The Guardian, 25 July 2014*

[21] *Bennet. A, 2012, 'National Front Used Football Grounds as Recruitment Grounds', The Guardian 15 May 2012*

[22] *Domeneghetti. R, 2017, 'From the back page to the front room', Ockley Books, Huddersfield, p185*

[23] *Winter. H, 2013, 'Margaret Thatcher scored political own goal with her attitude towards football', The Independent, 9 April 2013*

to bemoan the thuggish behaviour of a generation: "Many of the 16 to 25-year-olds involved in these disturbances have a latent capacity for violence. Toughness is a proof of manhood. Drink removes their inhibitions and pushes them over the edge. There are few internal disciplines or external restraints to rein them back. Their parents are at home in front of the TV and their upbringing and education have failed to give them self-discipline, a sense of social responsibility or much in the way of interest except having a good time".[24] Hurd identified the causes of this anger and violence as the result of those responsible having "no sense of social responsibility", but utterly failed to make the connection to his own government's policies. After all, it was Thatcher herself who had earlier told *Woman's Own* magazine; "There's no such thing as society".[25]

As identified by Paul Elliot, football terraces swarming with racist hooligans were not the cause of the ugliness of society they were a symptom of its creation at the top of government. As Football Association Secretary Ted Crocker told Thatcher in response to her criticism of football's hooligan problem: "Get your hooligans out of my game".[26]

It was in this climate that a chant began life on the terraces which would reach far beyond the stadium and back to the Houses of Parliament:

> *"There ain't no black in the Union Jack,*
> *Send those niggers back,*
> *If you're white you're alright,*
> *If you're black, send 'em back"*

As with 'You're Going Home in a Fucking Ambulance', the chant found an audience outside football and, cementing the links between the two, was adopted by first the National Front and then the far-right British National Party as their party slogan. Such was the popularity

---

[24] Harris. D, 2016, 'Margaret Thatcher's government thought football fans so violent she set up a war cabinet', The Independent, 19 February 2016

[25] Bourne. J 2013, 'May we bring harmony', Institute of Race Relations, 11 April 2013

[26] Domeneghetti. R, 2017, 'From the back page to the front room', Ockley Books, Huddersfield, p179

and reach of 'Ain't No Black in the Union Jack' that the UK's national flag became seen as an overtly racist symbol. Footage of fans celebrating England's World Cup win in 1966 exclusively features fans waving Union Jacks, but the pervasiveness of the chant into Britain's social consciousness led to 1982 Decathlete Daley Thompson's refusal to carry the flag after winning Gold at the Commonwealth Games.[27] The power of the chant to taint the Union Jack has pervaded for three decades, and to this day the majority of England fans shy away from the Union Jack in favour of the cross of St George, although it is beginning to make a reappearance as racial tensions rise following Britain's vote to leave the European Union in 2016.

Around the same time that 'Ain't No Black in the Union Jack' was infecting terraces up and down English football, West Bromwich Albion, inspired by a trio of black players; Laurie Cunningham, Cyrille Regis and Brendon Batson (collectively christened 'The Three Degrees' by their manager Ron Atkinson) enjoyed one of the most successful periods in the club's history. Cunningham moved to Real Madrid in 1979, but by then the levels of vitriol were already rising and the rare collection of three black players in one side made West Brom's fixtures a magnet for racists.

Batson provided *The Guardian* with an eye-opening description of matchdays at the time: "We'd get off the coach at away matches and the National Front would be right there in your face. In those days, we didn't have security and we'd have to run the gauntlet. We'd get to the players' entrance and there'd be spit on my jacket or Cyrille's shirt. It was a sign of the times. What shocked me when I joined West Brom was the volume. The noise and level of the abuse was incredible. At times, it was almost like surround sound in the grounds. But it was such a regular occurrence, you almost got used to it".[28] Paul Elliot agreed; "The ritualistic abuse was utterly unacceptable" describing horrific racist abuse including 'monkey-chants'.[29] When Paul Canoville became the first black player to play for Chelsea in 1980, his own fans

[27] Gilroy. P, 1987, 'There Ain't No Black in the Union Jack', Routledge Classics, p69

[28] Rees. P, 2014, 'We got off the coach and the National Front was there', The Guardian 25 July 2014

[29] Bennet. A, 2012, 'National Front Used Football Grounds as Recruitment Grounds', The Guardian, 15 May 2012

would boo his every touch and chant:

> **"White team in London,**
> **The only white team in London"**

Chelsea were far from alone in this. For example, during a late 1970s Leeds United v Norwich City game in which the both sides featured a black player (Terry Connor for Leeds and Justin Fashanu for Norwich) the Leeds fans saluted their own player by singing:

> **"One fucking nigger,**
> **There's only one fucking nigger"**

As late as 1988, the black Liverpool player and England international John Barnes was famously photographed nonchalantly back heeling a banana that had been hurled at him during the Merseyside derby at Goodison Park, while Everton's fans chanted:

> **"Everton are white,**
> **Everton are white"** [30]

It is little wonder then that Lord Herman Ouseley, Chairperson of English football's leading anti-racism campaign group 'Kick It Out' has since said: "Going to football as a black man [in the 1970s and 1980s] was a very uncomfortable experience. You had to keep your head down and your wits about you".[31]

For many years racism was the dominant theme of abuse and was rife in chanting, even after society had long since grown up, but eventually more enlightened social attitudes on race began to filter through to the terraces. This was helped by fans self-policing and calling out their fellow supporters for unacceptable abuse, coupled with new powers given to the police to crack down. As historian and academic Paul Gilroy puts it: "Nobody post-Lenny [Henry], Lennox

[30] *Cunningham. S, 2009, 'Barnes; There are lots of bad white managers', The Independent, 18 August 2009*

[31] *Rees. P, 2014, 'We got off the coach and the National Front was there', The Guardian, 25 July 2014*

[Lewis] and Linford [Christie], Scary [Spice, Mel B], Denise [Lewis] and Naomi [Campbell], could doubt that there is, after all, some kind of black somewhere in or rather underneath the Union Jack." It is an argument supported by empirical analysis of British national identity beliefs, which show a sharp decline in the importance accorded to whiteness and British ancestry as markers of 'being British' among those born since mass immigration began.[32] Additionally, awareness of the use of the Football Offences Act 1991 is growing. The Act lists chanting of a 'racist or indecent nature' as an offence, triggered when any person is offended by the chant, even if it is not directed at them, as long as it occurs within the confines of a football stadium.[33] The legislation has been used frequently to ban individuals convicted of using racist language[34] and saw six fans jailed in 2013 for chants glorifying the racist murder of teenager Stephen Lawrence, which had been committed two decades earlier.[35]

This juxtaposition of societal condemnation with ongoing isolated incidents was seen in May 2014 in Spain in an episode reminiscent of the one involving John Barnes back in 1988. As Barcelona's Dani Alves went to take a corner a banana was thrown at him by a fan of Villareal. However, instead of kicking the banana away, as Barnes did, Alves picked it up and took a bite. Although the affair showed that racism has yet to be eradicated from football, it also drew support for the player particularly in an internet campaign inspired by Alves' response. Players, fans and pundits uploaded images of themselves eating bananas to Twitter with the hashtag #WeAreAllMonkeys. The fan who hurled the banana was subsequently identified through CCTV and permanently banned from attending matches.[36] Then in late 2018, Tottenham Hotspur fan Averof Panteli was given a four-year ban from attending football matches and fined £500 for throwing a

---

[32] Ford. R, 2008, 'Is racial prejudice declining in Britain?', The British Journal of Sociology, Volume 59, Issue 4, p611

[33] McArdle. D, 2000, 'Football Society and The Law', Cavendish Publishing, London, p80

[34] Banks. D, 2012, 'Can the CPS really crack down on football clubs for racist chanting by fans', The Guardian, 29 March 2012

[35] BBC Website, 2013, 'Football fans jailed for abusive Stephen Lawrence chants', 30 October 2013

[36] Wanga.J, 2014, '#WeAreAllMonkeys: Can a picture of a banana fight racism?', The Independent, 29 April 2014

banana skin at Arsenal's Pierre-Emerick Aubameyang after a judge dismissed Panteli's claim it wasn't racially motivated and merely the closest thing at hand.[37]

Earlier that year Chelsea had announced they were adopting a novel approach to holding their fans to account for racism, swapping banning orders for visits to Auschwitz to those repeatedly chanting anti-Semitic rhetoric during their games against Spurs. Chairman Bruce Buck told *The Sun*: "If you just ban people, you will never change their behaviour. This policy gives them the chance to realise what they have done, to make them want to behave better. In the past, we would take them from the crowd and ban them, for up to three years. Now we say: 'You did something wrong. You have the option. We can ban you or you can spend some time with our diversity officers, understanding what you did wrong'. It is hard to act when a group of 50 or 100 people are chanting. That's virtually impossible to deal with or try to drag them out of the stadium. But if we have individuals that we can identify, we can act. The trips to Auschwitz were really important and effective and we will consider more as well as other things that will affect people".[38] Their plan was endorsed by the Football Supporters' Federation and anti-racism campaign group Kick it Out whose Programmes Manager Keeley Baptiste said: "Kick It Out believes strongly in the use of education to tackle discrimination and we support Chelsea's efforts to encourage supporters who have engaged in anti-Semitism to change their behaviour".[39]

While the kinds of racism described by Brendan Batson and Lord Ouseley above have been on the decline on the terraces since the early 1990s, other examples of racism: anti-Semitism and xenophobia remain common. As recently as November 2014, England fans were being asked to refrain from singing *"No Surrender to the IRA"* 16 years after the Good Friday Agreement was signed. Furthermore, the row over Tottenham Hotspur supporters' use of the anti-Semitic term "Yid" in the self-referential chant *"Yid Army, Yid Army"* resurfaces every few

---

[37] Murphy. S, 2018, 'Tottenham fan banned for hurling banana at Arsenal's Aubameyang', The Guardian, 18 December 2018

[38] Lipton. M, 2018, 'Chelsea to send racist fans to visit Nazi death camp Auschwitz', The Sun, 11 October 2018

[39] PA Sport, 2018, 'Chelsea seek to educate racist offenders', Eurosport, 11 October 2018

years. It became national news in September 2013, when then Prime Minster David Cameron embroiled himself in a polarising debate on identity and offence. On the one hand opposition fans have long used the racially derogative term "Yid" to abuse Tottenham Hotspur fans who are based in a traditionally Jewish area of North London. Tottenham fans in turn adopted the word as a defence-mechanism, chanting *"Yid Army"* and *"Yiddos"* as positive expressions of their own identity. Some Jewish groups, however, felt the term was too rooted in anti-Semitic abuse and was thus offensive in any context. Cameron was asked his view, responding: "You have to think of the men's motivation. There's a difference between Spurs fans self-describing themselves as 'Yids' and someone calling someone a 'Yid' as an insult. You have to be motivated by hate. Hate speech should be prosecuted, but only when it's motivated by hate." Cameron's approach was in direct opposition to the Football Association's stance of zero-tolerance for the word, whoever sung it and in whatever context.[40]

Commentator Lee Barnett thought the FA had taken the correct stance, writing in *The New Statesmen* at the time:

"Yid. A hideous word, chanted by Mosley's blackshirts in the 1930s as they marched through the East End, now chanted every week by non-Jews in a way that's frankly indistinguishable. Chanted again and again, reinforcing the ordinariness of the word, making it okay for anyone and everyone to use it in whatever circumstances they choose. That's the point: in such a combative atmosphere, the word "yid" becomes normalised; its very usage allows, if not actively encourages, others to use it in a less than complimentary manner. It encourages other teams' supporters to use the word and fling it back at Spurs' supporters. That may not be the aim, nor the intention, but it's as an inevitable a consequence as shouting the ref is biased when he rules against your team. It beggars belief to suggest that the Y-word has been reclaimed by Jewish fans, since it's not Jewish fans in the main who are screaming it out loud; this must be the first time in history that "reclaiming" a word has been advanced as an argument by people who don't own the word. It's nonsense. It's equally ludicrous

---

[40] *Wilson. J and Dominiczak. P, 2013, 'David Cameron embroiled in race row over Tottenham Hotspurs' Yid chant', 17 September 2013*

to complain about others shouting the word when you've thrown it out there as a challenge to them in the heated atmosphere of a football match. There's no hope of ridding football of anti-Semitism if, as part of that, you have to reserve one team's right to chant an anti-Semitic epithet, because 'oh, we're doing it nicely—it's our 'identity'".[41]

Following the warnings from the FA, and despite the inherent historical inference, during Tottenham's next match, a comfortable 2-0 Premier League home win over Norwich City, Spurs fans flouted the FA warnings with frequent renditions of '*Yid Army*' and the defiant:

> *"We'll sing what we want,*
> *We'll sing what we want,*
> *We're Tottenham Hotspur,*
> *We'll sing what we want,*
> *Yid Army, Yid Army, Yid Army"*

Six years on, in December 2019, Spurs released the results of a survey on the use of the term 'yid', which garnered more than 23,000 responses and highlighted the split. Despite 94% acknowledging it could be considered a racist term against a Jewish person, 55% of respondents reported that they were "happy with its use within football". That left 45% unhappy. The 45% was further split with 22% wishing it abandoned altogether, with the other 23% somewhat confusingly requesting it was "used less", although no explanation was given for how that might work, or what was an acceptable number of uses. The survey also highlighted the differences in behaviour provoked by football, with 33% of respondents saying they used the word "regularly" in a football context, but only 12% also used it outside of football.[42]

The matter was further complicated in February 2020 when recognised English language authority, the *Oxford English Dictionary* added "a supporter of or player for Tottenham Hotspur" to their definition of "yid".[43] The response was mixed. The BBC quoted *Jewish*

41 Barnett. L, 2013, 'We can't rid football of anti-Semitism unless Spurs fans stop chanting "yid army"', New Statesman, 29 September 2013

42 Welch. B, 2019, 'Most Tottenham Hotspur fans, Jewish and non-Jewish, support 'Y-word' chants', The Jewish Chronicle, 16 December 2019

43 BBC, 2020, 'Dictionary includes Spurs fans in Yid definition', 12 February 2020

Chronicle editor Stephen Pollard, who told them that in his opinion Spurs' fans use of the word was "not controversial among many of the Jewish Spurs supporters, such as myself, who are proud to be Yiddos".[44] Tottenham Hotspur's own response was less positive however, saying "We find the Oxford English Dictionary's definition of the word misleading given it fails to distinguish context. As a club we have never accommodated the use of the Y-word on any club channels or in club stores and have always been clear that our fans (both Jewish and gentile) have never used the term with any intent to cause offence".[45] For their part the *Oxford English Dictionary* released a statement noting "We reflect, rather than dictate, how language is used which means we include words which may be considered sensitive and derogatory. These are always labelled as such", adding that the term was used as a "self-designation" by some fans.[46]

The debate over the use of the word "yid" and the idea that fans can *"sing what we want"* is not a new one, as journalist Tom Lamont notes:

"Football fans have never been afraid to be tasteless, and there aren't many topics they shy from, be it run-ins with the law; *"Robinho, she said no, Robinho, she said no"*, shortly after the Brazilian's arrest on suspicion of rape – no charges were brought, mental health problems; *"Two Andy Gorams, there's only two Andy Gorams"*, after the goalkeeper was reported to have schizophrenia, or global conflict, [such as the chant aimed] at Liverpool's Israeli player Yossi Benayoun; *"the Gaza's not yours, the Gaza's not yours".*[47] While in Israel itself, during the Tel Aviv derby, fans of Hapoel greeted the Maccabi goalkeeper with a barrage of plastic child dolls after his troubled wife nearly killed their own child after throwing the infant out of a second-floor window".[48]

Even with backing from the Prime Minster and despite the assertion of fans, they do not, and should not, enjoy carte blanche to chant whatever they like and Humphrey's assertion that football fans

[44]   BBC, 2020, 'Dictionary includes Spurs fans in Yid definition', 12 February 2020

[45]   TalkSPORT, 2020, 'Tottenham blast 'misleading' Oxford English Dictionary definition of 'yiddo' and 'yid'', 13 February 2020

[46]   BBC, 2020, 'Dictionary includes Spurs fans in Yid definition', 12 February 2020

[47]   Lamont. T, 2009, 'The chant-makers of English football', The Guardian, 3 May 2009

[48]   Mitten. A, 2008, 'Mad For It – From Blackpool to Barcelona, Football's Great Rivalries', Harper Sport, London

are guilty of hate-speak is beginning to be recognised by both the fans themselves and the authorities. As Lamont notes: "opinion has shifted, hardened, perhaps, by the abuse of England's black players on visits to Spain in 2004 and Croatia in 2008, or the allegations of Islamophobia against Newcastle fans in 2007 for chants about Egypt striker Mido. Football spectators, once able to blare whatever they liked from the stands, are increasingly being held to account for the content of their chants".[49]

This process of supporters self-policing was highlighted after footage of Chelsea fans racially abusing Raheem Sterling, during their club's 2-0 Premier League win in December 2018, was widely shared on social media by fans, who predominantly called on Chelsea to take action against the perpetrators. Within days Chelsea had reviewed the social media footage and banned four fans from attending games at Stamford Bridge.[50] The online outrage made it a national story, leading to Sterling himself taking to Instagram to highlight the role the media has played in normalising the treatment of black footballers. Sterling vividly illustrated his point with two *MailOnline* stories of young Manchester City players purchasing homes for their parents. The story on the white Phil Foden was headlined: "Manchester City starlet Phil Foden buys new £2m home for his Mum," while the story about his black teammate, Tosin Adarabioyo, was titled: "Young Manchester City footballer, 20, on £25,000 a week splashes out on mansion on market for £2.25m despite having never started a Premier League match".[51]

Part of the process of fans beginning to hold each other to account and self-police, was the rise of football fanzines, which came about as a direct result of the same disillusion created under Thatcher that also fuelled increased racism. Continuing football's links with music, the first fanzines were edited by punk rock music fans, a trend highlighted by the emergence of national fanzine *When Saturday Comes* in 1986,

[49] Lamont. T, 2009, 'The chant-makers of English football', The Guardian, 3 May 2009

[50] BBC, 2018, 'Chelsea fans suspended for alleged abuse of Man City forward', BBC, 11 December 2018

[51] Sterling. R, 2018, 'Sterlling7', Instagram, 9 December 2018

initially as an off-shoot of punk fanzine *Snipe*.[52] Co-Founder Andy Lyons picks up the story:

"I was working in a record shop in London, with Mike Ticher and we were talking about football as much as we were music. The 'zine culture in music had been established since the 1970s, so when the idea of doing an equivalent for football came up, it was natural to include it as a supplement within a music 'zine. At the time, there were football publications, but these were aimed at either teenagers or older people, there wasn't really anything around for fans aged between 20 and 40. For the first issue we just photocopied 100 or so copies of this supplement, one of which made it to *The Guardian*. They liked it enough to publish our details and we were quickly inundated with requests, so had to fire up the photocopier for a bigger run".[53]

Other titles began appearing at the same time, including *The End*, founded by Peter Hooton who would later form part of band *The Farm*, and *Boys Own* which covered football and music.[54] Richard Haynes, in his study on the rise of football fanzines *The Football Imagination* stresses that their rise can be attributed to a desire to voice an alternative view of football acting in effect as a defence mechanism and expressing discontent with the portrait of football fans presented in the mainstream media, which painted anyone who liked the game as a hooligan by default. Andy Lyons agrees: "I think they took off because people wanted to have their voices heard. Partly to counter the view that we were all hooligans, but also to protest at the treatment of fans by the government at the time and also highlight mismanagement of clubs by their owners".[55] Three decades on they retain that function, as highlighted by Paul O'Dowd, co-editor of Leeds United fanzine *The Square Ball*, who told the BBC: "Some of the best fanzines have some of the worst [football club] owners".[56]

[52] Haynes. R, 1995, 'The Football Imagination; The Rise of Football Fanzine Culture', Fan magazines, p39

[53] Lyons. A, 2018, Email interview, 15 November 2018

[54] Domeneghetti. R, 2017, 'From the back page to the front room', Ockley Books, Huddersfield, p190-192

[55] Lyons. A, 2018, Email interview, 15 November 2018

[56] McKenzie. C, 2017, 'I'm surprised that football fanzines have survived', BBC, 25 November 2017

In the aftermath of Heysel, a group of fanzine editors, including Lyons, met with other concerned fans and, led by Liverpool fan Rogan Taylor, formed the Football Supporters' Association. In 2002 the body became the Football Supporters' Federation following a merger with the National Federation of Supporters' Clubs. The first edition of *When Saturday Comes* to be published in the aftermath of Hillsborough set the tone, stating that football fans were "deemed to be passive accomplices to the sociopathic minority. The police see us as a mass entity, fuelled by drink and single-minded resolve to wreak havoc by destroying property and attacking one another with murderous intent. The implication is that 'normal' people need to be protected from the football fan. But we are normal people".[57]

While fanzine writers, were normal people, they were also frequently left-wing. The founders of *The End*, for example, claimed their biggest compliment was being labelled a "lefty pink pop mag indoctrinating the youth of [Liverpool]" and used their platform to speak out about racism, sexism and homophobia[58] and highlight fans' treatment by an administration seemingly determined to hold them up as a cause of the country's ills. Their voice was increasingly being heard and the idea of creating your own publication caught the public's imagination.[59] As fanzine numbers grew from 22 in January 1988 to over 300 by the early 1990s,[60] their dissenting voice was amplified, uniting like-minded fans of clubs around the country and ultimately helped lead to the formation of Kick it Out in 1993, initially as a small independent charity, but later formalised as a body responsible for tackling all aspects of inequality and exclusion in the English game.[61] This process happened on a national level, but also on a local level as individual clubs, particularly in the non-league game, became magnets for fans eager to experience football in a different, less toxic way.

---

[57] Domeneghetti. R, 2017, 'From the back page to the front room', Ockley Books, Huddersfield, p185

[58] Domeneghetti. R, 2017, 'From the back page to the front room', Ockley Books, Huddersfield, p187-192

[59] Edwards. R, 2015, 'The worst five months in English football', FourFourTwo, 14 January 2015

[60] Domeneghetti. R, 2017, 'From the back page to the front room', Ockley Books, Huddersfield, p194

[61] Kick it Out, 2018, 'About Kick it Out', Kick it Out website, Retrieved 12 October 2018

Tom Lamont describes this process occurring at non-league club Dulwich Hamlet, who are in the sixth tier of English football. "Something unusual was happening—a younger, liberal outlook bleeding into the usual sporting tribalism, so that the terraces started policing themselves of a common blight [racism, homophobia, misogyny], which in turn encouraged more casual attendees. Gates kept rising, with crowds at some games pushing up to the ground's 3,000 capacity. As one fan described it, Dulwich offered 'a beers-in-the-air intensity, minus the toxic shit that normally goes with it'".[62]

A similar thing has happened at Eastbourne Town, three divisions below Dulwich Hamlet, where a group of younger fans disillusioned by the expense of league football, set-up the fantastically named ultra group *Pier Pressure* in 2017. As with their Dulwich counterparts the group wanted to create a boisterous and carnival atmosphere at the football but refused to leave politics at the turnstiles, highlighted by their chant; *"Eastbourne Town is anti-faschistische"*.[63] The group are also active outside football running collections for local charities and food banks. The group actively champion diversity and inclusivity, while some supporters helped successfully campaign to oust the local Conservative MP at the 2017 General Election.[64] Founder Leon Jervis explained: "The main focus of the group is just to be open to everybody. We'd let anyone come and join us, even if it looks a bit mental, we're here to have fun, maybe let off a few smoke bombs and mainly be passionate about the place that we live".[65] Fellow Eastbourne fan Tracie Searle agreed, adding "Being a woman watching football, I feel my opinion is valued by other people [here] and I am a lot more vocal. Previously, for a very long time, I had felt like it wasn't. I love the little jokes, I love the community, I love the chants, everybody gets involved, it's like a party on a Saturday afternoon".[66] Alongside their 'Anti-faschistische' chant, *Pier Pressure* celebrate their home town with:

[62] Lamont. T, 2018, 'Dulwich Hamlet; the improbable tale, The Guardian, 26 October 2018

[63] Cop1 90, 2020, 'Pints, Pier Pressure, and Passion', Copa90, 4 February 2020

[64] Carmichael. C, 2020, 'How ultras fan culture took hold at Eastbourne Town', The Guardian, 13 February 2020

[65] Cop1 90, 2020, 'Pints, Pier Pressure, and Passion', Copa90, 4 February 2020

[66] Cop1 90, 2020, 'Pints, Pier Pressure, and Passion', Copa90, 4 February 2020

"Oh Eastbourne Town,
Is wonderful,
Oh Eastbourne Town is wonderful,
It's full of old people and seagulls,
Oh Eastbourne Town is wonderful" [67]

By 2018, times had changed enough across English football that fans were being praised on national TV news bulletins when footage emerged of Liverpool fans' new chant in homage to their Egyptian striker Mohammed Salah, a practicing Muslim, at a time when Islamophobia was on the rise in the country at large. To the tune of Dodgy's 1996 hit 'Good Enough', the fans sang:

"If he's good enough for you,
He's good enough for me,
If he scores another few,
Then I'll be Muslim too,
If he's good enough for you,
He's good enough for me,
Then sitting in a mosque is where I wanna be...
Mo Salah, la la la la,
La la la la la la"

Muslim actor and broadcaster Adil Ray told *Channel 4 News*: "If you bear in mind that the Muslim community are often accused of not being integrated, not being part of the mainstream and yet we have probably the best player in the Premier League right now, is a Muslim. Equally, and unfairly, if you want to call it the 'white, working class' who you might associate with football traditionally are often accused of being racist or prejudiced, or not welcome to the Muslim community and yet here we have both of those situations merging together"[68]

Meanwhile the 'Ain't No Black in the Union Jack' chant has since been reclaimed in a single by Ebony Bones, who in 2018 released

---

[67] *Cop1 90, 2020, 'Pints, Pier Pressure, and Passion', Copa90, 4 February 2020*

[68] *Channel Four News, 2018 'Channel Four News', Channel Four, 15 February 2018*

her pop version featuring Enoch Powell's 'Rivers of Blood speech' and referencing the BNP's modern-day equivalent, Britain First. The chorus of Bones' version includes the lyrics:

"There ain't no black in the Union Jack,
Send 'em back, send 'em back
No black in the Union Jack,
Send 'em back, send 'em back,
Red, white and blue,
Let them in to sponge the system,
Now the country is screwed,
Red, white and blue,
Britain First, go join the back of the queue"

Bones' single was released in the aftermath of Britain's 2016 referendum on whether or not to leave the European Union. The vote occurred four years after the then Conservative Home Secretary, Theresa May, told *The Daily Telegraph* she wanted to create a "hostile environment" for illegal immigrants.[69] Those two events were followed by a revival of racism in football stadia, just as Thatcher's policies had 20 years earlier. The link between the Conservative government's decision to implement a hostile environment in 2012 and the rise of racism is clear. That year saw Kick it Out report its first rise in racist incidents, since its inception in 1993, a trend that has continued every year since May's speech. That increase jumped again following the Brexit referendum in 2016, with reports of discrimination up 38% from 2017 to 2018 alone[70] and jumping another 11% during 2018, leading to their spokesman Troy Townsend calling the climate "our most worrying period of time within the game".[71]

Just as it was with hooliganism and racism in the 1980s when Ted Crocker told Thatcher to get her hooligans out of his game, racism

---

[69] Grierson. J, 2018, 'Hostile environment; anatomy of a policy disaster', *The Guardian*, 27 August 2018

[70] Henry. M, 2018, 'Kick it Out finds 38% increase in discrimination in Premier League and EFL', BBC, 7 February 2018

[71] Magowan. A, 2018, 'Kick it Out says reports of racism and homophobia continue to rise', BBC, 28 November 2018

isn't a football problem but a societal one that is most visible, and audible, in chanting. As John Barnes noted in the aftermath of the hostile environment Raheem Sterling faced at Stamford Bridge: "if you silence all the racists in a stadium, you will still have a stadium full of racists".[72] Days later, journalist Barnay Ronay wrote on similar lines: "The lesson of the rise in reported abuse, and of viciousness in all its forms, is that our society is producing racists. Football doesn't make this happen. But it does provide the most visible public space where people get together and shout their brains right down the lens of a TV camera".[73] Kick it Out echoed that message, saying: "Racism is both a football and societal issue, and it is clear that we are living in a climate of rising hatred and tribalism across the world. In this country, the situation is no different and the language of division has become normalised within our political debate—and our politicians must take the lead in countering that. In that context, it is no surprise to see a rise in reported incidents in English football. But it is also important to note that racism in the game has now become a far more mainstream topic—which we believe is encouraging supporters to take action and report abuse they see or hear".[74]

While overt racism and racist chanting had fallen prior to May's introduction of the hostile environment for immigrants, homophobic abuse continued largely unabated and partially filled the void. A 2009 Stonewall survey on homophobia in football found that while 61% believed there is less racist abuse in contemporary football compared with 1989, just 31% believed there was less homophobic abuse.[75] A British Social Attitudes Survey recorded that just 17% of Britons believed that homosexuality was "not wrong at all" in 1983, climbing rapidly to 47% in 2018.[76] That increase in support for LGBTQ+ equality has led to an increase in fans self-policing, just as they have done

[72] Barnes. J, 2018, 'If every racist was silenced stadiums would still be full of racists', The Guardian, 12 December 2018

[73] Ronay. B, 2018, 'Football shouldn't carry the can for society's ills', The Guardian, 14 December 2018

[74] Bassam. T, 2020, 'Sharp rise in football racism as incidents go up by more than 50% in one year', The Guardian, 30 January 2020

[75] BBC, 2009, 'Football failing on homophobia', BBC, 12 August 2009

[76] British Social Attitudes, 2018, 'British Social Attitudes 30; introduction', Retrieved 19 September 2018

with racism. However, at the time of writing in July 2020 no official anti-homophobic chanting law exists and unacceptable homophobic abuse continues to be aired in stadia.

The recorded lag between societal rejection of first racism and then homophobia, and the ongoing verbal abuse that persists within grounds, coupled with the nature of football chanting in drawing on topical events for their inspiration, means chants are unlikely to act as a progressive tool for change within society. However, the chants do play a role in raising awareness and starting conversations on issues that remain prevalent in areas of society, despite perceived mainstream acceptance. The Dani Alves and Pierre-Emerick Aubameyang incidents, plus the ongoing abuse of Raheem Sterling, shows that racism has still not been eliminated from the game, and by extension society. Yet all three also prompted widespread public declarations of support which spread across football and society at large, with former England women's player Eniola Aluko going as far as to call the public outcry over the abuse dished out to Sterling as: "very positive" and "a genuine step forward [because] Sterling has managed to turn something outrageous into a catalyst for long, overdue change".[77]

The pressure to do something about homophobic chanting became amplified after a single chant aimed at Sol Campbell in December 2008, which brought the themes of racism and homophobia together and broke enough societal taboos to spark a noticeable sea-change in the attitude towards football chanting from fans and the general public alike.

---

[77] *Aluko. E, 2018, 'Sterling's racism ordeal was ugly but the reaction has been positive', The Guardian, 13 December 2018*

7. HOMOPHOBIA

'SOL, SOL, WHEREVER YOU MAY BE'

Homophobic abuse in football chanting is not a new phenomenon, but sadly it is an enduring one. In 1968, a year after homosexuality was decriminalised in the UK, author Arthur Hopcroft noted that chants such as *"Ey-ay-addio the Goalie is a Queer"* and *"Where's Your Handbag Gone?"* occurred at every league game, at every league ground, in the UK.[1] While Liverpool's renditions of The Beatles hit 'She Loves You' were also not always as tuneful sing-song *Panorama* portrayed them as. Renditions would frequently accompany a physio helping an injured player leave the pitch with the implication being that the necessary close physical contact of having an arm around each other was worthy of mocking.

Like racism, homophobia on the terraces became increasingly frequent as the mood on the terraces and across the nation darkened into the 1980s, but unlike racism, there was little concerted effort to challenge it in the following decades. This lack of response from the authorities led to social equality campaign group Stonewall denouncing football as "institutionally homophobic" in 2009 after a survey they conducted with over 2,000 fans found 70% reporting they had heard homophobic abuse in the previous five years, with more than half feeling the authorities hadn't done enough to challenge it.[2]

A year later, in 2010, the Football Association announced they had been unable to find a player from the Premier League willing to endorse a video designed to discourage homophobic chanting. Lacking support from within football the project was abandoned, prompting journalist Eamon McCann to question what was different about homophobia within football: "Players queued up to be associated with the 'Kick Out Racism' campaign a decade ago. But [there's been] no takers for kicking out bigotry aimed at gays. Can it be that football, the most representative expression of popular mood the world over, is uniquely out of step with changing attitudes sweeping across the rest of society? Or could it be that football,

[1] *Hopcroft. A, 1968, 'The Football Man', CPI Group, London, p194*

[2] *BBC, 2009, 'Football failing on homophobia', BBC, 12 August 2009*

on account of its particular authenticity, provides a context for the expression of attitudes and values which remain widespread and deeply felt in society?"[3]

If one chant sums up the problem, and the depths of homophobic hatred fans were able to express through the medium of chants, it was the one aimed at Sol Campbell by Tottenham Hotspur fans during their Premier League meeting with Portsmouth at Fratton Park in December 2008.

Campbell was a firm favourite with Spurs fans after coming through the club's youth ranks, but he incurred their wrath by winding down his contract and leaving on a free transfer for their arch-rivals Arsenal in 2006. On his return to White Hart Lane with Arsenal, Campbell expected to receive some stick but was surprised by the level of hatred he encountered, including 4,000 white balloons and countless cards and flags emblazoned with the word 'Judas' in a bold blue typeface. Among the fans releasing the balloons and holding the cards, Campbell saw his own brother, telling FourfourTwo: "I don't think he was chanting, no—that would have been too much. But he was in there, and I couldn't believe it. It's amazing really, he could have been sat anywhere that day, but I happened to pick his face out".[4]

If that was a shock, the level of abuse which Campbell continued to receive even after leaving Arsenal for Portsmouth took it to another level. When Campbell next faced Spurs, this time at Portsmouth's Fratton Park, he was met with a chant for which four people were arrested and later banned from attending any football match for three years, while seven others had bans overturned on appeal. To the tune of 'Lord of the Dance' they sang:

> **"Sol, Sol, wherever you may be,**
> **Not long now until lunacy,**
> **We won't give a fuck if you're hanging from a tree,**
> **You're a Judas cunt with HIV"**

---

[3]   *McCann. E, 2010, 'Why are gay footballers still hiding in locker room closets', Belfast Telegraph, 9 July 2010*

[4]   *Gaghan. C, 2014, 'Sol Campbell: One on One', FourFourTwo, 22 June 2014*

The official reason the police gave for the arrests was that the chant was homophobic, which it undoubtedly is, but it could have been for any number of other offensive elements. Taking each in turn, the chant first abuses Campbell for a perceived mental illness, likely a reference to a match between Arsenal and West Ham in 2006 in which a clearly distressed Campbell asked to be substituted at half-time. After the game, his manager Arsène Wenger explained to the media the defender had told him he felt guilty about his first-half performance, Wenger agreed to substitute him, and Campbell promptly left the stadium. Later, his teammates admitted Campbell had "worries" in his private life, which were interpreted by some outsiders to mean he was gay and struggling to deal with it.[5]

The third line continues the mental health theme by referencing suicide but also refers to Campbell's race and alleged homosexuality. It recalls the death of Justin Fashanu, the only professional footballer in England to have come out as gay while playing, who took his own life by hanging and who like Campbell was black. Furthermore, the reference to *"hanging from a tree"* simultaneously conjures images of lynchings, the historical treatment of black men, particularly in the United States, which were themselves public spectacles designed to create maximum intimidation of minority groups by larger mobs. After a brief deviation into religious language to label Campbell a 'Judas', after the disciple who infamously betrayed Jesus, the chant returns to homophobia with the reference to HIV, a disease Campbell doesn't have but which historically disproportionately affects homosexual men.

The Campbell chant was widely seen as a watershed moment. Although, remarkably, the police's initial response to the Campbell chant was to pass the buck back to the Football Association by claiming that because the chant emanated from a crowd they couldn't risk intervening for fear of creating "further problems". Campbell's manager at the time Harry Redknapp spoke out telling the assembled media: "This kind of thing has no place in football, no place in life. Somebody has got to make a stand. It is way out of order. You can go to places and see people saying filthy things, even though they have got kids with them. What sort of example is it to set kids?" Campbell

5   McCarra. K, 2006, 'The strange case of Sol Campbell, still missing in action', 3 February 2006

himself called it a "human rights situation" adding "If this happened on the street you would be arrested".[6] Eventually, following official complaints about their lack of response, the police investigated, ultimately making the 11 previously mentioned arrests.

As well as highlighting the authorities' apparent lack of desire to get involved, the Campbell chant sparked a crackdown on abusive chanting from the fans themselves. Stonewall's homophobia in football survey a year after the Campbell chant found 85% supported the eventual action taken by police against the fans involved[7] and the season after the chant, banning orders in English football shot up 15% from the previous season, to 3,391 bans following a rise in fan-reported incidents.[8]

While diminishing, homophobic chants remain commonplace, particularly in games involving Brighton and Hove Albion. Gay Spurs fan Darryl Telles, author of *We're Queer and We Should Be Here,* wrote about his experience of following his team at Brighton when his fellow Tottenham fans sung their way through a homophobic repertoire: "Some may see it as banter and when it's written down here it looks like a bad joke; *'Does your boyfriend know you're here?'* or *'We can see you holding hands'.* However, when it's hundreds of fans singing the same chant, you suddenly, as a gay man, feel vulnerable and isolated. It re-affirmed the notion that I didn't belong—certainly not there among a crowd whose side I was supposed to be on".[9]

Four years after the Campbell chant, the Brighton and Hove Albion Supporters Club and the Gay Football Supporters' Network teamed up and collated a dossier of abuse, which they submitted to the FA and the Football League, noting they had already spent more than 15 years trying to get the authorities to take the abuse seriously. The dossier recorded homophobic specific chants by 72% of opposition fans over the course of the 2012-13 season, including: *"Town full of faggots"*, *"We can see you holding hands"*, *"We always shag girls"*,

6   Wilson. J, 2008, 'Police called in over Sol Campbell abuse by Tottenham Hotspur fans at Fratton Park', 1 October 2008

7   BBC, 2009, 'Football failing on homophobia', BBC, 12 August 2009

8   Data.gov, 2015, 'Statistics on football banning orders', 26 November 2015

9   Telles. D, 2017, 'We're Queer And We Should Be Here', 2017, Memoirs Publishing, p113

"What's it like to suck a cock?" and *"You're Queer and you know you are"*.[10]

The dossier, alongside a campaign called 'Right Behind Gay Footballers' for players to wear rainbow coloured laces over one weekend in September 2013, drew support, as well as some criticism, from fans, players and Gay Rights groups.[11] Criticism for the campaign came from fellow equality group Football v Homophobia, who expressed concern over the language used in the campaign, stating: "We applaud the sentiments behind the idea central to the 'Rainbow Laces' campaign, namely solidarity with gay players. [But] it is incongruous to run a campaign aiming to change football culture while using language which reinforces the very stereotypes and caricatures that, in the long term, ensure that homophobia persists".[12] While not perfect, the campaign did succeed in bringing the prevalence of homophobic abuse back to national attention and helped shine a spotlight on the ongoing problem with homophobia in football. In-turn, the renewed focus on homophobic chanting in the national consciousness helped to kick off a campaign for homophobic abuse to be given the same legal classification as racist abuse.

A year after the dossier was handed to the FA and Football League, Colin Kazim-Richards became the first footballer to be charged by police with using abusive or insulting behaviour. The former Brighton player, returning with Blackburn Rovers mimicked pulling down his shorts and covering his buttocks during a game at Brighton's Amex home. After Kazim-Richards was found guilty and fined £750, PC Darren Balkham, Sussex Police's football liaison officer for Brighton and Hove Albion, told the BBC: "Brighton fans have been subjected to a lot of homophobic abuse over many years. We are where racism was 20 years ago".[13] That same season Channel 4 show *Dispatches* recorded men, women and children at Crystal Palace v Brighton singing

[10] Sharpe. R, 2013, 'The shocking list of alleged homophobic abuse suffered by Brighton supporters', 3 April 2013

[11] Magowan. A, 2013, 'Rainbow laces: Anti-homophobia group criticised by campaigners', 19 September 2013

[12] Magowan. A, 2013, 'Rainbow laces: Anti-homophobia group criticised by campaigners', 19 September 2013

[13] BBC, 2014, 'Colin Kazim-Richards guilty over homophobic gesture', BBC, 9 April 2014

to the tune of the hymn 'Kumbaya My Lord':

"Up the arse,
My lord,
Up the arse"

As a result, the following month East Midlands police warned Leicester's fans that such chants would not be tolerated ahead of the club's meeting with Brighton.[14] Frustratingly, East Midlands police's zero-tolerance approach was not carried out nationwide and a further three years on Brighton in particular were still suffering. Liz Costa from the Brighton and Hove Albion Supporters Club told the BBC in 2017: "We have been fighting it for more than 20 years. Some stewards over the years have thought it was funny, even some of the police. People said we would never get anywhere, that it was just banter. I'm sorry, I don't class it as that. If you were talking about black people rather than gay people, they would be whipped out of the stadium before their feet touched the floor. It starts with *"We can see you holding hands"* or *"Does your boyfriend know you're here?"* From there it can get more graphic or dark, such as *"You're from a town full of gays and we hope you all die of Aids"* [for example]". Abuse at one ground was so bad that BBC Sussex had to turn off a crowd microphone, while outside two fans were attacked.[15] The same year in a BBC Radio 5 Live survey, 8% of fans were still insisting that they would stop supporting their team if one of their players came out, while other respondents went as far as to say they are repulsed by seeing their club's badge on a rainbow backdrop.[16]

Brighton are far from being alone as the subjects of this abuse, just as Sol Campbell is not the only former Arsenal player to be taunted in this way. His former teammate Ashley Cole also become a target for abuse after he left the club on a free transfer for Chelsea in similar circumstances to Campbell's own switch to the Gunners from Spurs.

---

[14]   *Pink News, 2014, 'Police warn Leicester City fans: 'We won't tolerate homophobic chanting at Brighton match'', 8 April 2014*

[15]   *Henson. M, 2017, 'Homophobia in football', BBC, 17 August 2017*

[16]   *Henson. M, 2017, 'Homophobia in football', BBC, 17 August 2017*

As with Campbell, time was no healer and despite Cole having left the club nine years earlier, in 2015 mobile phone footage emerged of Arsenal fans singing their own version of Lily Allen's single 'Smile' ahead of their FA Cup semi-final with Reading:

"Ashley Cole,
Is a Chelsea batty boy,
He's a Chelsea batty boy,
He's a Chelsea batty boy"

Chelsea fans are also targeted with repeated homophobic chanting, with one chant in particular continuing to get frequent airings:

"Chelsea rent boys,
Chelsea rent boys,
Ohhh oooohh,
Ohhh oooohh"

The 'Chelsea rent boys' chant is believed to have originated in the 1980s after a newspaper reports of a police-raid on the home of a known hooligan from the Chelsea Headhunters. The officers were alleged to have found its target in bed with a male prostitute and led to fans adapting the infamous Headhunter chant from the time: *"Chelsea aggro, Chelsea aggro"*.

Three decades on, it is only the *'Chelsea rent boys'* version that remains heard on the terraces, despite it being repeatedly reported to the authorities. Tim Rolls, chair of the Chelsea Supporters Trust described the reception he received when he reported the chants to stewards at Manchester City's Etihad stadium and Liverpool's Anfield stadium: "At the Etihad the police just laughed. At Anfield I was told that the stewards in our section were policing us, not Liverpool supporters, and that if I persisted in complaining I would be ejected from the ground. I am not aware of stewards taking action against the chants at any ground".[17]

17 Lo. J, 2014, *"Chelsea rent boys' football chant accused of homophobia amid World Cup furore'*, Pink News, 17 July 2014

Then in 2016 Luton Town announced that they were investigating their own fans for homophobic chanting in a game at Leyton Orient. During that game, a section of Luton fans spotted two men watching from one of the surrounding flats, leading to chants of *"Do you take it up the arse"* and the slightly contradictory: *"We know what you're doing"*. Five days later, and only after being approached by a number of media organisations, Luton Town released a statement which threatened consequences for anyone found guilty. However, just as the police did in the Campbell incident, they passed the buck and placed the emphasis on fans to self-police and report incidents, saying:

"The Club was contacted by the media to respond to allegations that a small number of Luton Town fans made homophobic chants towards people occupying the flats that form part of the stadium. Luton Town take such allegations very seriously and were extremely disappointed to learn of these allegations which can tarnish the reputation of our club. We do not wish to be associated with anyone who believes such actions are acceptable. Unfortunately, the chanting was not reported by any spectator to police officers or stewards on duty at the time. With the incident not being reported to anyone within the stadium at the time, it makes retrospectively identifying and punishing any individual or group of individuals very difficult. Each club has received observations from supporters and from these communications it would appear that some good-natured exchanges between Luton fans and the occupants of the flats strayed into totally unacceptable homophobic chants. There can be absolutely no excuse for discriminatory chanting or gesturing of any kind. If any Luton Town supporter is proven to have taken part in any form of discrimination they can expect to be banned from attending matches at Kenilworth Road. Any supporter, should they see or hear of any such behaviour should inform a steward or club official in order that action can be taken against the culprit immediately".[18]

Other clubs have made more proactive steps towards turning the tide of homophobia in the game. For example, when Norwich City announced their support for Norwich Pride a few months before the

18 *Luton Town FC, 2016, 'Club Statement: Leyton Orient Incident', LutonTown.co.uk, 20 October 2016*

Luton incident, the club's official social media feeds received a backlash from some fans. One fan tweeted the club asking: "What the hell has this to do with football?". To their credit, the club immediately replied with the simple, but effective: "Everything".[19]

The fact Justin Fashanu made his name at Norwich, where he remains a cult hero, not least for his spectacular volley against Liverpool in 1980 which won BBC *Match of the Day's* Goal of the Season award, coupled with openly gay comedian and actor Stephen Fry's spell on the club's board, marks Norwich, along with Brighton, as a target for homophobic abuse. A minority of Ipswich fans, as part of their East Anglian rivalry have been known to chant celebratory songs regarding the death of Fashanu in games between the sides:

"He's gay,
He's dead,
He's hanging in the shed,
Fashanu, Fashanu"

To their credit, both Ipswich Town Football Club and a large section of their fans have condemned the chanting and in recent years it has been aired much less frequently.

Homophobic abuse at games is also often cited as the reason that there are, at the time of writing, no openly gay footballers playing in England's top-flight. Fashanu himself said in his suicide note that: "being gay and a [public] personality is so hard".[20] Fashanu's death led to the formation of 'The Justin Campaign', which joined forces with 'Pride Sports' to form 'Football v Homophobia', and 18 years after his death still has to include in its aims: "We want football to take a clear stand against homophobia and transphobia so that everyone can enjoy the beautiful game and so that football leads the way in removing discrimination and prejudice based on sexual orientation and gender identity".[21]

[19] Cunningham. D, 2016, 'What the hell has this got to do with football?', AlongComeNorwich, 30 July 2016

[20] Watson-Smyth. K, 1998, 'Fear of arrest led to Fashanu hanging himself', The Independent, 10 September 1998

[21] Football v Homophobia, 2018, 'Our Story', FootballVHomophobia.com, Retrieved 4 December 2018

Three years after the Campbell chant The Secret Footballer used his column in *The Guardian* to describe the environment from a player's perspective and highlighted the mirror of society that chanting holds up:

"If we apply the law of averages theory, it is highly likely there are gay players among the professional ranks of football. The reality is that I don't "officially" know any gay footballers. What we are all agreed on, however, is that there is principally one very good reason that gay players would keep their sexual allegiance firmly in the locker: the fans. For the most part football supporters give out stick that qualifies as banter. But every now and again an element will cross the line. Would you come out and then travel around the country playing football in front of tens of thousands of people who hate you? I wouldn't. I would be in the dressing room feeling hugely depressed that certain components of our great game make it all but impossible for me to do anything other than keep quiet. Sadly, I'd say the general abuse players receive hasn't got much better. It is very rare that there is any appreciation of the opposition's great play, a stunning goal is normally met with a thousand hand gestures from the stands and our best talent is routinely booed with the sort of vigour and hatred that, I feel, offers us a precious insight into society as a whole. The changing room is a very harsh place to survive— say what you like about footballers' lack of intelligence (and people often do), the banter is razor-sharp and anything out of the ordinary is seized upon in a flash. But this is precisely the reason why a gay player would feel comfortable coming out here. A footballer is a footballer, it doesn't matter if you are black, white, straight or gay, players are at ease in this environment, where they are used to piss-taking. But the terraces are a different ball game. We are not at home here and are very much on our guard around fans. The changing room offers a strange, familiar sanctuary where the preferred etiquette is to have a quick laugh, look as if you know what's going on and get on with things".[22]

Sadly, the safe, comfortable environment in changing rooms described by The Secret Footballer is not always reflected out on the pitch. As with the Manchester United-Liverpool rivalry, which

[22] *The Secret Footballer, 2011, 'Fans stop gay players coming out', The Guardian, 12 March 2011*

descended into violence on and off the pitch, football's problem with homophobia has spilled from the stands to players and back again. Di Cunningham, organiser of Norwich City LGBTQ+ Supporter Group Proud Canaries and Chair of Pride in Football, explained in Norwich City fanzine *Along Come Norwich*, why she felt this was.

"Given the homophobic abuse routinely heard from the stands and seen on social media (and that's in the absence of any confirmed gay player) it's not hard to figure out why being closeted is preferable. It's clearly not only supporters who perpetuate football's casual homophobia; [a recent] Chelsea v Spurs Premier League clash saw Coventry City defender Chris Stokes deride players as "Faggots" on Twitter, later suggesting he'd been shocked to learn what the word meant. Ex-Birmingham and Derby defender (now manager of the Guayana national team) Michael Johnson who branded homosexuality "detestable" on Nicky Campbell's *Big Question* television show. I was devastated to hear that Martin O'Neill joked at Euro 2016 about being thought of as "queer" for spending too much time with Roy Keane. While Stokes received a minor rebuke, a penalty from his club, and Equality Training from the English FA, the FA of Ireland haven't taken issue with O'Neill and are yet to act in response to grotesquely racist and homophobic tweets made during the Euros by League of Ireland Premier Division Manager Murt O'Connor; who tweeted an image of an ape he tagged '[Raheem] Sterling' and reported that the Orlando Massacre murderer wasn't 'a Straight Shooter'."[23]

For his part Michael Johnson went on to apologise for his comments, which he called "naïve" and blamed on his Christian views and a lack of education at the time.[24] Yet, while openly gay players may be invisible on the pitch, LGBTQ+ supporter groups are becoming increasingly visible in the stands. Cunningham's own efforts include establishing first Norwich's 'Proud Canaries' and then an England equivalent named '3 Lions Pride', for the 2018 FIFA World Cup in Russia, which she attended despite death threats. 'Gay Gooners', 'Canal Street Blues' and 'Proud Lilywhites' soon followed at Arsenal,

[23] Cunningham. D, 2016, 'What the hell has this got to do with football?', AlongComeNorwich, 30 July 2016

[24] Fisher. B, 2018, 'Michael Johnson: I stopped counting after 42 rejected job applications', The Guardian, 18 November 2018

Manchester City and Tottenham respectively and have been joined by more than 30 groups across the 92 Football League clubs, with Leeds and QPR among the most recently established. They are an active, visible opposition to a terrace culture that has ranged from unwelcoming to outright hostile to the thousands of, often unseen, gay fans in their midst. As Cunningham explains:

"Advances in rights and changes in public attitudes have made it easier for LGBT people to be open with family and work mates about who they love [and] there's an obvious feedback cycle: as more sports professionals and celebrities come out they become role models and inspire others to be honest with themselves and others about their sexual orientation. And the openness helps, mentally and physically. In the absence of a strong line from the game's guardians to address this systematically, LGBT+ supporters themselves have taken on homophobes and trolls—with groups at clubs around the country asking fellow fans to ally up and challenge abuse in stadia if they feel safe to do so with Pride in Football's #CallitOut campaign. A simple, 'We're better than that' or 'Show some respect' or even 'Yes, actually my boyfriend does know I'm here'. Promotion of diversity and inclusion at clubs can't just be left to fans. It's the responsibility of the FA and the Leagues to ensure that values are systematically embedded in club policies (including HR) and seen to be followed through with".[25]

Gay Gooners Chairman Dave Raval told the BBC: "We are treading the same path of anti-racism campaigners maybe 20 or 30 years ago. We are getting there a bit faster, but there is still a way to go".[26] Raval is right when he says there is still a way to go and levels of abuse remain so bad that as early as 2014 the Liberal Democrats announced at their Party Conference that they were putting policies in place to ensure homophobic chanting is classified and punished in the same way as racist abuse as part of their 'Reclaiming the People's Game' policy proposal. In announcing the move John Leech MP commented: "In the 21st century, football grounds need to be a place where everyone feels comfortable, regardless of whether they are black or white, straight or gay. Football has worked hard to try

[25] Cunningham. D, 2018, 'What's Wrong with Football?!', AlongComeNorwich, 2 May 2018

[26] Henson. M, 2017, 'Homophobia in football', BBC, 17 August 2017

and kick racism out of the game. The Liberal Democrats want to see the same effort put in dealing with homophobia".[27]

Six years on and progress has been painfully slow, and when a section of Mexico fans were recorded singing homophobic chants in their 1-0 win over Germany in the 2018 FIFA World Cup, Conservative MP Damian Collins announced he had teamed up with former Wales Rugby Union captain Gareth Thomas to renew the push for amendments to the 1991 Football Offences Act:

"The time has come to move from acknowledgement to action. That is why Gareth and I are seeking to amend the Act to make chanting or gesturing of an indecent nature with reference to sexual orientation or gender identity against the law. When the Football Offences Act came into force, it made racialist abuse within football stadia illegal. The proposed amendment seeks to extend that legal protection to LGBT+ players and fans. If enacted, the bill would protect LGBT+ fans and players in the UK, recent events, including at the World Cup, have once again demonstrated that homophobic abuse takes place at football matches the world over. FIFA and other sports governing bodies should take the necessary steps to ensure that homophobic abuse will never be tolerated, and that action will be taken against people that engage in activities like these, no matter where the game is played. We hope that the bill will soon become law and will contribute to making football a sport that is truly open to everyone".[28]

Around the same time and a decade on from the Campbell chant, which had by then fallen into disuse, Spurs supporters remained unforgiving of their former captain, with some still singing a chant taunting him. While it was not overtly racist and homophobic like the 2008 offering, the chant, based on Leicester City's 'Jamie Vardy, he's having a party' song, still wished him dead:

**"When Sol dies,
We're having a party"**

---

[27] Leech. T, 2014, 'Homophobic chanting to be a criminal offence', Liberal Democrats website, Retrieved 19 September 2018

[28] Greenfield. P, 2018, 'MP aims to ban homophobic chants at football matches', The Guardian, 23 June 2018

As of early 2020, no progress has yet been made on Collins' and Thomas' bill as British politics became bogged down in leaving the European Union.

A couple of months later West Ham United fanzine *Pride of Irons* documented both their experience of homophobic chants being sung in the away end during the Hammers 1-0 Premier League defeat to Brighton and Hove Albion, and the reaction they received after drawing attention to it on their social media channel. Their experience is eye-opening and highlights how much work remains to be done:

"During Friday's match, two chants made an appearance ('*We can see you holding hands*' and '*Does your boyfriend know you're here?*'). Not really a surprise. Last season a few lads behind us tried to get one of the chants going. A few of us turned around, politely asked them to leave it out and it was over. Done. No aggro, no arguing and we carried on watching the game. This time though, it was different. It wasn't a small group of lads. We were surrounded by a wall of noise both in front and behind us. From where we were standing, it felt like the whole away end was joining in. Now despite what some might think looking at some of the comments on social media, our precious snowflake hearts didn't melt. We didn't run out crying or contact the stewards to grass anyone up. We looked at each other, rolled our eyes and shook our heads. Sure, it was disappointing, but as LGBT people, we've all dealt with much worse. At that particular moment I was most concerned about the young lad who was with us. He's approaching 10 and as you can imagine is football mad. He's like all kids at that age who are mad about football and having the opportunity to go to a Friday night game at that age and stay up late was almost too much excitement to take. The reason I was concerned about him is he has two Dads. Did he know what the chants meant? Was he okay? Looking at his expression I could tell he'd heard and he understood, but importantly he was okay. You see, kids from LGBT families aren't sensitive snowflakes either.

"We tweeted: "*Does your boyfriend know you're here?*" Sang loudly by the majority of frustrated West Ham fans. Pretty disappointing.' That's it. Disappointing. No-one claimed to be the victim of a hate crime or anything extreme. Just the general feeling among our group. Whilst I know there are plenty of people out there just gagging to tell me exactly how I should feel about the chants—and many have—or to tell me that it's 'just banter', let's be clear; calling someone gay or insinuating that they are as a form of insult isn't 'just banter'. The intention is to insult. If you're reading this and you disagree, then have the courage of your convictions and go speak to a gay friend or family member. Tell them you think the song is banter and then convince them. After all, if it's not a problem they won't have an issue with it, right? Don't have any gay friends to talk to about it? Maybe that's something to think about. Honestly though. It's a little ironic that we're the snowflakes for being disappointed by a chant, yet overreacting to our disappointment is totally reasonable.

"Responses to our tweet included: 'I'm only 27 and since I've left school you can no longer say; "you've dropped your gay card" or; "is that your best mate or your boyfriend?" Actually, you better not call yourself "Pride of Irons" because Irons is slang for poofs. To think Jesus died for this fucking generation...' I'm sure the Messiah would be horrified to find out that he gave his life and yet poor 27-year-olds can't go around mocking gay people. [Another read:] 'I do believe that political and rights activists groups should be kept out of football. Why does sexuality have to be constantly defined? You're just humans attracted to other humans. You're not special or hated... that taboo is long gone'—entirely missing the point that the chant had been sung to do the exact opposite, suggest that homosexuality is somehow different and thus worthy of ridicule.

"I've met so many West Ham fans over the years and none have ever had an issue with me being gay. Not to my face anyway. I don't think our fans are bigots and I'm confident the vast majority of those singing the chants aren't homophobic. They probably had a few beers and got swept up in the moment. And that's why we're disappointed. Because we know what it means to be West Ham. We know that's not what our club is about. 'West Ham Family' remember? Let's just hope next time we face Brighton the rest of the family remember us. It's strange. We're often told that we shouldn't bring sexuality into football. Groups like 'Pride of Irons' are regularly criticised for speaking out and told we'd be respected and left alone if we're quiet and don't draw attention to ourselves. Yet when LGBT people are dragged into football's spotlight through stuff like this, we're still the villains. We literally can't win. I guess the ultimate irony of this whole episode is that with the current attitudes towards us in football, you really can't see us holding hands. Most of us wouldn't dare".[29]

As the *Pride of Irons* article shows, despite widespread revulsion at the treatment of Sol Campbell, homophobic abuse has not been eradicated from English football stadiums. That said, it has at least led to it being toned down, without losing the competitive ridicule and subsequent humour. This is important because if football is to be made a sport that is open to everyone, there is a vital balance that needs to be struck between humour and offence. After all, humour plays a key role in football chanting and the creation of positive 'us' identities, because it is closely tied to the idea that success isn't important. Psychologist Dr Christina Fominaya sums it up: "the action people remember isn't the successful one, but the failed one. The power of the stories lies in their ability to provoke laughter and a shared sense of identification with the participants".[30]

In this way, humour helps foster and maintain a sense of identity and status, particularly in England and the UK. As social commentator AA Gill wrote: "Jokes are the English social currency, making mates and strangers laugh has a higher status in England than it does in almost any other country. Having a laugh isn't just a national cultural affinity, it's a large part of [our] behaviour and motivation".[31]

[29] *Pride of Irons, 2018, 'You can't see us holding hands', Pride of Irons website, 8 October 2018*

[30] *Fominaya. C, 2007, 'The Role of Humour in the Process of Collective Identity Formation', Cambridge University Press, Cambridge, p253*

[31] *Gill. AA, 2005, 'The Angry Island', 2005, Orion Books, London, p104*

8. HUMOUR & OFFENCE

'YOUR TEETH ARE OFFSIDE'

Humour, like identity and rivalry, is a key ingredient of football chanting, particularly in Britain. However, the use of humour, by its very nature, can lead to people being offended and the relationship between humour and offence is so intrinsic that social commentator AA Gill defines the former as "the sound of the bullies"[1] and it is fair to say that many football chants are often exaggerated insults and deliberately offensive in order to further foster the 'us v them' mentality.

Because both humour and offence are highly contextual and personal, something can be both funny and offensive at the same time, even to the same person. Linguistics expert Barry Blake sums up the difficulties of classifying something as being either funny or offensive when he says: "humour is universal, although what strikes some people as funny will not strike others in the same way".[2] Or, as British comedian Jimmy Carr and writer Lucy Greeves point out in an article on how to be funny: "the who, where, when, what and why of a joke's telling can be more significant than its topic, and no single theory—from Freud's notion of the joke as a release of suppressed sexual neurosis to Schopenhauer's definition of humour as a reaction to incongruity—can explain how jokes work".[3]

Importantly, humour and offence are often mutually dependent and as Jim Holt, who has written a history of jokes, notes: "the whole point of humour is to take a threatening, disquieting something and by a clever twist make it okay".[4] Social commentators and folklorists Alan Dundes and Thomas Hauschild agree: "Nothing is so sacred, so taboo, or so disgusting that it cannot be the subject of humour. Quite the contrary—it's precisely those topics culturally defined as sacred, taboo or disgusting which more often than not provide the principle grist for humour mills,

[1]   Gill. AA, 2005, 'The Angry Island', 2005, Orion Books, London, p112

[2]   Blake. B, 2007, 'Playing with Words', Equinox, London, p3

[3]   Carr. J and Greeves. L, 2006, 'How to be Funny', The Telegraph, 29 October 2006

[4]   Winterman. D, 2008 'Why is Russell Brand Funny?', BBC News, 3 November 2008

[after all] comedy and tragedy are two sides of the same coin".[5]

Football chanting can be described in similar terms to those ascribed to humour and offence above. Like jokes, chants can spring unbidden and unrehearsed, inspired by their context and their target. Chants are polarising because they depend on the team you support and also highly contextual. They often take their inspiration from societally taboos and are frequently laden with offensive language, which is included as an easy way to shock and to add immediate humour and offence. As Carr and Greeves note: "Surprise is the fundamental joke mechanism. A very cheap and easy way of making people laugh is to throw in some swear words. It's become something of a tradition among the more iconoclastic comics to write a routine that is ostensibly aimed at depriving taboo words of their power to shock, but which conveniently harnesses the power of shocking words to make us laugh".[6]

Writer David Shariatmadari argues that we have a uniquely visceral and emotional response to swear words that enhances their power:

"Most of the time, words behave themselves. They're just a useful arrangement of sounds in our mouths, or letters on a page. They have no intrinsic power to offend. If I told you that 'skloop' was a vile swearword in some foreign language, with the power to empty rooms and force ministerial resignations, you might laugh. How could an arbitrary combination of sounds have such force? But then think of the worst swearwords in your own language and you quickly understand that something else is at play here. Our reaction to them is instant and emotional. [Swear words] get dragged out of the linguistic realm, and into the emotional [realm]. People who have experienced brain damage in certain areas of the left hemisphere, which is the seat of language in most right-handed people, may find themselves unable to form sentences, but able to swear. They might retain the ability to shout words like 'Goddamit', even phrases like 'Heavens above' or worse. While parts of the highly evolved cortex may have been destroyed, areas that developed earlier in our history—the

---

[5]   Dundes. A and Hauschild. T, 1988, 'Auschwitz Jokes' from 'Humour in Society', Powell. C and
      Paton. G Eds, Macmillan, Basingstoke

[6]   Carr. J and Greeves. L, 2006, 'How to be Funny', The Telegraph, 29 October 2006

limbic system and basal ganglia, which mediate emotion and habitual movements—remain intact. This is where swearwords seem to live, in the animal part of the brain that once gave rise to howls of pain and grunts of frustration and pleasure. There's a time and a place for swearing, and a sense of taboo can help [us] understand that society expects different standards of behaviour in different surroundings".[7]

Swear words are also incredibly versatile, as linguistic expert, and Countdown regular Susie Dent wrote in *The Independent*: "How many other words can act as a noun: 'he doesn't give a fuck'; an adjective: 'not a fucking clue'; verb: 'I fucked up'; intensifier: 'it's gone fucking mad', and; everyday filler: 'abso-fucking-lutely'?".[8] The word 'fuck' is so versatile in fact it can do all of those jobs in single a sentence: "fuck the fucking fuckers".

Once you add the aspects Carr and Greeves note as being essential in the creation of humour to the emotional connection we have with swear words described by Shariatmadari and the high-octane context of a match day with all its incumbent joy and frustration, it becomes clear why swearing is such an integral part of football chanting. When included in football chants these qualities of humour can allow fans to ridicule people, organisations and social situations in a relatively harmless way, depending on your definition of harmless.

Journalist Mike Ward highlights both how football fans regard chanting as a genre, for humorous abuse and competitive one-upmanship, and how this may not be the case in the outside world:

"Correct me if I'm wrong but you've never had sexual intercourse with a sheep, right? Nor, for that matter, do you lick your lips at the prospect of munching on a deceased rodent retrieved from a domestic refuse receptacle. Splendid. Because countless football fans have been falsely accused of these and other unsavoury activities. Not just recently but for decades. I'm talking about the time-honoured taunts of rival fans. In that first instance, it's the trusty old chant of *'Sheep-sheep-sheep-shaggers'* directed towards fans of clubs from rural locations or supporters who follow teams located in Wales. In the second, I'm referring to the ditty which traditionally targets fans

---

[7] Shariatmadari. D, 2014, 'This is why your brain wants to swear', The Guardian, 22 April 2014

[8] Dent S, 2018, 'F-Word; You won't believe what it used to mean', The Independent, 4 July 2018

based on Merseyside, suggesting not only do they *'look in the dustbin for something to eat'* but that if they *'find a dead rat [they] think it's a treat'*. Ha ha. OK, so these and other taunts are all in jest. Harmless wind-ups and only someone with a triple sense-of-humour bypass would allow themselves to get offended by such cruelty, bigotry or statistical inaccuracy, right?"[9]

Ward's deliberation over whether the songs are mere "jest" shows how difficult it can be to classify the relative levels of humour and offence within chants, and as Gill wrote, they can contain both in equal measure: "The terraces are really, really funny and really, really horrible, both at the same time. It's the volume and the power, the huge wattage of anger, sharpened with malevolent wit".[10]

While not easy to define, there must be a line with acceptable mocking jest on one side and hateful abuse on the other. One suggestion is that the existence of laughter in and of itself makes any offensive content acceptable, but by that standard if a single person laughed at the Sol Campbell chant it is automatically rendered tolerable. Writer Paul MacInnes suggests three starting points for comedic content that would differentiate between humour that is both offensive and acceptable and hateful abuse: power, choice and originality. This is based on the assumption that those with more power and wealth have more advantages and therefore more choices. The logic being that mocking something that has been chosen, is acceptable. For example, it is fine to mock someone's choice of clothing or favourite band, but not the colour of their skin or sexuality.[11] As an example, take another chant born in the Manchester United-Liverpool rivalry: 'Your teeth are offside'. Aimed at then Liverpool striker Luis Suárez. The chant began at United and spread across fans of Premier League clubs during the 2013-14 season in the aftermath of Suarez being banned for ten matches for biting Branislav Ivanović and just two years after the Uruguayan received an eight-game ban for racially abusing United's Patrice Evra. Thus, Suárez was picked on for a combination of his buck-toothed appearance, his tendency to stray offside and his

[9]   Ward. M, 2003, 'Same Old Cliché, Always Boring?', *Four Four Two Magazine*, August 2003

[10]   Gill. AA, 2005, 'The Angry Island', 2005, Orion Books, London, p112

[11]   MacInnes. P, 2010, 'Can you define offensive comedy?', *The Guardian*, 9 April 2010

biting ban with another reworking of the Beach Boys' 'John B Sloop':

"Your teeth are offside,
Your teeth are offside,
Oh Luis Suárez,
Your teeth are offside"

Taking MacInnes' suggested starting points of offensive comedy that is acceptable, the chant picks on someone with power and wealth for his choice to both bite people and repeatedly be caught offside within a game. You could go as far as arguing that because Suárez was earning more than £100,000 per week at Liverpool, he had also made the choice to not pay for cosmetic dental work.

While undoubtedly potentially offensive, 'Your teeth are offside' mocks Suárez in an original and ridiculous way. The potential for offence is not in the same league as the chant which Spurs fans taunted Campbell with, or those Manchester United and Liverpool fans indulged in about Munich, Heysel and Hillsborough.

Aided by social media and having been immediately picked up by television 'Your teeth are offside' spread like wildfire across Premier League grounds as the season went on. The chant was also well-received in Europe and cited as an example of chanting and English humour at its best, with *L'Équipe* quoting the song and noting: "You can say what you like about England, there is a real football culture. And in the stands, humour inspired by Monty Python, silly, wicked and so funny".[12] The French broadcaster RMC picked up on the key roles played by humour and offence in football chanting during their coverage of the game and declared that thanks to that chant, Manchester United fans had won the battle of the terraces.

Less well known is the Liverpool fans' immediate response to *'Your teeth are offside'*, which used the same tune:

"He bites who he wants,
He bites who he wants,

[12] *Sport Witness, 2013, 'Manchester United chat about Suarez impresses French media', Sport Witness, 15 January 2013*

Oh Luis Suárez,
He bites who he wants"

Tottenham, taking inspiration from Manchester United's taunts of their rival's star player, created their own version of the song to taunt Arsenal's German playmaker Mesut Özil:

"His eyes are offside,
His eyes are offside,
Oh Mesut Özil,
His eyes are offside"

'His eyes are offside' aptly highlights the importance of context and the wafer-thin line between football chants being funny and offensive, or just the latter. While on the face of it, *'His eyes are offside'* is identical to *'Your teeth are offside'* in mocking somebody with wealth and power for their personal appearance the chant aimed at Özil is mocking an aspect of the person in which they have no choice. Suárez's consistent history of biting opponents, which is his choice, arguably makes mocking his teeth more acceptable.

It is never quite that clear-cut, however, and the large grey area that exists is highlighted in two more examples both involving Liverpool players at the time and using the same call and response-style tunes.

The first is part of a series of chants, aimed at Peter Crouch, who stands 6'7" tall:

"Does the circus,
Does the circus,
Does the circus know you're here?
Does the circus know you're here?"

Early in his career Crouch was subjected to the circus chant week-in, week-out, along with the even less sophisticated; *"Freak, freak, freak"*. Crouch later recalled how during his formative footballing years he would sometimes come off the pitch at half-time and find his dad tussling with groups of fans who'd spent the last 45 minutes abusing the player. It's also worth highlighting that Crouch was receiving this abuse at the start of his career, long before his footballing ability brought him wealth or power. Crouch, for his part, never seemed to let his unusual height bother him and used it to his advantage in his career. When he published his autobiography in 2018, Crouch also noted an interesting aspect of British polite society and how height is a physical characteristic that as a society we find it acceptable to point out and mock: "If you have a big nose, you don't get people coming up to you in the street and shouting 'Bloody hell, look how big your nose is' [but] I always wanted to be a footballer. Not a basketball player as I get asked on a daily basis, or a roofer who doesn't need a ladder, or a zookeeper who can talk to the giraffes face-to-face. I like being tall. I wouldn't change it for the world. I was born tall and I carried on being tall".[13]

When Crouch joined Liverpool in July 2005, following their incredible European Cup comeback win against AC Milan, his height was again the inspiration for the chants directed at him, but this time they were more affectionate in nature:

"He's big,
he's red,
His feet stick out the bed,
Peter Crouch, Peter Crouch"

Another example of a physical characteristic which is deemed fair-game to mock comes from a 2013 Premier League match in which West Ham fans taunted Liverpool's young midfielder Jonjo Shelvey, who is completely bald due to alopecia. While Shelvey was warming up in front of them, they sang:

"He's coming for you,
He's coming for you,
Oh Harry Potter,
He's coming for you"

In video footage capturing the chant, Shelvey appears to immediately

---

[13]   *Crouch. P, 2018, 'How to be a footballer', Random House, London, p1-6*

find it funny, rather than offensive and after a couple of renditions during which he laughs along with his fellow Liverpool subs, Shelvey makes a point of applauding the West Ham fans for their inventiveness. However, while Shelvey appears to find the chant funny, as already discussed the presence of laughter alone, even when it is the intended subject or victim of the chant, should not be enough to render something abusive as acceptable. It is also important to note that the motivation for Shelvey's laughter at the chant is unclear. It could be that he genuinely found that chant funny, but at the same time, the phenomenon experienced and described earlier by Spurs fan Darryl Telles who points out that when hundreds of fans are pointing at you and singing the same rhythmic chant, there is the potential for you to feel vulnerable and isolated. It is therefore not inconceivable that Shelvey's laughter was a defence mechanism rooted in his feeling uncomfortable, which he then masked by his applause.

That said Shelvey has been vocal in his comfortableness with having alopecia, opening up to *The Guardian* about it later that year:

"[It] is something I was born with, [then] I fell down the stairs when I was a baby and fractured my skull and I think that made it worse. I think I always stressed myself out as a kid, and alopecia can be caused by stress. I tried things [to cure it] when I was younger. I tried this ointment that you used to rub into your head and you had to sleep in a woolly hat for three months. I got to about the fourth day and it was just roasting. I took the hat off and thought: 'If you don't like it, don't talk to me'. When I was with Arsenal [as a nine-year-old] I used to go into training with a baseball cap on, because I was so scared of what people were thinking when I was growing up. I remember walking through Romford with my sister and I had my bald head and people would stare. My sister would get upset about it and ask people what they were looking at. Now, I've got to the stage that I don't even bother shaving it some days. This is just the way I am, I suppose".[14]

West Ham's 'Harry Potter' chant doesn't just exemplify the fine line between humour and offence, but is also an example of a

[14] James. S, 2013, *'Jon-Jo Shelvey; growing up was rough, people were getting stabbed'*, The Guardian, 20 December 2013

chant which, like the Brighton dossier of homophobic abuse, helped highlight alopecia as a condition in the national consciousness.

In 2012, with chants established in the public consciousness as being deliberately offensive, both in subject and language, a tongue-in-cheek social media campaign to make well-known football chants politically correct caught the public imagination. Thousands of people posted reworked versions of their favourite chants, stripped of their crudity with the hashtag #PoliticallyCorrectFootballChants:

"You portly gentleman,
You portly gentleman,
You seem to have eaten all the pies".

Or the profanity shorn:

"Your footballing ability is not to a high enough standard,
And you are aware of this"

The latter chant went viral for its ability to retain its power to communicate the basic truth at the heart of the original while somehow becoming more amusing despite being stripped of its offensive language. Chanting doesn't rely solely on swearing to express culturally taboo masculine identities, highlighted by one chant submitted to the hashtag, which retains its offensive heterosexual and misogynistic content, regardless of the language used:

"Please remove your brassiere,
And display your mammary glands,
To the gentlemen" [15]

Chants can be funny, they can be offensive and often they are both, but their target is not always the opposition.

[15] *The Telegraph*, 2012, *'Twitter trend renders football chants politically correct'*, *The Telegraph*, 8 November 2012

9. THE ART OF SELF-DEPRECIATION

'WE LOSE EVERY WEEK'

If you rank English football clubs by the number of major honours they have won over the course of their history, Arsenal are third behind Manchester United and Liverpool, yet Arsenal fan Nick Hornby famously and evocatively recalled his experiences of his first ever football match in less than glowing terms:

"What impressed me most was just how much most of the men around me hated, really hated, being there. As far as I could tell, nobody seemed to enjoy, in the way that I understood the word, anything that happened during the entire afternoon [...]. The natural state of the football fan is bitter disappointment. I'd been to public entertainments before of course; I'd been to the cinema and the pantomime and to see my mother sing in the chorus of *The White Horse Inn* at the Town Hall. But that was different. The audiences I had hitherto been a part of had paid to have a good time and though occasionally one might spot a fidgety child or a yawning adult, I hadn't ever noticed faces contorted by rage or despair or frustration. Entertainment as pain was an idea entirely new to me, and it seemed to be something I'd been waiting for".[1]

New York Times journalist Rory Smith observed a similar phenomenon to Hornby, in which experiencing pain is considered both desirable and even necessary for an authentic part of the football fan experience. Smith, who had just covered the 2018 Champions League final in which Liverpool had been defeated by Real Madrid, tweeted afterwards: "[Some people claim] losing a final doesn't count for anything. It does. Maybe nobody remembers second place. But a) the relevant fans remember finals, and football is about memories. And b) losing a final is better than losing in the quarters. More painful, but better".[2]

In describing the essence of suffering as being at the heart of what it is to be a football fan, Smith and Hornby are echoing the assessment of a cultural shift, originally identified by German sociologist Gerhard Schulze, who found that in Western societies having an authentic

[1]   Hornby. N, 1998, 'Fever Pitch', Riverhead Books, London, p110-111

[2]   Smith. R, 2018, '@RorySmith', Twitter, 26 May 2018

"experience" has become a focus of social, economic, and cultural activity, resulting in a strong focus on experience for the construction of our social identities.[3] In a 2008 survey of over 2,000 fans across Europe, three-quarters reported that the atmosphere was as important to them as the game.[4] As any fan can confirm football is not always good. It's not even often good. It can be dull, and it is certainly increasingly expensive. However, as fans we keep coming back and a large part of why we keep coming is the ability to make our own fun, despite, or even because of, the frequent frustrations and heartbreak.

Success is immaterial to the experience of being a football fan. As the Social Issues Research Centre in their study on passion in football put it: "loyalties are demonstrated and reinforced and in the strong sense of belonging that goes with being a 'true' fan" with 90% of fans surveyed, agreeing with the statement 'I associate football with passion and dedication'.[5] Note the prominent role played by aspects like "loyalty" and "dedication" in the fan experience, things that can't be demonstrated without enduring a period of hardship. Nick Hornby's description of his experience as a fan chimes with Schulze's finding, noting "it simply doesn't matter how bad things get, results have nothing to do with anything [...] I would like to be one of those people who treat their local team like their local restaurant, and withdraw their patronage if they're being served up rubbish. Unfortunately, there are many fans like me. For us consumption is all; the quality of the product is immaterial".[6]

Psychologist Dr Christina Fominaya found that "the action people remember isn't the successful one, but the failed one. The power of the stories lies in their ability to provoke laughter and a shared sense of identification with the participants".[7] Sports historian Richard Holt expressed a similar sentiment when he said: "inhabitants of big cities need a cultural expression of their urbanism which goes beyond the

[3]   *Von Hantelmann. D, 2014, 'The Experimental Turn', Walker Art Organisation, Retrieved 25 September 2018*

[4]   *Social Issues Research Centre, 2008, 'Football Passions', Social Research Centre, London, p11*

[5]   *Social Issues Research Centre, 2008, 'Football Passions', Social Research Centre, London, p9*

[6]   *Hornby. N, 1996, 'Fever Pitch', Indigo, London, p150*

[7]   *Fominaya. C, 2007, 'The Role of Humour in the Process of Collective Identity Formation', Cambridge University Press, Cambridge, p253*

immediate ties of kin and locality. This need for rootedness as well as excitement is most evident in the behaviour of football crowds".[8] For football fans the experience of attending matches and thus remaining part of this community is what sustains their support of the club, not how successful that club is.

This is most starkly illustrated in a study on the economics of football carried out in 2014 which found that the longer a club had existed the more loyal, measured by average attendances over a 50-season period and weighted relevant to that club's on-field success, their fans tended to be, concluding: "Duration of membership [of the Football League] is a significant determinant of loyalty. These results suggest that clubs which joined the league early continue to enjoy significant 'first-mover' advantages, in many cases more than a century after they first gained membership. It is evident that sporting history and tradition remain important factors in shaping patterns of demand for attendance at English football, even in the modern era".[9] The emphasis is on football fandom as an authentic and lived experience: being there, playing your part by chanting and understanding what being a fan is all about are crucial to this.

In their wide-ranging research into what sustains passionate loyalty to football clubs among fans, the Social Issues Research Centre concluded: "Emerging throughout these discussions about what constitutes a 'real' fan was the idea that it required both work and the acquisition of knowledge and skills. You can't simply walk into a stadium and immediately be accepted as a fellow fan. There are chants and songs to learn and an appreciation of 'proper' attitudes and modes of behaviour to be developed. Status positions with the main group of fans need to be identified and respected—your own status will ultimately rely on the extent to which your group membership has been earned in such ways".[10]

This process, which includes reference to the unwritten rules that govern expected codes of behaviour at football, is strengthened by

[8] Irwin. C, 2006, 'Sing When You're Winning: Football Fans, Terrace Songs and a Search for the Soul of Soccer', Carlton, London, p112

[9] Dobson. S, and Goddard. J, 2014, 'The Economics of Football', Edward Elgar Publishing, p372

[10] Social Issues Research Centre, 2008, 'Football Passions', Social Research Centre, London, p18

eliminating those aspects that make the individuals within a football crowd strangers to each other, and in-turn making the shared bonds—location and support of a football team—sacred.

Chanting is a way to recognise and vocalise those shared bonds and experiences. Communal strength can be derived from those shared agonies, even in the face of on-field adversity, enhancing the pain they have endured together in becoming loyal fans of their club and thus celebrating their 'us' identity. As *Guardian* journalist Andrew Harrison notes: "As anyone who has ever stood in a crowd knows, chanting is exhilarating. There's a binding joy to be had from singing together, be it a song as moving as 'You'll Never Walk Alone' or something as daft as aiming 'Your teeth are offside' at Luis Suárez. Chants can create unity".[11]

In recognising, vocalising and celebrating those bonds, fans are also taking strength from them, partly due to a sense of safety in numbers but also because, as noted earlier, singing makes us feel good, releases endorphins and gives us something else to focus on, with a particular power to quell anxiety.[12] In the immediate build up to the 2018 Champions League Final, Rory Smith wrote about how Liverpool fans had sung in order to help each other—fans and players alike—to get-through the nervous agony of a tight semi-final v Roma: "In those last, fretful minutes in Rome, when every second felt like an age and the final whistle seemed as though it would never come, Liverpool's fans sang to stave off the nerves. It was ritual, distraction and prayer: They started with 'You'll Never Walk Alone' the club's hymn, switched to 'The Fields of Anfield Road' and then, finally, sang, 'We Shall Not Be Moved'. When the game ended, Liverpool's players ran over to the corner of the Stadio Olimpico where the traveling fans had been corralled, another song started, much louder this time, more joyous".[13] Chanting had worked, the team had won and now it was time to celebrate together.

As well as distraction, chanting can be used to comfort, in the same

[11] Harrison. A, 2017, 'Oh Jeremy Corbyn; how Seven Nation Army inspired the political chant of a generation', The Guardian, 8 October 2017

[12] McLean. T, 2008, 'Choral singing makes you happy', Sydney Morning Herald, 10 July 2008

[13] Smith. R, 2018, 'How an Italian Disco Hit Became Liverpool's Champions League Anthem', New York Times

way that 'You'll Never Walk Alone' was used to provide solace to a recently bereaved Jean in *Carousel*. Particularly useful as a soothing, verbal comfort-blanket is the self-depreciating chant, which is one way in which togetherness in the face of adversity can be expressed *en masse*, or as journalist Paul Doyle writes, the self-depreciating chant shows that "unity in glorious nihilism is strength".[14]

For the most common example of this type of comforting, self-depreciation chanting, take the tune of old favourite 'Sloop John B':

> *"We lose every week,*
> *We lose every week,*
> *You're nothing special*
> *We lose every week"*

'We Lose Every Week' is painfully blunt in its assessment of the performance of the fan's team, but this bluntness acts to bring together a community of disparate, frustrated and angry people. Note how, even given the calamitous state of affairs on the pitch, the crowd continue to identify as one with the under-performing players, through the personal pronoun "we".

Context is again crucial and frequently the more embarrassing the on-pitch performance, the louder and more heartfelt, the chant. Just as it brings those singing it together, '*We lose every week*', simultaneously works to take the shine off the opposition's glee, by stating that by winning, the opposition are just like everyone else and "nothing special". Then, in addition to taking the joy of victory away, the subtext of the chant is essentially: 'Sure, we lose every week, but we lose together as a tight-knit community. Furthermore, despite losing every week, we still come and watch, which in turn makes us real fans, more worthy of respect than glory-hunting, plastic, fans. Those fans, the ones that frequently taste victory, might get to win matches, but they don't get to belong, and belonging is much more important than winning anyway'.

Assigning credit for starting chants is always difficult, but '*We lose every week*' appears to have first been sung by West Ham fans

---

[14] *Doyle, P, and Glendenning. B, 2016, 'The Joy of Six: Football Chants', 6 May 2016*

in January 2014 while 3-0 down to Nottingham Forest, who were in the division below, in an FA Cup third round match they lost 5-0. The Hammers, then sung it again later that season as they lost 6-0 to Manchester City in the League Cup semi-finals. Two months on, Norwich City fans sung it in response to Arsenal fans gloating about taking a 2-0 lead at Carrow Road, in a game that would ultimately relegate the Canaries from the top-flight. Social media is also full of clips of fans from almost every club having cause to break into 'We lose every week' at some stage since, which highlights the pride felt by supporters up and down the land in supporting their team, despite their on-field woes.

This reverse pride garnered from abject performances is further highlighted by the number of different examples, which all do the same thing. For example, take these three chants, sung in quick succession by Tottenham Hotspur fans after falling 4-0 behind at Anfield:

> *"You've only scored four,*
> *You've only scored four,*
> *How shit must you be?*
> *You've only scored four"*

'You've Only Scored Four' like 'We Lose Every Week', is set to the tune of 'John B Sloop', but with adapted words to fit the specific context of the situation. Again, the purpose is to derive strength from the adversity bringing together the fanbase while, more overtly here, taking the shine off the celebrations of the Liverpool fans.

'You've Only Scored Four' was soon followed by:

> *"5-4,*
> *We're gonna win 5-4,*
> *We're gonna win 5-4,*
> *5-4,*
> *We're gonna win 5-4,"*

The '5-4' chant signals a switch in emphasis, which is matched in a switch in tune and an increased tempo. Having taken the shine off Liverpool's 4-0 lead and galvanised themselves in the process, the Spurs fans then adopt a more optimistic and positive outlook, demonstrating the indefatigable hope that sustains fandom, in a sport in which success, even for top sides is rare. As the work conducted by the Social Issues Research Centre says: "[Supporting a team] is rarely straightforward [and it is] often emotionally fraught, but at times [you are rewarded with] the most intense and beautiful of experiences".[15]

Unsurprisingly, the hoped comeback didn't materialise, but the Spurs fans continued to make their own entertainment, moving on to another chant, sung to the tune of Welsh hymn 'Bread of Heaven' and popular with clubs when losing heavily and playing poorly:

"Let's pretend,
Let's pretend,
Let's pretend we scored a goal,
Yeeeeaaaaaahhhhh"

Adding some much-needed additional joy, 'Let's Pretend' comes complete with mock goal celebration, complete with cheering, fist-pumping and the hugging of the stranger enduring the same agony next to you.

To emphasise the point that there is pride in displaying loyalty through adversity these chants are accompanied with fans displaying that overt pride through their body language: making themselves appear as large as possible by standing straight with their arms out-stretched up and away from them. According to Professor Krauss Whitbourne these are an archetypal sign of unwavering confidence, pride and control, whereas "a sagging posture, tells other people that you don't feel very good about yourself. Keep yourself upright, but not ramrod stiff, and you let the world know that you feel comfortable in your body and, by extrapolation, good about yourself".[16]

With its roots in pride, it is no surprise that a posture of outstretched arms, raised in a 'V for Victory' salute above your head, is hard-coded into our evolutionary make-up rather than a learned behaviour. Scientific studies of victorious athletes in the Olympics and Paralympics observed that blind athletes use the very same gestures as their sighted

[15] *Social Issues Research Centre, 2008, 'Football Passions', Social Research Centre, London, p13*

[16] *Whitbourne. SK, 2012, 'The Ultimate Guide to Body Language', 30 June 2012*

peers, even though they have never seen anyone else do it. The psychologists involved in the study, Dr Jessica Tracy of the University of British Columbia and Professor David Matsumoto of San Francisco State University, suggested the reason such behaviour became hardwired into us, is because they were universal signs of dominance and submission among our ape relatives and ancestors. They concluded: "When competitors make these gestures after a competition, they are confirming their place in the pecking order". Dr Tracy added: "anecdotal evidence suggests, the human pride and shame displays are very similar to non-human displays of dominance and submission, seen in a wide range of animals. Pride and shame would have been powerful mechanisms in enhancing or inhibiting an individual's social status".[17]

In evolutionary terms, by adopting the victory sign, you make yourself appear larger but are thus more visible to any would-be predators. Therefore, in raising your arms you demonstrate that you feel confident enough to boost the risk of attack. As such, by adopting this position on the terraces, fans are communicating their disregard for the perceived danger, albeit in this context of being embarrassed by their team's shoddy efforts, rather than eaten. Furthermore, if fans did the opposite of this, and slumped quietly into their seats, this would convey an acceptance of defeat and a lack of fight or desire to regain the upper hand, something they would deem unacceptable in their team and therefore by extension apply that standard to themselves.

It is this idea of supporting through the bad times, being more important than on-field success that is behind other frequently heard chants like:

> *"You only sing when you're winning,*
> *Sing when you're winning,*
> *You only sing when you're winning"*

And:

> *"Where were you when you were shit?*
> *Where were you when you were shit?"*

---

[17] *Highfield. R, 2008, 'Victory salute hardwired into our genes', 11 August 2008*

Precisely because the success of their club is immaterial to the experience of being a football fan, there is a vast camaraderie and mutual respect between fans of different clubs, which exists, like an iceberg just below the surface of the fierce, visible tribal loyalties. This was highlighted in the work conducted by the Social Issues Research Centre which concluded: "Supporters who desert their teams when they are underperforming are simply not 'real fans'. In fact, the 'fair-weather' fan is the most widely derided type of football supporter. Being a fan means accepting emotional risk and being prepared to 'suffer'".[18]

The concept of being a real fan, or a set of real fans, is an important one because when times get hard it is frequently to this sense of authenticity to which fans turn to provide both comfort and a perceived moral victory that is more important than whatever is happening on the pitch. As writer Pete Miles wrote about the vocal "Ultras" at clubs around the world: "The ultras are not just about the here and now, their displays can evoke memories of not only the club's history but also the story of the town or the area. Cultural identity plays a huge part in their rabid support of a club".[19]

This sense of cultural identity is particularly pronounced among away fans who, by virtue of spending more money and time on following their club around the country, are frequently the most devoted, passionate and therefore vocal fans. The presence of away fans also helps increase the atmosphere among the home fans because the 'us' and 'them' identities become more pronounced and thus more fierce. This was one of the reasons the Football Supporters' Federation (FSF) fought for cheaper tickets for away fans in their 'Twenty's Plenty' campaign.[20]

Kevin Miles, Chief Executive of the FSF, explained the rationale behind the campaign, saying: "Away fans in particular bring noise and colour to grounds, adding to the spectacle immeasurably. But following your side on the road can be expensive and, despite football being wealthy we believe very little of it is used to reduce costs for

[18] Social Issues Research Centre, 2008, 'Football Passions', Social Research Centre, London, p13

[19] Miles. P, 2016, 'Beyond the Turnstiles', Ockley Book, Huddersfield, Yorkshire, p22

[20] Gibson. O, 2013, 'Atmosphere and fans' role in Premier League games becoming a concern', The Guardian, 16 November 2013

match-goers".[21] Journalist David Edwards went as far as to label away fans "the lifeblood of our national game" adding: "take them away and see what atmosphere you are left with".[22]

The reason away fans sacrifice so much time and money on following their team around the country is a sense of identity and belonging, frequently expressed through their chanting, no matter what is happening on the pitch. As one Coventry City fan put it: "What is important is to be there to let the others know that you are not just a 'home fan' that goes only to home matches when things are going well. The bloke in the pub who never goes who starts telling you how Coventry City should be playing [...] It's like people who talk politics but don't vote. It's important to be there because you represent the group and the city, always and no matter what".[23]

Coupled with this, away fans are corralled into a smaller area of the stadium and thus, you have those people who want to sing and chant, physically located closer to one another and in turn able to sustain and grow those first murmurings of a chant. Author Tim Marshall highlights how this can help teams with large home grounds, across which their vocal support is too thinly spread to kick-start any chanting: "[there are only] a limited number of people prepared to sing at the Emirates Stadium. Sometimes you can't hear the songs for the noise of children crunching and slurping overpriced crisps and fizzy drinks. You have to travel away from London N7 if you really want to hear the Arsenal fans singing".[24]

Not all self-depreciating chants require a team to be playing poorly and on occasion it is the unexpectedly good performance of a side that can inspire their fans to indulge in a self-depreciating sing-song. A frequent example, which again uses 'Sloop John B' (how The Beach Boys must wish that chanting counted toward chart position or resulted in royalties), is a classic of the self-depreciating chant genre:

[21] *Edwards. D, 2017, 'Premier League away fans to pay only £20 for tickets', The Telegraph, 7 April 2014*

[22] *Edwards. D, 2017, 'Premier League away fans to pay only £20 for tickets', The Telegraph, 7 April 2014*

[23] *Social Issues Research Centre, 2008, 'Football Passions', Social Research Centre, London, p12*

[24] *Marshall. T, 2014, 'Where do chants come from', The Telegraph, 1 August 2014*

"We're winning away,
We're winning away,
How shit must you be?
We're winning away"

'We're Winning Away' celebrates support in adversity, specifically away support, which is more difficult logistically, more expensive and therefore less likely when a club is doing badly, while also managing to fit in a quick taunt of the opposition.

Another example takes a swipe at modern football lexicon, with Aston Villa's away support heralding an early season 1-1 draw at Championship rivals Bristol City in September 2018. They reworked terrace favourite 'We're Gonna Win the League' with the rather more prosaic:

"And now you're gonna believe us,
And now you're gonna believe us,
And now you're gonna believe us,
We're there or thereabouts" [25]

A final example, sung by AFC Wimbledon in their FA Cup second round tie vs MK Dons in 2012, is both self-depreciating and existential.

The AFC Wimbledon-MK Dons rivalry is unlike any other in English football, born from one club becoming two. Founded in 1912 as Wimbledon Old Centrals, Wimbledon Football Club spent the 65 years scrabbling around in non-League football before finally being elected to the Football League in 1977. Within just nine years the club had risen through the top four divisions, winning promotion to the top-flight in 1986.[26] Two years later the Dons won their first and only major honour when a Lawrie Sanchez goal and a Dave Beasant penalty save—the first ever in an FA Cup Final—helped clinch a 1-0 FA Cup Final win over Liverpool. Within days of winning the cup, the issue of their Plough Lane home that would ultimately see the club dissolved 16 years later, began to rear its ugly head. Initially plans were

[25] Kendrick. M, 2018, '@MatKendrik', Twitter, 29 September 2018

[26] The Guardian, 2004, 'Wimbledon becomes MK Dons', 21 June 2004

submitted for Wimbledon to build a new all-seater stadium within their home London borough of Merton, but no site could be found. Then in 1991, following the production of the Taylor Report into the Hillsborough disaster, the need for a new ground re-emerged as Plough Lane was written off as too expensive to renovate.

Consequently, the club was forced to leave their home of 79 years in 1991 and become lodgers at Selhurst Park, the home of Crystal Palace. The arrangement was planned to be temporary but a decade on no local solution had been found and to almost universal horror, in 2001 the owners announced that they were planning on moving the club 56 miles north to Milton Keynes.[27] Despite opposition from across football the move was sanctioned on appeal in 2002.[28] Immediately a group of Wimbledon fans broke from their former club and despite warnings from the FA Commission who rubber-stamped the move that "resurrecting the club from its ashes [was] not in the best interests of football",[29] began a breakaway club of their own. The new club was named AFC Wimbledon and formed an agreement with Kingstonian FC to play at their Kingsmeadow ground, which was as close to Wimbledon's former home in Merton as possible. Breaking from the old club, which had just been relegated to League 1 (the third tier of English football), AFC would start in the Combined Counties League (the ninth tier).

Having begun in the worst possible way, the new club thrived thanks to the Herculean efforts of a raft of fiercely determined volunteers who used the adversity to their benefit. One co-founder of the club, Ivor Heller, told *The Daily Telegraph* that his instinct urged him to head across to the FA's headquarters in Soho Square and "smash the FA to pieces", but instead he channelled his energy into a more productive avenue, forming a new club: "I said to Kris Stewart, then Chairman of the Wimbledon Independent Supporters Club: 'Kris if you walk through those doors at 9am tomorrow morning I'll know we are on our way'. He was early. [At the meeting] I turned to a very good friend of mine and said: 'In ten years' time, we are going to get

----

27   BBC, 2001, 'League warns Dons over move', 10 August 2001

28   The Football Association, 2002, 'Summary of the Commission's Decision', 30 May 2002

29   Doyle. P and Glendenning. B, 2016, 'The Joy of Six; Football Chants', 6 May 2016

into the First Division and win the FA Cup'. Everyone turned around and said I was mad—which was quite right—but who is ever going to tell me or anybody else who follows a club called Wimbledon what to dream or what not to dream? We have already smashed everybody's expectations to pieces and we will carry on doing that for as long as we have breath in us".[30] Six weeks after that first meeting, AFC Wimbledon were playing their first match. The club mirrored the rapid rise of its first incarnation, winning five promotions in nine years. They didn't quite match Heller's bold claim but did achieve a remarkable return to the Football League by 2011, surviving their first Football League season comfortably.

In 2011/12 the club were celebrating their first decade since they formed, when the FA Cup draw paired them with their old club, the now renamed MK Dons, who were at the time only one division above. The draw was an exciting one for neutrals, but uncomfortable for AFC Wimbledon fans, as journalist Paul Doyle explains: "It was the draw everybody wanted, and nobody wanted. Far from viewing it as an excellent opportunity to bloody the nose of a club they refer to as Franchise FC, many AFC Wimbledon fans were appalled when news of the fixture broke. Now these [fans] were confronted by the prospect of having to muddy their spats on a visit to the ground of a club most held in contempt and whose existence many of them refuse to acknowledge".[31] The game was an eventful one, with MK Dons taking the lead before being pegged back. Finally, and only seconds away from a replay at Kingsmeadow, a loose ball flicked the heel of MK Dons defender Jon Otsemobor and looped up and over the stricken goalkeeper into the AFC Wimbledon net, giving MK Dons a 2-1 win. The real highlight came in the stands however, where on surveying the home fans, the travelling AFC Wimbledon fans asked:

> *"Where were you, when you were us?*
> *Where were you, when you were us?"*

MK Dons' move out of London also highlights the solidarity between

[30] Wilson. J, 2016, 'AFC Wimbledon's rise from the ashes', 29 May 2016

[31] Doyle. P and Glendenning. B, 2016, 'The Joy of Six; Football Chants', 6 May 2016

long-suffering fans. When the news of the plans were announced, the backlash from fans of all clubs was immediate and boycotts of Wimbledon home games by both home and away fans meant the average attendance at a Wimbledon game dropped from 18,000 to 3,000 almost overnight. The boycott lasted well beyond the club's eventual move from Selhurst Park to Stadium MK in 2004, following a four-year sojourn to the National Hockey Stadium. Bradford fan and sports journalist David Hobbs summed up the ongoing sentiments of many when he admitted: "Come five o'clock and *Final Score* on a Saturday I know where my sympathies lie and if MK Dons have lost, it feels like another small triumph, another dig in their ribs has been applied from all those 'real' fans who wish they weren't there. Childish maybe, but so is much of life as a football fan." He went on to add his admiration for the magazine *When Saturday Comes*, which has never featured an MK Dons fan in their season preview, instead leaving the space blank, but for the words "No questions asked".[32]

Co-Founder and current Editor Andy Lyons explains why the fanzine initially took and continues to hold this stance: "Through MK Dons, Milton Keynes essentially brought a football club and took it away from the people it really mattered to. If the town and its people had wanted a Football League club of their own, they could have built one from the existing clubs in the areas and climb the leagues, just as AFC Wimbledon have been forced to do. That process of taking a club away from its roots and artificially implanting it somewhere else, will always rankle with fans so as an editorial decision it's unlikely to change. They always will have stolen the club and no amount of time can change that".[33]

To this day fans of MK Dons' opponents will sing;

"Shit club,
No history,
Shit club,
No history"

---

[32] *Hobbs. D, 2013, 'MK Dons; Should I be over this now?', 19 November 2013*

[33] *Lyons. A, 2018, Email interview, 15 November 2018*

Meanwhile AFC Wimbledon fans, buoyed by Merton Borough Council's 2017 decision to grant planning permission for a new stadium back at Wimbledon's old Plough Lane site,[34] have a new song[35] to the tune of 'Show Me the Way to go Home':

> *"Show Me the Way to Plough Lane,*
> *I'm tired and I want to go home,*
> *I had a football ground 20 years ago,*
> *And I want one of my own"*

Through these self-depreciating examples, it is clear that when things go wrong, which as Hornby described and as all football fans know they frequently do, chanting can be a positive tool for bringing disparate people together and a source of comfort, albeit one laced with an unmistakably tribal, piss-taking nature.

---

[34] *The Guardian, 2017, 'AFC Wimbledon given permission to build a new ground at Plough Lane',*
      13 December 2017

[35] *Wilson. J, 2016, 'AFC Wimbledon's rise from the ashes', 29 May 2016*

10. IT'S NOT ALL VOCAL 1

'CLAPS, CLAPPING, CLAPPERS AND A THUNDERCLAP'

Many chants are not just vocal but are almost a dance of choreographed rhythmic clapping and gestures, which together form part of the overall performance. Academic studies have gone as far as to describe the complex and co-ordinated routines as rituals to explain fan behaviour that works to further strengthen those bonds of community within a fanbase, and which, like both chanting and football, have their roots deep in our ancestral pasts.

The study by the Social Issues Research Centre found that: "Rituals of various kinds are a common feature of every known human society, past or present, and they may be performed on specific occasions by a single individual or by an entire community. Rituals serve to express group obligations, strengthen social bonds within the group, state one's affiliation as a member of a group, or just for the sheer pleasure of the ritual itself. The matches are rife with ritualised behaviour such as chanting and flag-waving".[1] In Italy these rituals are almost militaristic, with groups of Ultras known to publicise their arrival in the stadium via choreographed drills and salutes, as well as through their flags, banners, chants, and flares.[2]

In some chants, clapping acts almost like punctuation, either as commas, which allow participants to pause for breath, or as exclamation marks accentuating points. Numerous chants combine the two. Sometimes the clapping can provide a rhythmic pulse to the chant, keeping the group in time and together. Examples include chants like Norwich City's 'Yellow Army', shortened by the tendency when using the Norfolk dialect to run words together and drop consonants to simply:

"Y'army,
(clap),
Y'army,
(clap),
Y'army,

[1] *Social Issues Research Centre, 2008, 'Football Passions', Social Issues Research Centre, London, p25*

[2] *Jones. T, 2016, 'Inside Italy's ultras', The Guardian, 1 December 2016*

(clap)
Y'army,
(clap)"

The 'Y'army' chant is one which most clubs have a version of with just the colour changing and which can continue on loop for five or ten minutes, acting almost as background noise between more complex or punchy chants. To allow it to perform this function, chants like 'Y'army' use clapping as both rhythm and punctuation. The clapping is an essential component because longer chants like this feature alternating voices in a call-and-response style in which one group will do the first 'Y'army', with a second group doing the next and both groups providing the clapping. The clapping between each line allows both groups to stay in time and provides a neat audible punctuation mark between lines. Furthermore, by using a call-and-response style and taking a breath between alternate lines, chants like 'Y'army' can continue for longer but maintain high-tempo, because everyone involved has time to get their breath back between each burst of noise. Note, too, the militaristic use of the word "army", which is one example of a fully-stocked armoury of war-based terminology that echoes across football chanting and is strongly linked to ideas of traditional masculinity in terms of fighting, strength and bravery,[3] which characterised those early hooligan firm chants of the early 1970s.

The most famous clapping chant of all, however, has not been around long, but provided the soundtrack to Euro 2016: 'The Thunderclap', which instantly became synonymous with Iceland, despite beginning life on a different shore years before.

The intimidating slow clap-based chant is simple in its construction, featuring a single booming clap alongside a deep vocal grunt that can most closely be represented on a page as *"huh"*. Alongside the clap and *"huh"* the chant calls for a bespoke style of clapping, with fans holding their arms aloft and straight and drawing their straightened arms together in a high-arc, creating a visual spectacle every bit as impressive and intimidating as the accompanying noise. Initially the gaps between the claps are long drawn-out silences, but as the chant

---

[3]   *Chilton. P, 2004, 'Analysing Poltical Discourse', Sage, London, p48*

progresses the gap between each clap shortens slightly, building to a crescendo and culminating in one final thunderous clap, followed by a massive cheer and a more traditional round of bent-arm applause. Given its intimidating sound and appearance the chant has been described as a 'Viking war chant' and it was almost immediately mythologised as an ancient pre-battle ritual, akin to that used by Heraclius.

However, according to Icelandic publication *Morgunblaðið*, Icelandic club Ungmennafélag Stjarnan adopted the song after being introduced to it during a Europa League game at Fir Park against Scottish Premier Division side, Motherwell.[4] "It's been popular here for a few years but I'm not sure quite when it started", Motherwell fans' representative Dave Wardrope told *The Guardian* in 2016. "No-one is certain, but we don't think our fans took it from another club's supporters. They made it up themselves".[5]

Rather than Vikings, the most frequently given explanation for how the thunderclap arrived at Fir Park is that Motherwell fans took it from the 2006 film *300* about a different warrior race: the Spartans. In the film Scottish actor Gerard Butler plays the lead role of King Leonidas who leads his army into a battle against the Persians. Along the way Butler is challenged on the diminutive size of his army by a rival general, Daxos, at which point Leonidas questions the troops of his rival, asking each in turn "What is your profession?" In each case the answer comes back; "potter", "sculptor", "blacksmith". Leonidas turns to his men and asks; "Spartans, what is your profession?" the answer comes back en masse; *"Huh, huh, huh"*, accompanied with a bang on their shield each time and increasing in tempo with each burst and mimicking the finale of the chant.[6] By answering in rhythmic unity, the power of the message is clear, we are one entity, united together and thus stronger than an army of any size constructed from individuals.

As with many chants there is no easy way to prove authorship of the thunderclap chant. However, a *Guardian* investigation into its origins uncovered footage of Middlesbrough supporters thunderclapping back

4   Davis. C, 2016, 'The origin of Iceland's Viking Thunderclap', The Telegraph, 8 July 2016

5   The Guardian, 2016, 'Iceland, Motherwell, Lens, where did the thunderclap originate?', The Guardian, 13 July 2016

6   Butler. G, 2006, '300', Warner Bros, USA

in 2013, while French football fan Yves Reny noted that an initially slow but quickening clap-based chant has been commonplace at Ligue 1 grounds for some time. This is especially the case in northern France, with RC Lens supporters having led the way by clapping in unison for more than two decades.[7]

Stjarnan's other claim to fame is their elaborate choreographed goal celebrations. In 2010 they were awarded the prize of 'Best Goal Celebration Ever' by Sky Sports for a routine in which the goalscorer become a fisherman hauling in and landing a prize fish played by a teammate, who was then hoisted up and held lengthways by the team for the traditional catch photograph.[8] After beating Motherwell they went on to beat Poland's Lech Poznan (whose fans are famous for their own backs-turned goal celebration: 'The Poznan') before eventually falling to defeat against Inter Milan. Following their Europa League success, Stjarnan fans introduced their newly adopted chant to their national side. From there 'The Thunderclap' first came to international attention following Iceland's last-gasp goal against Austria at Euro 2016, which secured qualification for the last 16. The celebration has gone on to prove so popular that it was quickly adopted by other European nations at the tournament. Wales followed up their quarter-final win over Belgium with an impromptu version of the Icelandic celebration, before hosts France decided to mark their semi-final victory over Germany with a rendition of the chant.

For their part Motherwell's slow-cap then evolves into their anthem *'Since I Was Young':*[9]

> **"Since I was young,**
> **I followed on,**
> **Motherwell FC,**
> **The team for me,**
> **Ooooohhhh, oooohhh, oooooohhhhh,**
> **Ooooohhhh, oooohhh, oooooohhhhh"**

---

7   *The Guardian, 2016, 'Iceland, Motherwell, Lens, where did the thunderclap originate?', The Guardian, 13 July 2016*

8   *Blount. L, 2010, 'Is this the best goal celebration ever', Sky Sports News, 28 July 2010*

9   *Davis. C, 2016, 'The origin of Iceland's Viking Thunderclap', The Telegraph, 8 July 2016*

Motherwell's 'Since I Was Young' was soon picked up by Hearts fans at Fir Park who adapted it to: "I followed Hearts, HMFC...", before it made its way south where versions were adopted by fans of Derby County, Huddersfield Town, Bradford City, Southend United and Plymouth Argyle.

As well as supplementing chants, clapping alone can be enough to create a powerful atmosphere. Leicester City tried to harness its effect when they introduced cardboard clappers at their King Power Stadium in a bid to give them the edge in a relegation survival battle at the tail end of the 2014-15 season. About 30,000 clappers, constructed from thick cardboard, folded in a concertinaed pattern to maximise their 'clappiness' when thwacked against an open palm were placed on seats ahead of their crunch home game with West Ham United. Having gone nine games without a win a late Andy King goal gave Leicester a vital 2-1 win and boosted their chances of avoiding relegation.[10]

Leicester won again the following Saturday, this time 3-2 at West Bromwich Albion, and with relegation rivals Swansea City next up at the King Power Stadium the clappers were back. Leicester won again (2-0) and then again (1-0 at Burnley) and after seven wins in their final nine games, Leicester had survived and a tradition had been born. Former Leicester captain Matt Elliot had no doubt where the credit for the revival came from: "Everyone is sitting there banging these clackers, you've got 30,000 people all involved buzzing and singing, something as basic as that has changed [their] form", thoughts echoed by a club spokesman who told *The Daily Mail*: "Senior management at the club feel this helps create a very positive atmosphere at the stadium. 'It is quite an undertaking to place clappers on 30,000 seats but we think it is well worth it. The clappers allow the supporters to make a big difference on match day. They can all join in and make as much noise as they want to support their team'".[11]

The emphasis on clappers allowing everyone to join in with the noise and moving away from audible support being drawn purely

[10] Whitwell. L, 2015, 'Are cardboard clappers the secret behind Leicester's success', The Daily Mail, 30 December 2015

[11] Whitwell. L, 2015, 'Are cardboard clappers the secret behind Leicester's success', The Daily Mail, 30 December 2015

from the cliquey lad culture described by Anthony King was deemed a big part of their success. Another former Leicester City player, Alan Birchenall, who now works as an official ambassador for the club and as the stadium announcer on match days, explained why to *The Leicester Mercury*: "The idea of giving the fans something to make a noise with is not new. But something special has happened with these clappers. They were a hit immediately with the kids and the mums but now the dads have joined in too. When I go out onto the pitch before kick-off when the teams are in the tunnel, the sheer noise makes the hairs on the back of my neck stand up".[12]

Elizabeth Skoglund Johnsen, in her published thesis on fan culture in Norway, emphasises the important role of physical activity during a match, when fans all join together in a show of support, such as clapping in support of their team. "This physicality acts as a unifying phenomenon, during which lawyers and teachers rub shoulders with manual labourers and retirees, moving in the same ways and working towards the same goal. Fans in such situations generate a mindset in which they can, and do, have a positive influence on the game".[13]

When Leicester returned to action in August 2015, the club decided to keep the feel-good factor going into the new season, and the clappers returned for their opening game against Sunderland. Another win, 4-2 this time, was the beginning of a fairy-tale season for the Foxes who suffered only one home defeat all season, and despite odds of 5,000-1[14] would go on to clinch the Premier League title. An analysis of the points earned by Leicester after the introduction of the clappers found they won 1.35 points per game more when the clappers were used compared to the equivalent games without them. They cost £12,000 per game to produce, or £228,000 over the season,[15] a drop in the ocean in Premier League financial terms which had other clubs casting envious glances at the East Midlands.

[12] Whitwell. L, 2015, 'Are cardboard clappers the secret behind Leicester's success', The Daily Mail, 30 December 2015

[13] Social Issues Research Centre, 2008, 'Football Passions', Social Issues Research Centre, London, p22

[14] BBC News, 2016, 'Leicester City clapper ban fans not so happy', BBC News, 24 November 2016

[15] Whitwell. L, 2015, 'Are cardboard clappers the secret behind Leicester's success', The Daily Mail, 30 December 2015

Across the Midlands and inspired by Leicester's relegation survival act, West Bromwich Albion introduced clappers for their Premier League relegation six-pointer with Brighton and Hove Albion in January 2018. Again, the clappers appeared to have an immediate impact as the Baggies ended a 20-game winless run, stretching back to the previous August, with a 2-0 win. Straight after the game captain Chris Brunt hailed their impact. "There was a good atmosphere and the clappers seemed to work," he said. "That was money well invested so the crowd were right behind us." Brunt's praise was matched by goalscorer Craig Dawson, who said: "The fans played a massive part and the atmosphere was brilliant. We've got to keep doing that every week. They were the added man. Hopefully it will be the same again for the next home game".[16]

Unfortunately for West Brom lightening didn't strike twice. Although they followed up their win over Brighton with a creditable 1-1 draw at Everton, they then lost 3-0 to eventual Champions Manchester City and followed that up with a 3-2 defeat to Southampton when they returned to the Hawthorns, eventually succumbing to relegation in May.

Despite their success at Leicester and initial impact at West Brom, there remains a vocal opposition to clappers being introduced across English football. Complaints centre around the synthetic nature of the type of atmosphere they produce and include a tone of lament that they are required in the first place. As one anonymous fan wrote about Leicester's King Power Stadium: "Clappers are ten times worse than vuvuzelas, which at least had some cultural significance at the [2010] World Cup in South Africa. Cardboard clappers are an attempt to manufacture atmosphere, effectively the club's owners spending money to say: 'Listen guys, you really aren't making enough noise'. Any self-respecting supporter should be hot pink with shame".[17]

Similar sentiments have been expressed at other grounds where they have been introduced. Steve Bruce, who was managing Aston Villa at the time, labelled them "ridiculous" after Birmingham City handed them out ahead of the Second City derby in October 2017

[16] Wilson. M, 2018, 'West Brom expected to keep cardboard clappers for rest of season', Express and Star, 14 January 2018

[17] Football 365, 2017, 'Premier League Hall of Shame; Leicester CIty', Football 365, 4 April 2017

and some were screwed up and hurled at Villa players during their 0-0 stalemate. Villa's marketing manager, Adam Lowe, used their introduction as an opportunity to score points over their local rivals by telling *The Birmingham Mail*: "We have never felt the need to artificially generate atmosphere with clappers and the like. We know that the Villa fans are more than capable of generating that noise".[18] The decision to introduce clappers into the heightened tensions of a derby fixture was also criticised by West Midlands Police. When asked if they knew the clappers might be introduced and whether they had considered what might happen if they were screwed up and turned into missiles, a spokesman responded: "No, we didn't [know they were going to be introduced] and had we known we would have advised against it. Awful and naïve idea".[19]

Even after Leicester's title-winning success, the same fate eventually befell clappers at the King Power Stadium. A section of the ground was banned from having them ahead of a Champions League game with Club Brugge after complaints a minority of fans had thrown their clappers into the away end. The club wrote to more than 500 fans, who sat in Block L of the East End, the closest to the contingent of away fans, explaining the decision: "Due to the behaviour of a small number of individuals, the distribution of clap banners in Block L at the King Power Stadium will regrettably be suspended for the foreseeable future. The football club places the safety of its supporters among its highest priorities and, with that in mind, we have been left with little alternative than to remove the clap banners from Block L".[20]

In response to the decision, the chairman of Leicester City's Official Supporters Club highlighted how successful the clappers had been at uniting a broad demographic of Leicester fans, but also acknowledged that some of his fellow fans had a tendency to inappropriately launch them skywards: "I sit in the L Block section, it's the noisiest part of the ground and it's fair to say the fans are incredibly passionate. But we are not hooligans. There are women and children in Block L as

[18] *Dicken. A, 2018, 'We don't need clappers', Birmingham Mail, 21 May 2018*

[19] *Murphy. D, 2017, 'Bloodied Glenn Whelan pelted with clappers in fiery Second City derby', Joe. com, 29 October 2017*

[20] *Lovett. S, 2016, 'Fans banned from using clappers at King Power Stadium', The Independent, 25 November 2016*

well as pensioners. I'm 66 myself and there are fans in there who are older than me. Yes, I've seen people throwing them around, but it's nothing particularly malicious. They are pieces of cardboard after all—how much damage are they going to cause? And it's not only Block L where it happens. I've seen them come flying over from Block K next to us".[21]

The fate of the clappers at Birmingham and Leicester is similar to that of the old wooden rattles, which started life as a way of warning of gas attacks in warfare, before becoming what Jonathan Liew described as being "as common at football grounds as flat caps and Bovril".[22] Unfortunately for fans of the ratchet-style noise the rattles created, like that of thousands of excited crickets, the wooden rattles were banned from English Football League grounds in the 1970s due to their ability to double up as a hefty handheld weapon.[23]

Clapping, like the arms-raised, chest-out gestures humans use to express victory, appears to also be an innate human instinct that has been hardwired into us through evolution. References to clapping can be found in the Bible, such as this: "O clap your hands, all ye people; shout unto God with the voice of triumph" from Psalm 47.[24]

The history of clapping is also deeply intertwined with conflict and violence having been used to bring communities together and to try and intimidate others for millennia. As Megan Garber explains:

"In the seventh century, as the Roman empire was in decline, the emperor Heraclius made plans to meet with a barbarian king. Heraclius wanted to intimidate his opponent, but he knew that the Roman army, in its weakened state, was no longer terribly intimidating, particularly when the intended intimidatee was a barbarian. So, the emperor hired a group of men to augment his legions—but for purposes that were less military than they were musical, he hired the men just to applaud. Heraclius's tactic of intimidation-by-noisemaking did nothing to stanch the wounds of a bleeding empire. But it made a fitting postscript

[21] Lovett. S, 2016, 'Fans banned from using clappers at King Power Stadium', The Independent, 25 November 2016

[22] Liew. J, 2010, 'FA consider banning vuvuzelas', The Telegraph, 20 July 2010

[23] Ashdown. J, 2010, 'Which odd items have been banned from football grounds', The Guardian, 21 July 2010

[24] Makovsky. K, 2013, 'The Origins of Applause', Forbes.com, 25 March 2013

to that empire's long relationship with one of the earliest and most universal systems people have used to interact with each other: the clapping of hands. Applause, in the ancient world, was acclamation. But it was also communication. It was, in its way, power. It was a way for frail little humans to recreate, through their hands the thunderous rumbles and smashes of nature. We find ways, in short, to represent ourselves as crowds—through the very medium of our crowd-iness. [Over time] applause became a way for leaders to interact directly (and also, of course, completely indirectly) with their citizens. One of the chief methods politicians used to evaluate their standing with the people was by gauging the greetings they got when they entered the arena and leaders became astute human applause-o-meters, reading the volume—and the speed, and the rhythm, and the length—of the crowd's claps for clues about their own political fortunes".[25]

By the time the Romans and Greeks were spreading their version of civilisation around their empires, communication via clapping had evolved to convey specific messages through different variations of rhythm, sometimes coupled with shouts, similar to how we use slow clapping to indicate impatience and can easily distinguish between applause as acclamation and ironic applause. "The coding [of applause quickly became] a pretty sophisticated thing," explains History Professor Gregory Aldrete.[26] Eventually, applause spread from the battlefield to the soapbox and the stage and soon found a natural home in football. The growth and transition of football chanting from piano to terrace has at its heart the idea that through chanting we, as fans, are participating in the game we love—we are helping our team to win.

For the same reasons, chanting found a natural bedfellow in clapping because the act of clapping evolved a similar function. As Garber notes: "we become part of the performance simply by participating in it, demonstrating our appreciation—and our approval—by amplifying, and extending, the show. But our claps matter more now, in many ways, because they are no longer ephemeral. They are performances

[25] Garber. M, 2013, 'A Brief History of Applause', The Atlantic, 15 March 2013

[26] Aldrete. G, 1999, 'Gestures and Acclamations in Ancient Rome', John Hopkins University Press, London, p70

in themselves, their praises preserved, their rhythms tracked, their patterns analysed and exploited. They send messages far beyond the fact of the applause itself".[27] "When we applaud a performer," explains the Desmond Morris, author of *The Soccer Tribe*, "we are, in effect, patting him on the back from a distance".[28]

Within football, this is most frequently exhibited by applauding good, or unlucky play: the thundering tackle, the thumping header, the thwacked effort that whistles over the bar, all draw immediate and instinctive applause regardless of how successful they are, and to the extent that in his newspaper column The Secret Footballer alluded to the fact that players, just like the politicians of Ancient Rome, will play less effectively for the team by seeking easy applause, which in-turn validates how they feel they played. "During our games it is noticeable that every 50-50 challenge is met with a roar of approval from the crowd and even if you don't win the ball, often there is a ripple of applause. For some players it is how they're accepted and how they judge whether they've had a good or bad game".[29]

Clapping is one way to create an atmosphere, on its own or by supplementing and facilitating chanting. Clapping also allows fans the opportunity to perform rituals that strengthen their bonds both with each other and with their club, all while presenting a united and intimidating front to the opposition. But there are other, quieter ways to present a similarly united front.

---

[27] Garber. M, 2013, 'A Brief History of Applause', The Atlantic, 15 March 2013

[28] Morris. D, 1971, 'Intimate behaviour', Random House, London, p110

[29] The Secret Footballer, 2012, 'It is time we gave up our tackle obsession', The Guardian, 13 January 2012

11. IT'S NOT ALL VOCAL 2

'SILENCE'

Chanting does not only act as a source of comfort for when things go wrong, it can also alert a broader audience to what is going wrong and help fix it. Just as fans weaponised the abusive nature of chants in order to threaten and intimidate opposition fans, chanting and even the act of chanting—or not chanting—has been turned into a stick with which to beat people and organisations in positions of power.

Stephen Reicher discussed the power of crowds to strip individuals of aspects of their identity, in turn potentially exposing their sense of race. This helped to make football terraces a breeding ground for racism in the 1970s and 1980s as a reaction to perceived concerns around the rise in multiculturalism, in an increasingly fractured society under Margaret Thatcher. However, that doesn't tell the full story of what Reicher found when investigating the power of crowds. He argued: "They are not only shaped by society but also [...] they in turn bring about social change". He later went on to add: "Empirically, it rapidly became clear that, if deindividuation produced behavioural changes it didn't necessarily lead to anti-social behaviour. Indeed, at times people may become more generous and more affectionate to others under deindividuated conditions".[1] Football fans continue to use chanting and the anonymity provided by crowds and their highly visual and thus powerful massed ranks to protest.

The starkest examples of chanting, or the lack of it, as a form of protest come from Germany, a nation with a thriving fan scene, albeit one that that supporters perceive as being under attack from the German Football Association, the DFB. The catalyst for the initial protests was a paper published by the DFB in the summer following the 2011-12 season, provocatively titled: *Safe Stadium Experience* immediately implying stadiums were at that point unsafe because of fan behaviour. The document was itself a response to a media storm of condemnation after a pitch invasion and widespread

[1] *Reicher. S, 2018, 'The Psychology of Crowd Dynamics', University of St Andrews, Fife, Retrieved 12 October 2018*

use of flares and smoke bombs in a tense relegation play-off game between Fortuna Düsseldorf and Hertha Berlin at the culmination of the domestic league season the previous May.

Despite police figures which showed there was no statistical basis for the assertion that German football fans were heading back to the dark violence-laden hooligan days of the past, the media uproar to the televised scenes from Düsseldorf created an intense pressure for German politicians and the DFB to do something in response. The document released by the DFB drew heavy criticism from fans and clubs alike and led to a hastily rehashed version being released in November 2012, ready for a vote a month later. The new document, under the same name, was more palatable for the majority of clubs, but fans remained sceptical. Only six clubs wanted to seek further consultation, including FC St Pauli who lived up to their anti-estab-lishment identity.[2] Two weeks before the clubs were due to vote on the DFB proposals, German fans across the country united in a powerful protest and agreed to all stay resolutely silent for the first 12 minutes and 12 seconds of the next round of games, referencing the date the clubs were due to vote on the proposals: 12 December 2012.

The Guardian sent its sports correspondent David Conn to report on the protest. Conn chose to visit the Bundesliga's flagship atmo-spheric stadium, Signal Iduna Park, home of Borussia Dortmund and their 'Yellow Wall', a single terraced stand that holds 25,000 home fans. He saw a 1-1 draw, ironically against the team that had survived relegation in the game with Hertha Berlin that ignited the whole situation: Fortuna Düsseldorf. Conn's account of the game paints a vivid picture of the vibrancy that fans and chanting add to the matchday experience:

"As the match kicked off that vast wall of 25,000 up-for-it Borussia fans did indeed keep their sound to a low murmur, even as [Jurgen] Klopp's fast young side, with its complement of home-developed young stars, zipped the ball around and immediately attacked. Eventually the clock on the video screen clicked round to 12 minutes, 12 sec-onds. A young guy next to me smiled and said: "OK, it was nice to

2   StadiumDB, 2012, 'Controversial safety regulations approved, what now?', StadiumDB.com, 13
     December 2012

meet you, goodbye", then launched into 77 minutes and 48 seconds of constant roaring, bellowing and chanting. Huge yellow flags unfurled, and the ultras, on a platform facing the thronging terrace, urged and led the fans' singing with a megaphone, literally banging the drum. After the game, Düsseldorf fans in red and white were drinking with Dortmund supporters in the Westfalenstadion Strobels bar [and] there was not a breath of trouble all night".[3]

Note Conn's use of the word "eventually" when describing the switch from silence to incessant chanting, which it can be inferred drastically reduced the enjoyment and excitement of the opening period of the match, despite the action on the pitch being described in terms you would associate with football excitement: fast-paced, high-tempo and attacking. The silence's deafening effect was not just felt by Conn, but also the players with Borussia Dortmund captain Sebastian Kehl later telling the writer it was a "funny feeling" playing in front of silent stands, despite them holding over 80,000 fans".[4]

Despite the protests, the new measures were passed by a large majority of Bundesliga and Bundesliga 2 clubs, pacified first by the tweaks made to the original document and, secondly, the promise of future dialogue with fan groups. While the protests seemingly failed, fan groups had succeeded in changing the tone of the debate and in doing so, managed to positively affect the way in which the German media represented them, winning praise for their creative and peaceful campaign.[5]

Six years later Bundesliga fans meted out the silent treatment again, as relations between them and the DFB disintegrated once more. This time a range of issues led to the fans' discontent, ranging from the chaotic rollout of the Video Assistant Referees (VAR) and increased ticket prices, through to increasingly large numbers of games being rescheduled for television. The protests concerning more and more games being moved to Monday nights for TV dated back to the middle

[3]   Sky Sports, 2012, 'German Bundesliga fans hold silent protest at grounds to show displeasure at security proposals', Sky Sports, 28 November 2012

[4]   Sky Sports, 2012, 'German Bundesliga fans hold silent protest at grounds to show displeasure at security proposals', Sky Sports, 28 November 2012

[5]   StadiumDB, 2012, 'Controversial safety regulations approved, what now?', StadiumDB.com, 13 December 2012

of the 2017-18 season and included televised games at Dortmund and Mainz being disrupted by thousands of tennis balls being lobbed onto the pitch from the terraces.

Then in August 2018, on the eve of the 2018-19 season, a collection of fan groups led by VfB Stuttgart and Hertha Berlin released a statement lamenting the way the game was being systematically "torn even further away from its cultural and social roots and gutted on the altar of profit and greed".[6] Talks between the fan groups and the DFB broke down at the end of August, so once again supporters came together to make their voices heard—silently. This time fan groups called for a 20-minute silence at all grounds in the midweek round of fixtures in late September 2018 during *Englische Woche* (English Week – the term given in German football to describe a week in which teams play at the weekend and then again midweek, a common occurrence in England, particularly outside the top-flight but rare in Germany). Alongside the silence, banners appeared at stadiums across Germany including one at Werder Bremen reading: *"Football is for you and me, not for fucking pay tv"* which donned the front pages of most newspapers covering the protest.[7]

The following day Dortmund took to the field to face Nurnberg at Signal Iduna Park. This time *The Guardian* sent its football reporter Andy Brassell to cover the game. Brassell's report documents a very similar experience to that of David Conn six years earlier:

"It was almost surreal. Signal Iduna Park, that fullest and famously atmospheric of European grounds, was reduced to a murmur on match night. You could repeatedly hear the sound of boot on ball as a crowd of 75,000 sat in near silence, a vigil only broken for a modest cheer as Jacob Bruun Larsen scored to give the hosts an early lead. The fans' statement, short and to the point, was reprised on banners in enclosures at both ends of the stadiums: 'DFB, DFL and Co. *Ihr werdet von uns hören, oder auch nicht*' [translating as] 'You will hear from us, or not'. After the silence was broken at Westfalen on Wednesday, those fans showed exactly what everyone

[6]   *Brassell. A, 2018, 'Bundesliga fans give DFB the silent treatment', The Guardian, 27 September 2018*

[7]   *Washington Post, 2018, 'Bundesliga fans protest commercialisation with silence', Washington Post, 25 September 2018*

had been missing for those opening 20 minutes, raising the roof".[8]

Again, note the language Brassell uses in regard to the atmosphere, or lack of it, concluding with that fact that everyone missed it, fans, players, managers, and the television companies.

The fans' protests continued through the autumn of 2018 with displays across the Bundesliga. Eintracht Frankfurt fans displayed a collection of banners in their 2-1 win over RB Liepzig, the first of five Monday-night fixtures which sparked the protests. In front of the watching television audience for which the game had been moved, the banners included numerous examples with *"Montag* (Monday)" crossed out one that said *"Eintracht says no to Mondays"* and one inspired by the Boomtown Rats 1979 No. 1 single 'I don't like Mondays'. In terms of audible protesting, fans of both clubs accompanied their banner displays by ensuring the game kicked off under a chorus of boos, and then whistled throughout[9] and ultimately forced the DfB to climb-down and abolish Monday night games from the slots on offer when they renewed their TV deals for the 2021-22 season onwards.[10]

By uniting and remaining silent, fan groups were able to highlight in the starkest way how important the atmosphere created by fans is to the wider game and thus how important it is to maintain and facilitate fans to continue to create it. Philipp Markhardt, spokesman for the ProFan group who helped organise the protest explained to *The Guardian* at the time: "The protest is to show the clubs what it would be like if we were not there".[11] Football is big business, particularly in terms of television broadcasting rights and the significance of chanting and the atmosphere fans create was highlighted by Premier League Chief Executive Richard Scudamore on the eve of the 2013-14 season when he said fans were an integral part of the Premier League "show" being sold around the world: "We can't be clearer. Unless the show is a good show, with the best talent and played in decent stadia with

[8] Brassell. A, 2018, 'Bundesliga fans give DFB the silent treatment', The Guardian, 27 September 2018

[9] World Soccer, 2018, 'Boatend gives Frankfurt win as fans protest Monday football', World Soccer, 19 February 2018

[10] DW Sports, 2018, 'Bundesliga Monday games to be discontinued after fan protests', DW Sports, 21 November 2018

[11] Conn. D, 2012, 'Germany's Bundesliga takes a stand by keeping faith with noisy fans', The Guardian, 2 December 2012

full crowds, then it isn't a show you can sell".[12] This febrile, tribal atmosphere associated with the English game has helped see the value of the TV rights explode from £191m in 1992 to £5.14bn, or around £11m per game, for the 2016-19. package.[13] As it is with the Premier League, so it is with the Bundesliga, whose rights for 2017-18 leapt to £4.64bn over four seasons, breaking the €1bn per season barrier for the first time,[14] while promoting itself around the world extremely effectively for its enjoyable matchday experience[15]

Two years before the protest, Bundesliga Chief Executive Christian Seifert, told *The Guardian* that the success of the Bundesliga is because its clubs all have what Seifert described as a "core value" of putting fans first: "Borussia Dortmund has the biggest stand in the world. The Yellow Wall holds 25,000, and the average ticket price is €15 (£13) because they know how valuable such a fan culture and supporter base is".[16] Dortmund for their part helped maintain that link by providing logistic support, including official club staff to the fan groups and doing all they could to enable their protests. Jens Volke, Dortmund's official Supporter Liaison Officer, who previously stood on the Yellow Wall as one of the club's ultras, explained why it was vital to establish and maintain those links: "This [protest] is their opinion, so we believe we should support free speech. It is a policy of the club, we want young people to come here, to feel included, and we work with them, to help them use their energy in a positive way. They are not outsiders; they are part of the club".[17]

The relationship between clubs and protesting fans in Germany is not always so cordial however and the sometimes-uneasy relationship

[12] Gibson. O, 2013, 'Atmosphere and fans' role in Premier League games becoming a concern', The Guardian, 16 November 2013

[13] Wilson, B. 2018,' Premier League Football TV rights deal to be decided', BBC News, 9 February 2018

[14] Uersfeld, S, 2016. 'Bundesliga clubs say new TV rights deal closes gap to Premier League', ESPN, 9 June 2016

[15] Brassell. A, 2018, 'Bundesliga fans give DFB the silent treatment', The Guardian, 27 September 2018

[16] Jackson. J, 2010, 'How the Bundesliga puts the Premier League to shame', The Guardian, 11 April 2010

[17] Conn. D, 2012, 'Germany's Bundesliga takes a stand by keeping faith with noisy fans', The Guardian, 2 December 2012

came to a dramatic head in the spring of 2020, with a string of protests aimed at TSG 1899 Hoffenheim owner Dietmar Hopp.

German ultras have long protested against Hopp, who is described by journalist Andreas Sten-Ziemons as "for his detractors [personifying] the commercialisation of football"[18] and by Andy Brassell as "an affront to the traditional values of German football, of paying one's dues" to those opposed to his presence in German football[19] by side-stepping the 50+1 ruling that governs professional football in Germany. The rule is designed to prevent a situation whereby one individual can hold a majority share of a club ensuring fans retain ownership of their club and excessive commercialisation, like that seen in England's Premier League, is avoided.

Hopp began investing in Hoffenheim in the 1990s, at which point they were in the regionalised eighth tier of German football. By 2008, with estimates suggesting Hopp had invested around €350 million,[20] Hoffenheim made it to the Bundesliga. Immediately Hopp became the target of protests, particularly on Dortmund's 'Yellow Wall' who greeted Hoffenheim's first visit with banners reading '*Gegen den modern fussball* (Against modern football)' and '*Hasta la vista Hopp*' below an image of Hopp behind the crosshairs of a sniper.[21] Similar banners followed at Hoffenheim games around the Bundesliga, but Dortmund fans didn't let it go and ensured Hopp was targeted at almost every game between the clubs over the next decade. By February 2020, the DFB decided enough was enough, fining Dortmund €50,000 and imposing a two-year ban on their fans attending matches in Hoffenheim,[22] despite promising in 2017 to no longer impose these types of collective punishments.[23]

A week later anti-Hopp banners re-emerged among ultra-groups at other clubs, including FC Köln and Union Berlin, where fans showed

---

18 Sten-Ziemons. A, 2020, 'Why do so many fans hate Dietmar Hopp?', DW, 3 March 2020

19 Brassel. A, 2020, 'Chaos caused by Hopp banners raises questions about Bundesliga priorities', The Guardian, 2 March 2020

20 Sten-Ziemons. A, 2020, 'Why do so many fans hate Dietmar Hopp?', DW, 3 March 2020

21 Sten-Ziemons. A, 2020, 'Why do so many fans hate Dietmar Hopp?', DW, 3 March 2020

22 The Observer, 2020, 'Bayern fans' offensive Hopp banner causes farcical finish at Hoffenheim', The Observer, 29 February 2020

23 Sten-Ziemons. A, 2020, 'Why do so many fans hate Dietmar Hopp?', DW, 3 March 2020

their solidarity with their Dortmund counterparts. Things escalated further when Borussia Monchengladbach fans used their home game with Hoffenheim to display banners that displayed some support for Dortmund fans, albeit tinged with rivalry reading; *'Sons of bitches, insult a son of a bitch and get punished by sons of bitches'*,[24] alongside the image of Hopp behind crosshairs. The Sporting Director at Borussia Mönchengladbach, Max Eberl came out after the game and attacked the actions of the ultras, saying "We come out against racism and discrimination before a game—and then 50 idiots put up a banner like that. It's madness. The club [will] do their all to identify the perpetrators".[25]

The protests came to wider attention a week later when, in the presence of Hopp himself, defending German Champions Bayern Munich visited Hoffenheim for a Bundesliga match. Having gone 6-0 up with 20 minutes left to play, Bayern Munich's fans picked up the Gladbach ultras' baton by unfurling a banner in the away section which read *'Du Hurensohn'* (You son of a bitch),[26] mimicking those which had seen Dortmund punished and Monchengladbach criticised. On seeing the banner, the referee followed UEFA's recently developed three-step protocol for 'discriminatory incidents', taking the players off the pitch and suspending play. Presumably hoping to get the game going again, and led by their visibly angry former Hoffenheim manager, Hansi Flick, the Bayern players approached their fans asking them to take the banner down. With it removed and 13 minutes remaining, the game resumed but seemingly in protest at what they'd read, both sets of players agreed to stop playing competitively and instead passed the ball among themselves. When the clock finally reached full-time, Hopp was led onto the field by Bayern supremo Karl-Heinz Rummenigge, to applause from both sets of players in a symbolic act of support.

After the game, criticism of the ultras came from all angles. The German FA president Fritz Keller branded the events in Hoffenheim:

[24] Honigstein. R, 2020, "Crosshair' banner was in bad taste but Ultras have right to protest', The Athletic, 27 February 2020

[25] Honigstein. R, 2020, "Crosshair' banner was in bad taste but Ultras have right to protest', The Athletic, 27 February 2020

[26] Brassel. A, 2020, 'Chaos caused by Hopp banners raises questions about Bundesliga priorities', The Guardian, 2 March 2020

"The lowest point", adding "It can't go on like this".[27] Monchengla-dbach's Max Eberl followed up his comments from a week earlier by insisting: "They have a voice. Protest is OK, but not in this way",[28] while Rummenigge went further and labelled the ultras "idiots".[29]

One of the ultra-groups responsible for the banners in the Bayern end were *Schickeria*, which in 2014 were recognised by the DFB with the Julius Hirsch Prize which is handed to clubs, players and fan groups that take a stance against racism, antisemitism and discrimination.[30] In response to the storm of criticism, they released a statement of their own;

"We used the words 'son of a bitch' in a banner today. This is not normally the language we'd use but would not be worth mentioning as it is. Similar terms are used quite often at a football game. You can ask the Borussia Dortmund fans, for example, who are titled every game as 'BVB, sons of bitches' [...] The word became a big topic only with the criticism of Hoffenheim and its owner Dietmar Hopp, which was excessively exaggerated [...] The DFB has broken its word to refrain from collective punishments. Even if the punishment does not concern us and the topic of Hopp is not so relevant to us, we see this as an attack on fan rights in general. It is a topic we cannot leave unanswered. You do not have to approve of the wording, but there was no alternative for us as this is the only way to get necessary attention. If you want to interrupt football matches whenever such insults are expressed, you will no longer be able to play a game over 90 minutes. The interruption today was excessive and absurd. Football remains dirty—Fans remain rebellious—Against collective punishments—Fuck you DFB".[31]

A key issue for the fans was the suggestion from Eberl as well as the DFB and some parts of the media that their response to the

[27] Brassel. A, 2020, 'Chaos caused by Hopp banners raises questions about Bundesliga priorities', The Guardian, 2 March 2020

[28] Brassel. A, 2020, 'Chaos caused by Hopp banners raises questions about Bundesliga priorities', The Guardian, 2 March 2020

[29] Tamsut. F, 2020, '@ftamsut', Twitter, 3 March 2020

[30] Tamsut. F, 2020, '@ftamsut', Twitter, 3 March 2020

[31] Unsere Kurve ist die Süd, 2020, 'Statement – Spruchband Erklärung', Facebook, 29 February 2020

banners was a crackdown on what Keller termed "discrimination and personalised threats".[32] That suggestion was backed up in comments made by Bayern player Thomas Müller, who took to his Twitter account to call for an end to "hate campaigns, racism, antisemitism, homophobia and all other forms of hate".[33] The problem with lumping protests against Hopp in with racism, homophobia and other forms of discrimination, was best articulated by *Unsere Kurve* (Our Curve), an advocacy group for the wider community of German ultras in a statement which argued: "Personal insults, however inappropriate or clumsy, should not be compared to structural discrimination forms such as racism, which are anchored in our society. Dietmar Hopp is by no means affected by discrimination, as a rich, white man".[34] In a stance different to most of their counterparts, German newspaper *Die Tageszeitung* agreed, saying that the unconnected issues had been mixed up in "a morality cocktail", before pointedly querying why instances of actual racism had not drawn the same criticism and adding that by treating attacks against Hopp differently, the DFB were in fact confirming what led to the initial protests, the perception that he was receiving preferential treatment.[35]

Ultra groups across Germany felt the same, and a wave of anti-DFB banners were on display over the next weekend of fixtures. Dortmund's read: '*Cosying up to billionaires instead of finding solutions to societal issues – shit DFB*' alongside another set featuring the faces of Rumminegge, Hopp and Keller with the words '*The ugly faces of football*'.[36] In the capital, Hertha Berlin's fans went with a similar theme and chanted "*Shit DFB, Shit DFB, Shit DFB*" on repeat while displaying a banner reading: '*Bribes, collective punishment, deaths in Qatar. It's clear where the grotesque face of football is*'".[37] Similarly,

[32] *Tamsut. F, 2020, 'Fan protests against Dietmar Hopp: A story of broken trust', DW, 4 March 2020*

[33] *Tamsut. F, 2020, 'Fan protests against Dietmar Hopp: A story of broken trust', DW, 4 March 2020*

[34] *Tamsut. F, 2020, 'Fan protests against Dietmar Hopp: A story of broken trust', DW, 4 March 2020*

[35] *Honigstein. R, 2020, "Crosshair' banner was in bad taste, but Ultras have right to protest', The Athletic, 27 February 2020*

[36] *Ford. M, 2020, '@matt_4d', Twitter, 7 March 2020*

[37] *Fahey. C, 2020, '@cfaheyAP', Twitter, 7 March 2020*

Monchengladbach fans asserted: *'If there were collective punishments for corruption, the DFB HQ would be as empty as your promises'.*[38] Schalke fans displayed an apology which read: *'We apologise to all bitches for connecting them with Mr Hopp'.*[39] Wolfsburg fans went with; *'Fuck you DFB'* and an image of their logo behind crosshairs[40] and SC Freiburg's ultras declared the DFB; *'Dietmar's Fussball Bund* (Dietmar's Football Federation)'.[41] Eintracht Frankfurt took a lighter approach as their fans slowly unfurled a large banner, which ran across the front of the stand reading *'Dietmar Hopp you son of a...'* then dramatically pausing before unveiling the last word; *'mother'* followed by a smiling emoji.[42] Stuttgart's fans went with *"Dietmar Hopp is a Timo Werner"* in references to the infamous "Timo Werner is a son of a bitch" chant,[43] but the response by *Schickeria* at Bayern highlighted the contradiction in the DFB's stance best of all asking: *'Who do we have to insult for the EU to rethink its border policies?'.*[44]

The situation is different in England where the distance between club and fan group is more arms-length. That is apart from at a limited number of fan-run clubs including Exeter City, Newport County, Wycombe Wanderers and AFC Wimbledon where the co-founder Ivor Heller was directly involved in numerous fan protests ahead of the club being uprooted to Milton Keynes. These protests ranged from fans turning their backs on the action during matches *en masse* and lying down in front of coaches, through to simply arguing with the club's directors face-to-face at games.[45]

The issue of fans' interests being disregarded in pursuit of ever larger broadcast deals, coupled with rocketing increases in ticket prices and the resulting gentrification of football, is a common theme of fan protests and is frequently blamed for stifling the atmosphere

[38] *Ford. M, 2020, '@matt_4d', Twitter, 7 March 2020*

[39] *Murphy. R, 2020, '@swearimnotpaul', Twitter, 7 March 2020*

[40] *Rhind-Tutt. A, 2020, '@achiert1', Twitter, 7 March 2020*

[41] *Rhind-Tutt. A, 2020, '@achiert1', Twitter, 7 March 2020*

[42] *Tamsut. F, 2020, '@ftamsut', Twitter, 4 March 2020*

[43] *Murphy. R, 2020, '@swearimnotpaul', Twitter, 9 March 2020*

[44] *Tamsut. F, 2020, '@swearimnotpaul', Twitter, 8 March 2020*

[45] *Wilson. J, 2016, 'AFC Wimbledon's rise from the ashes', 29 May 2016*

at matches, particularly in England. In 2013 the Football Supporters' Federation launched their 'Twenty's Plenty' campaign calling for a £20 cap on ticket prices, particularly for away fans.[46] Chief Executive of the Football Supporters Federation Kevin Miles explained the reason for the campaign at the time: "There is a groundswell of opinion, now recognised by many clubs and managers, that one of the factors that has defined English football—its vocal, passionate crowds—is at risk of ebbing away if no action [on ticket prices] is taken. Premier League clubs had started to engage on away ticket pricing because they realised the impact it could have on the overall matchday experience and on television income if [crowd] numbers fell. The introduction of cheaper pricing and standing areas would go a long way to bringing back some of the atmosphere".[47]

Following the announcement of the record £5.14bn TV deal in early 2015, the campaign gathered pace and large banners began appearing at a number of Football League grounds. Crystal Palace fans displayed one of Premier League Chief Richard Scudamore re-imagined as an overweight pig in a suit, about to feast on a trough piled high with cash and bearing the label *"TV deal"*, while a longer banner beneath it read: *"£5billion in the trough yet supporters still exploited"*.[48] Arsenal fans, famous for paying the most of all supporters in the Premier League held one asking *"£5bn and what do we get? £64 a ticket"*.[49] A league below, fans of Championship Fulham held aloft a banner proclaiming: *"Working class game, business class prices"*, while Liverpool's Kop became a sea of banners and black flags in a number of protests, including one at home to Stoke City which detailed the ticket prices; *"1990; £4, 2000; £24, 2010; £43 and 2020; ??"* above the line *"Let me tell you a story of a poor boy..."*[50]

[46] Football Supporters Federation, 2018, 'Twenty's Plenty#', FSF website, Retrieved 5 October 2018

[47] Gibson. O, 2013, 'Atmosphere and fans' role in Premier League games becoming a concern', The Guardian, 16 November 2013

[48] Lewis. J, 2015, 'Share the wealth pigs; Crystal Palace fans in Premier League protest', Daily Star, 21 February 2015

[49] The Guardian, 2016, 'Premier League ticket prices fans verdict', The Guardian, 10 February 2016

[50] Taylor. J, 2014, 'Liverpool fans protest about soaring cost of football tickets', The Mirror, 29 November 2014

A couple of years later in response to a ticket price of £77, Liverpool fans staged a mass walkout on 77 minutes, having earlier displayed a number of banners, including one showing the Liver bird lifting a fan by his feet and shaking the loose change from his pocket. Another became a staple protest banner around the league, and simply read; "*Football without fans is nothing*" alongside one reading; "*£nough is £nough*".[51] The "*£nough is £nough*" banner was then used to highlight the universal nature of the campaign during a Premier League game between Manchester City and Liverpool. For the game, the banner was redrawn in blue and red and ahead of kick-off the Manchester City fans held the banner's blue end, which then reached across the border of high-viz stewards and police officers, into the segregated Liverpool end, where the away fans clasped the red end. The campaign achieved a measure of success with clubs agreeing to cap away tickets at £30 in March 2016.[52]

Banners haven't only been reserved for ticket-price protests, however, and thanks to their visual presence and easy-to-photograph message, they have become de rigueur for all sorts of issues across English and European football, from the implementation of Video Assistant Referees (VAR) in the Premier League to politics, mental health and inclusivity.

The introduction of VAR to the English Premier League in 2019-20 saw a wave of protest banners from fans disenchanted with the effect on the match-day experience. Four months into the season, the issue came to a head over the Christmas and New Year games. First, Norwich City fans held aloft a banner aping the Premier League's assertion that VAR would only intervene in cases where there had been a "clear and obvious error"[53] holding up a banner during their home draw with Tottenham Hotspurs which read: "*VAR – Clearly and obviously not working. Decision: Get in the bin*".[54] Three days later Manchester City was ordered by stewards to stop displaying a

[51] Netherton. A, 2016, 'Liverpool fans' protest admirable but not enough', Eurosport, 2 February 2016

[52] Football Supporters Federation, 2018, 'Twenty's Plenty#', FSF website, Retrieved 5 October 2018

[53] The FA, 2020, 'Laws of the Game and FA Rules', FA website, Retrieved 10 March 2020

[54] Southwell. C, 2019, "VAR - Clearly and obviously not working!' - City fans fed up with VAR after Pukki offside', The Pink'Un, 28 December 2019

banner reading: *"RIP football. VAR is here. Fans boycott?"*.[55] Anti-VAR banners began to spread. Crystal Palace fans hit the headlines next with a series of banners ahead of their Premier League clash with Arsenal which read: *"Killing the passion. Killing the atmosphere. Killing the game. End VAR now"*.[56] Accompanying the banners at games were frequent chants of *"Fuck VAR, Fuck VAR"* or *"It's not football anymore"*, often sung by fans of both clubs at the same time highlighting the issue as one that crossed tribal boundaries.[57]

The most frequent target of the protest banner is the current manager or owner and they will often call for regime change. These banners may simply be the name of the person, or group, the fans are unhappy with and "out". The popularity of these at Arsenal during the last few years of Arsène Wenger's reign was such that *"Wenger Out"* banners began propping up around the world including on the big screen in New York's Time Square, a Coldplay gig in Thailand, an Ethiopian league game, an Australian school photo and even in the background of a commercial for Pepsi.[58] As with chanting, however, they can often be more controversial in a bid to make the point more strongly. One of the most controversial examples of a regime change banner was held up by West Ham fans during a 4-1 defeat to Liverpool at Anfield and read: *"Brady, Sullivan and Gold you have done more damage to the East End of London than Adolf Hitler did. Out, out, out"*.[59] Then in February 2020 a West Ham season ticket holder was banned from attending any further games that season for wearing a t-shirt which read *"GSB OUT"* while volunteering as a flag waver for their home game against Liverpool. The club's rationale was that by wearing the shirt fan Cameron Robson "deliberately intended to incite the crowd".[60] Robson appealed the ban, which was initially rejected,

[55] Challies. J, 2020, 'Man City fan ordered to take down anti VAR banner during Everton FC clash', Manchester Evening News, 1 January 2020

[56] Dutton. T, 2020, 'Crystal Palace fans brand VAR 'failed experiment' as they promise more protests against technology', The Evening Standard, 11 January 2020

[57] FourFourTwo, 2019, 'Chris Wilder says fans are furious with VAR', FourFourTwo, 9 December 2019

[58] Innes. R, 2017, 'Wenger Out goes global', The Mirror, 3 May 2017

[59] Dawes. O, 2018, 'West Ham fans vent anger', HITC, 25 February 2018

[60] Steinberg. J, 2020, 'West Ham ban fan for wearing anti-board T-shirt at pitchside', The Guardian, 4 February 2020

before the club relented and overturned it, but not before Robson had missed two matches.[61] Elsewhere for comparison, Bayern Munich fans took aim at their board during the 2012 disagreement with the DFB, opting for a banner that unambiguously stated: *"The board are a whore, fucked by the police and the German FA"*.[62]

Newcastle United fans have also resorted to banners in a bid to rid their club of owner Mike Ashley. An early example was held up at Motherwell during a 2013 pre-season friendly and read: *"Support the team, not the regime"*. A year later change had not been forthcoming, and the tone strengthened to: *"Lies. Deceit. Lack of Ambition. Time for change"*.[63] Then, turning their ire on manager Alan Pardew during a trip to Swansea in October 2014, Newcastle fans went with: *"LLWDLLLWWLWLLLLLLWLLDDLD. Not a Welsh town. Our form in 2014."*[64] A section of Newcastle fans took their protests further in 2018, by staging and 11th minute 'walk-in' to mark the 11th year of Ashley's ownership. Adding insult to injury, the fans who waited to enter the ground found themselves walking in, just as Javier Hernandez opened the scoring for West Ham, in a 3-0 home defeat for the Geordies.[65]

Banners and chanting are not the only ways fans can express their discontent however and disrupting the game by lobbing items onto the pitch, in the manner of Dortmund and Mainz's tennis-ball protest mentioned earlier, has become increasingly common in the latter half of this decade. As early as 2002 Luton Town fans forced their new board to rethink the decision to appoint Terry Fenwick to replace the popular duo of Joe Kinnear and Mick Harford, who had been sacked—by post. The fans lobbed fruit at the new chairman and vice-chairman as they arrived at the ground as well as boycotting some matches. The show of fan power encouraged new owner John Gurney

[61] Steinberg. J, 2020, 'West Ham fan has ban for 'provocative' anti-board T-shirt lifted', The Guardian, 19 February 2020

[62] Honigstein. R, 2012, 'Ultras play with fire as Bundesliga engulfed by flares and violence', The Guardian, 26 November 2012

[63] Srnicek. P, 2015, 'Trust and respect are gone in football', Newcastle Chronicle, 15 March 2015

[64] @FootyAwayDays, 2018, 'Which is the best banner you've ever seen at a match?', Twitter, 9 October 2018

[65] Waugh. C, 2018, 'Newcastle United 0-3 West Ham', The Newcastle Chronicle, 1 December 2018

to run a public vote in the mode of the then popular TV show 'Pop Idol', to see who the fans did want as boss, if not Fenwick. Journalist John Ashdown called the resulting process "predictably chaotic" and ultimately resulted in the appointment of Mike Newell, by virtue of Newell being the only candidate involved in the public vote, who wanted the job.[66]

After Hull City fans failed to persuade their owners, the Allam family, to sell the club via traditional protest methods such as chanting, banners and boycotts, they took a cue from Germany and launched a barrage of stress balls onto the pitch during their Championship defeat to Nottingham Forest in October 2017.[67] Dan Collier, a member of the Hull Supporters Trust and Hull City Action for Change, explained: "we chose stress balls because we were stressed with the owners".[68] The shower of balls managed to get the game stopped for a few minutes, but the Allams remained. Six months later the fans tried again. The protest, led by Collier's group Action for Change, again included an avalanche of balls being launched onto the pitch, which held up their game against Sheffield United for two and a half minutes. This time the ball chucking was followed up by an orchestrated campaign of whistles and back turning which the group announced prior to the game, in a statement saying: "We ask those protesting to only blow their whistle at the 30-minute mark of the game, to effect as unified and effective protest as possible. This will allow play to continue on the pitch both before and after this point. Those supporters not wanting to blow a whistle, but who still want to participate in some form of protest, we encourage to turn their back on the game for one minute at the 30-minute mark of the game, as a form of visual protest".[69]

A few months later, Charlton Athletic fans, inspired by Hull's visual protest and equally determined to force regime change, staged a symbolic visual protest during their League One home game with

---

[66] Ashdown. J, 2018, 'The forgotten story of Luton Town's manager idol', The Guardian, 12 October 2018

[67] Swan. P, 2017, 'Protests were handled well and had nothing to do with Hull City defeat to Nottingham Forest', Hull Live, 29 October 2017

[68] Collier. D, 2018, 'Interview on Twitter', Twitter, 9 November 2018

[69] Rathborn. J, 2018, 'Hull v Sheffield United suspended after fans protest, The Mirror, 23 February 2018

Fleetwood Town. The protest, organised by the supporters' group Charlton's Coalition Against Roland Duchatelet (CARD), came following a report in *The London Evening Standard* in the build-up to the game that a member of the club's staff had been told to ask Human Resources whether or not he could eat crisps at his desk during his break, because the club had recently reduced their cleaning services in a cost-cutting measure. In response, CARD distributed packets of crisps to fans entering the Valley ahead of kick-off, suggesting they could either eat them, or throw them onto the pitch shortly after kick-off. Most fans chose the latter, holding the game up and immediately bringing the matter to national attention.[70]

In 2018, during their Europa League Group match against Red Bull Salzburg, Glasgow Celtic fans displayed a banner which read: *"Cut this BULLshit out of football"* alongside images of the Red Bull logo. It was a protest at the drinks company buying clubs and then changing their names, which they first did in 2005, changing Austria Salzburg to FC Red Bull Salzburg.[71] As a form of protest against Red Bull, Celtic's banner paled into insignificance compared to the severed bull's head that Dynamo Dresden fans hurled onto the pitch ahead of their domestic clash with Salzburg's commercial sister-club RB Leipzig in August 2016.[72]

In the same game, the Celtic fans showed that banners can be used for a different purpose. Demonstrating support for their striker Leigh Griffiths after he announced he was taking a break due to depression, they displayed a banner reading: *"It's OK to not be OK, You'll Never Walk Alone Leigh"*.

Other examples of fans using banners to promote inclusivity have come from Norwich City. Ahead of their Premier League fixture against Sheffield United in December 2019, they displayed a banner reading: *"Carrow Road – A home for everybody"*.[73] Alongside the words, the banner featured portraits of club legends Justin Fashanu,

[70] Treadwell. M, 2018, 'Charlton v Fleetwood held up by fans crisp protest', Sky Sports News, 25 August 2018

[71] Shotter. J, 2017, 'Red Bull and the fight for football's soul', Financial Times, 5 May 2017

[72] Shotter. J, 2017, 'Red Bull and the fight for football's soul', Financial Times, 5 May 2017

[73] Barclay End Norwich, 2019, 'Most of today was rubbish, but we're immensely proud of how this turned out....', Twitter, 8 December 2019

Ruel Fox, Mario Vrančić and Delia Smith. Fashanu had also been commemorated with a *"Norwich and proud"* banner, featuring a graphic of him celebrating his strike against Liverpool which was named the 1980 Goal of the Season, with his shirt number picked out in the rainbow flag ahead of the team's Championship clash with Rotherham United.[74] The goal itself was then celebrated when Norwich met Liverpool close to the 40th anniversary, with a 20-metre long banner recalling Barry Davies' Match of the Day commentary of the goal, in rainbow colours around Justin's face.[75]

Other banners have been less concerned with football and are more overtly political. For example, in 2015 and in response to a worsening situation for refugees fleeing conflict in the Middle East into Europe, a series of banners proclaiming *"Refugees welcome"* began to appear on the terraces at English football grounds, having been a mainstay in Bundesliga grounds for years. Dena Nakeeb, who helped to organise the campaign, explained why football crowds were the perfect place to display such banners, despite them seemingly having little to do with football: "It's not just the imagery behind manly blokes holding banners supporting an issue which is so poignant at the moment. It's the fact we as the British public are showing solidarity".[76] Swindon Town and Aston Villa fans led the way, but there were also banners displayed at Newcastle United's St James' Park, Arsenal's Emirates, Charlton Athletic's Valley and Norwich City's Carrow Road.[77]

In Europe Barcelona fans held up a banner which read: *"Catalonia is not Spain"* during their Spanish Super Cup tie with Real Madrid in 2012,[78] before escalating that to *"Only dictatorships jail peaceful political leaders"* ahead of their 5-1 La Liga rout against the same opposition in 2018, referencing the arrest warrant issued for Carlos

---

[74] Freezer. D, 2018, 'Canaries fans unveil Fashanu banner as part of work to promote LGBT+ inclusivity at Carrow Road', Eastern Daily Press, 1 December 2018

[75] BBC, 2020, 'Justin Fashanu: Fans remember Norwich City star's wonder goal', BBC, 15 February 2020

[76] Gibson. O, 2015, 'English football supporter' groups to show Refugees Welcome banners', The Guardian, 3 September 2015

[77] Nice One Mag, 2015, 'Banners of the week; Refugees Welcome', Nice One Mag website, 12 September 2015

[78] The Herald, 2012, 'A derby game between two great teams and a referendum on national identity, The Herald, 6 October 2012

Puigdemont, the Catalan independence movement leader.[79] While in Greece PAOK fans used their Europa League game against Chelsea to protest the potential renaming of the Republic of Macedonia in a deal with Greece. They displayed a prominent banner reading: *"Macedonia is only one and it's here"*, leading the club to make an official statement on the matter, saying: "As the biggest sporting and social movement of Northern Greece and Macedonia, established by people who suffered, chased away from their homes, PAOK cannot stand silent or unaffected by recent developments. Macedonia is our land, our home, our history. Historically there is only one Macedonia and it's Greek".[80]

Just as the fanzine scene sprung up in the 1980s in opposition to the way fans were being portrayed, the modern protest movement is following suit. As highlighted by the rise in the disruption of matches by fans throwing items onto the pitch, increasingly English supporters are looking further afield for inspiration and tactics to aid their cause. And it's not just in terms of protesting that English fans are taking their cues from Germany, but more and more fans across Britain are looking at Europe and all corners of the globe to inspire and reinvigorate the atmosphere in the increasingly sterile British football grounds.

[79] *Sport Archives 2018, 'Camp Nou banner during classic, Sport Archives, 27 October 2018*

[80] *PAOK, 2018, 'PAOK statement regarding Macedonia', PAOK website, Retrieved 30 October 2018*

12. EUROPE

'ALLEZ, ALLEZ, ALLEZ'

The history of chanting mirrors the history of football's development as a whole in that, while the basis of the modern game was invented in the UK, different styles have developed on different shores. Today, in many regards, the atmosphere at modern English grounds is distinctly lacking compared to other countries. The similarities between the growth and development of the game and the growth and development of chanting and terrace culture don't end there. Just as the quality of the English game on the pitch experienced a giant leap forward thanks to the influx of foreign talent in the 1990s, the rise of social media has seen increased cross-fertilisation of ideas, and English terraces are beginning to reap the benefits.

As with the rules of the game itself, Victorian England played an essential role in the birth of chanting, but the idea of creating an atmosphere in support of your team was not limited to England. For example, a full decade before Liverpool fans performed Cilla karaoke on the Kop, a group of Yugoslavia fans crossed the Atlantic to watch their side compete in the 1950 World Cup finals in Brazil. The Yugoslavians were so impressed by the carnivalesque atmosphere created by the home fans at that tournament, that when they returned to following their domestic club, Hajduk Split, they resolved to replicate what they had experienced. The new group, a forerunner to the modern-day ultras groups, took their name from the Brazilian fans who had inspired them: 'Torcida' and were responsible for introducing new concepts of unstinting support of their team regardless of the result into domestic football. Out went negativity and the hounding of underperforming players, and in came unceasing positivity, synchronised chanting, banners, smoke bombs and flares, which remain a mainstay of the continental ultras scene.[1]

The England football team slipped from being world beaters to also-rans, due to combination of wilful isolationism and wanton ignorance of the world game. Similarly, the atmosphere created by English fans went from being world-leading to one derided as the 'prawn sandwich brigade' due to a perfect storm of all-seater stadiums, colossal ticket

[1] Miles. P, 2016, 'Beyond the Turnstiles', Ockley Book, Huddersfield, Yorkshire, p21

price increases and, counter-intuitively, increased numbers of season ticket holders.

In response to the tragedy at Hillsborough, an inquiry was ordered to ascertain what had gone wrong. Overseen by Lord Justice Taylor, the report was published nine months after the disaster, in January 1990. Despite the perception that persists almost three decades on, Justice Taylor's report found no inherent safety problems with standing, as long as crowd numbers were managed to prevent overcrowding, concluding: "standing accommodation is not intrinsically unsafe"[2] and going as far as to recommend a maximum standing density of 47 people per 10 square metres.[3] However, in order to help prevent another Hillsborough-type disaster, Justice Taylor went on to recommend that stadiums, where appropriate and viable, be converted to all-seater as they would "bring benefits to spectator comfort, safety and crowd control".[4]

Taylor's interim report made 28 recommendations which give some indication to the lax levels of safety at grounds prior to Hillsborough, and included some fairly basic advice to clubs including suggesting that each ground must have a doctor present at every game, turnstiles should work, crush barriers should be checked for rust damage and that the police should get together with the clubs to formulate written agreements of where the responsibilities of each were held.[5] The report also called for an immediate nationwide reduction of capacity on terraces by 15%, meaning large terraced grounds experienced substantial drops in capacity, for example the capacity at Portsmouth's Fratton Park fell from 36,000 to 26,000 overnight.[6]

Taylor's ultimate proposal to make all grounds in the top-two divisions all-seater didn't come until the final report. This caused clubs in those divisions a headache because the banking and width of most of the existing terraced steps in their stadiums was insufficient to simply bolt seats onto, meaning clubs needed to drastically alter the designs

[2]   *Lord Justice Taylor, 1990, 'The Hillsborough Stadium Disaster', Home Office, London, p95*

[3]   *Lord Justice Taylor, 1990, 'The Hillsborough Stadium Disaster', Home Office, London, p29*

[4]   *Lord Justice Taylor, 1990, 'The Hillsborough Stadium Disaster', Home Office, London, p95*

[5]   *Harris. N, 1999, 'Long haul to implement Taylor Report', The Independent, 15 April 1999*

[6]   *Daly. J, 2010, 'The Taylor report unpicked', Daly History, 30 December 2010*

of their grounds. The Taylor Report recognised this and estimated the cost of these changes would be roughly £130m.[7] However this proved to be a substantial under-estimate.

Rather than alter their existing ground, many clubs upped sticks and moved home entirely. When Scarborough moved into their new home in 1988 they were the first club to relocate since 1955. After the Taylor Report was published a flurry of clubs followed Scarborough's lead. The first was Millwall, who left their infamous Den for the imaginatively named New Den in 1993, becoming the first new-build stadium to open after the Taylor Report. In the seven years following the Taylor Report's publication, a total of £507.8m was spent on football stadiums, divided between the clubs (£371.3m) and the Football Trust (£136.5m).[8] By the turn of the century, the figure had leapt to £560m[9] and the list of clubs who had moved home had swelled to include Sunderland, Middlesbrough, Stoke City, Manchester City, Wigan Athletic, Arsenal, Bolton Wanderers, Hull City, Reading, Derby County, Southampton, Leicester City, Chesterfield United, Oxford United, Coventry City, Cardiff City, Swansea City, Huddersfield Town and Doncaster Rovers to name but a few.

Lord Justice Taylor had the foresight to recognise some potential problems with all-seater stadiums, which have been realised. The first was that seating, by virtue of being both more comfortable and roomier, thus limiting capacities, would likely cause clubs to raise ticket prices. Taylor noted: "Spectators do not want to pay and, it is argued, many could not pay the substantially higher price of a seat as against the cost of standing".[10] Unfortunately, Justice Taylor dismissed the concern, citing the costs of seating tickets at Glasgow Rangers being £6, compared to £4 to stand.[11] Unfortunately, the situation at Ibrox proved to be the exception rather than the rule and as all-seater stadiums were introduced ticket prices skyrocketed by over 1,000% in just 20 years. The same seating tickets at Ibrox cited by Taylor had

[7]   Harris. N, 1999, 'Long haul to implement Taylor Report', The Independent, 15 April 1999

[8]   Daly. J, 2010, 'The Taylor report unpicked', Daly History, 30 December 2010

[9]   Harris. N, 1999, 'Long haul to implement Taylor Report', The Independent, 15 April 1999

[10] Lord Justice Taylor, 1990, 'The Hillsborough Stadium Disaster', Home Office, London, p13

[11] Lord Justice Taylor, 1990, 'The Hillsborough Stadium Disaster', Home Office, London, p13

themselves leapt to around £30 in late 2018, an increase of 400%,[12] while the standing option has gone.

Malcolm Clarke, chairman of the Football Supporters' Federation, complained about the rise in cost of enjoying live football by explaining the effect high prices have on the matchday crowd: "Some Premier League clubs do offer good deals, but the prices at the top clubs, and particularly London clubs, are mostly outrageous. They are beyond the reach of many younger people who used to have access to football and now, if they are interested, are watching the game in the pub. Football, by tradition, was always accessible to almost everybody, and in the current economic climate, with jobs and standards of living under threat, there is a great danger an increasing section of the community will be priced out".[13]

This is important from the point of view of creating an atmosphere, as the group being priced out are those who traditionally would be the ones singing and chanting. As David Conn wrote, the effect of pricing people out and in turn ruining the atmosphere in grounds, is a huge concern for Bundesliga fans: "In Germany they are tussling about flares, about managing the limits of a raucous and youthful fan culture they insist they want to nurture, not price out. On their monumental standing areas, with cheap tickets, and member-owned clubs whose executives hold forth about the game's soul, football in Germany speaks to us, of essentials we somehow managed to lose, of how football might be".[14]

As well as pricing people out, the other effect of all-seater stadiums is to physically stop the organic congregation of like-minded people. An open terrace would allow those people who wanted to sing to move around and come together, while those who wanted to enjoy the match in a less-boisterous way could freely move to more sedate areas. By allocating everybody a single, immovable spot in the stadium, this natural osmosis was prevented. In return, small clusters of groups, or individuals who want to sing, have increasingly found themselves

[12]   Rangers FC, 2018, 'Rangers FC ticket prices', Rangers.co.uk, Retrieved 17 October 2018

[13]   Boyce. L, 2011, 'Inflation-busting football', This is Money, 18 August 2011

[14]   Conn. D, 2012, 'Germany's Bundesliga takes a stand by keeping faith with noisy fans', The Guardian, 2 December 2012

strung out across an expanse of seats too disparate to be conducive to singing together. This problem has been exacerbated by the increasing number of season ticket holders at many grounds, who retain their spot season-after-season, in turn restricting the movement of fans around the ground on an annual, as well as a game-by-game, basis.

Lord Taylor also foresaw this could happen, but deemed it was a small price to pay for increased safety in grounds: "to many young men the camaraderie of singing together, jumping up and down, responding in unison to the naming of the players, their emergence on to the pitch, the scoring of a goal, an unpopular decision—all of these are an integral part of enjoying the match. They like being part of an amorphous seething crowd and do not wish to have each his own place in a seat. To such extent as the seating limits togetherness or prevents movement, that price is surely worth paying for the benefits in safety and control".[15]

This knock-on effect of forcing fans to sit in one place is another one of the key concerns of German fans, who have seen what has happened at English grounds and are desperate to avoid the same fate. Nicolai Maurer, 26, a member of Dortmund's largest ultra group *The Unity,* made up of 260 men and women mostly in their early 20s, explained: "If there are some problems at the stadium we do not believe the answer is repression. The politicians are threatening that Germany must have seats, and we are worried it will be like England, where the football atmosphere was famous but now it is so quiet. At Manchester City it was a little better, but at Arsenal, we could not believe you could watch football so quietly. We don't want that".[16]

While football grounds have proven to be safer since Lord Taylor's recommendations were implemented, they have also become more sterile. As a result, the atmosphere has suffered and as it has diminished over time people have begun to question if there is not a middle-ground to be found, one that retains the safety record but allows some of the fun, and in-turn the atmosphere the game is sold on, to return.

To that end, fans are now beginning to join forces with each other,

---

[15] Lord Justice Taylor, 1990, 'The Hillsborough Stadium Disaster', Home Office, London, p13

[16] Conn. D, 2012, 'Germany's Bundesliga takes a stand by keeping faith with noisy fans', The Guardian, 2 December 2012

and in some cases get tentative assistance from their clubs, to address this. One of the solutions has been to introduce 'singing sections' within grounds for cup-ties as these matches often aren't included in season ticket packages, so there is more freedom to pick and choose where groups of people can gather together. Manchester United were one of the first to get involved and trialled a singing section for their home Champions League tie with Real Sociedad in 2013. They advertised 1,500 tickets for the section and received more than 6,000 applications from fans wanting to be involved. Other clubs have followed suit and, frequently led by fan campaigns, singing sections have been used at games across the top two divisions of English football, including at Chelsea, Everton, Crystal Palace, Nottingham Forest, Norwich City, Cardiff City and Newcastle United.

Meanwhile, at Tottenham Hotspur, the club have engaged with a fan group called *The 1882 Collective*, who got together and initially enlivened youth team matches with their vocal presence, before the club initiated singing sections in their Europa League games and helped move fans who wanted to sing into the same block at White Hart Lane.[17] Recognising the restrictions of seating, the club have also installed rail-seating sections in their new Tottenham Hotspur Stadium to great acclaim. *The Guardian's* Barnay Ronay called it "an astonishing place, a giant, reverberating ball of air in a fine steel and glass case. It is a wonderfully open thing too, reaching up to the moon on all sides, but somehow also airy and uplifting". Ronay went on to describe how the design of a single-tiered rail-seated section, designed specifically with an integrated safety bar, to help improve the atmosphere worked: "From pitch-side the eye is drawn to the single tier stand at the south end, curving up to its central peak miles up in the sky above north London. In the course of this opening game it went from a pyramid of silent angst (one benefit of that noise-funnel design: we can hear the whining and whingeing a lot more clearly) to a bouncing, seething mound of human joy. The stands were already rocking half an hour before kick-off".[18] Manager Mauricio Pochettino

[17] Gibson. O, 2013, 'Atmosphere and fans' role in Premier League games becoming a concern', The Guardian, 16 November 2013

[18] Ronay. B, 2019, 'Astonishing new stadium brings hope and fear to Tottenham Hotspur', The Guardian, 3 April 2019

led the plaudits after the stadium opened with a 2-0 win over Crystal Palace in April 2019, saying: "For our opponents, it is going to be so difficult here. If I am playing for Tottenham, I am so quick and fast in that atmosphere. It was impossible not to be affected by the energy. If you are not motivated to play in this atmosphere, something is not right in your head".[19]

Another knock-on effect of English football's dampened atmosphere is a rise of fans looking to the Continent for their kicks. As Pete Miles describes in his essay which accompanies Leon Gladwell's groundhopping photo-diary: "A whole new branch of tourism has been generated by the clamour to attend the biggest and most boisterous matches across Europe".[20]

In Europe, the more vocal fans are known as the "ultras", a word said to have derived from the 19th century French term *'ultra-loyaliste'*, meaning 'beyond' or 'extreme' and initially applied to a right-wing political faction who supported the restoration of the Bourbon Monarchy following the fall of Napoleon.[21] Those very same Bourbons are better known now for having their name emblazoned across a chocolate biscuit.[22]

On the other side of the Alps from the Bourbons' home, it is Italy which boasts one of the strongest and most dedicated "ultras" culture, highlighted by the fact that the Italian word for fan, *'tifoso'*, translates as those who have typhoid.[23] The growth of the ultra culture and of chanting in Italy is remarkably similar to what happened in England in that it emerged from the 1960s and 1970s and spread via the railways.

The first groups of organised Italian ultras were young, mainly men, enticed to football by reduced price ticket campaigns, which saw them congregate in the cheapest areas of Serie A stadiums, principally located behind the goals. This new group of fans distinguished themselves from the more traditional Italian football fans by adopting the

[19] Hytner. D, 2019, "Tonight we touched glory': Pochettino on Spurs' perfect start at new stadium', *The Guardian, 4 April 2019*

[20] Miles. P, 2016, *'Beyond the Turnstiles', Ockley Books, Huddersfield, Yorkshire, p23*

[21] Hodges-Ramon. L, Girard. W and Morris. N, 2018, 'A culture of violence; How political and social turmoil gave rise to Rome's radical ultras', *The Gentleman Ultra, 1 May 2018*

[22] Chambers Concise Dictionary, 2014, 'Bourbon', Allied Publishers, London, p144

[23] Jones. T, 2016, 'Inside Italy's ultras', *The Guardian, 1 December 2016*

chanting, and massed ranks of raised scarves they'd seen on English terraces and the carnivalesque drums from Brazil that two decades earlier had inspired fans of Hadjuk Split.[24] From the arrival of the first ultra group, AC Milan's *Fossa dei Leoni* ('The Lion's Den', named after AC's former ground in 1968[25]), the ultras culture took off, and within a decade every major Italian club boasted at least one set of ultras.[26] As the groups became more organised they began to travel to games together and, as in England, the authorities soon implemented football special trains specifically to carry football fans and keep them separate from the travelling public as they criss-crossed the nation by railway.[27]

Quickly, Italian fans became renowned for their elaborate choreographed displays, now known as 'tifos' in England, which would feature widespread use of pyrotechnics, such as hand-held signal flares, smoke bombs, fireworks and coloured Bengal lights, all to bring an extra touch of liveliness to the terraces. The ultras saw themselves as a distinct and separate part of the club, just as groups of English fans began to around the same time. Yet while they were primarily focused on inspiring their team and intimidating the opposition during games, their identities were more overtly political than the hooligan firms that began to coalesce in England. However, as with English hooligan firms, violence was a key ingredient in the life of an ultra. After Liverpool fan Sean Cox was attacked and severely injured by ultras ahead of their 2018 Champions League semi-final against Roma, the fanzine *The Gentleman Ultra* provided a comprehensive report on how violence and politics were inextricably linked within the Italian ultra-culture:

"Violence, whether it be motivated by intra-club rivalries, political affiliations or the disaffection of a neglected social class, is part of the dark underbelly of Italian ultra-culture. In Italy, these groups have become extremely organised and a powerful element of civil society. Their identities are often underpinned by local and political

[24]   *Ed, 2011, 'History of Ultra movement in Italy', Libcom.org, 20 February 2011*

[25]   *Ed, 2011, 'History of Ultra movement in Italy', Libcom.org, 20 February 2011*

[26]   *Jones. T, 2016, 'Inside Italy's ultras', The Guardian, 1 December 2016*

[27]   *Ed, 2011, 'History of Ultra movement in Italy', Libcom.org, 20 February 2011*

loyalties and their support for their club is vehement. They are the fans who provide the enchanting match day atmosphere: the mass choreographies, the eclectic mix of banners, flags and flares, and the incessant wall of noise generated from the Curvas (the bends located in the south or north end of Italian stadia). But this social movement is also a product of its time, especially in Italy where the phenomenon originated in the late 1960s to '70s. It is impossible to detach violence from the political backdrop of an era known as the *Anni di Piombo* ('Years of Lead'). This civil conflict polarised Italian society into groups of politically active youths, pitting left-wing and right-wing paramilitary factions against each other. These tensions spilled over into football, leading to the presence of battle-hardened neo-fascists and communists in the stadia".[28]

In 2016 there were 382 ultra-groups in Italy, of which some are still explicitly political (40 far-right and 20 far-left)[29] and as *The Gentleman Ultra* outlined: "At AS Roma, for example, two groups of ultras were founded in the early 1970s, one with allegiances to the far-left (Fedayn) and the other to the far-right (Boys Roma). Both mixed politics, violence and football freely. Add to this the already combustible nature of *campanilismo* (local patriotism) and civic rivalry in Italy—sentiments underpinned by age-old parochial hostilities—and the picture of where this culture of violence originates becomes clearer".[30]

The 'Years of Lead' the fanzine refers to were a particularly violent episode of both Italian footballing and political history. Within football the violence was initially confined to the stadium and its immediate surroundings. However, while confined, the flare-ups were serious and included a number of stabbings, with incidents in a series of games involving Juventus, Napoli, Lazio and AC Milan. When Juventus hosted Atalanta in 1977, ultras clashed with iron bars and shortly afterwards the Milan derby between Internazionale and AC included a knife-fight. Then, on the 28 October 1979, the escalation of hostility

[28] Hodges-Ramon. L, Girard. W and Morris. N, 2018, 'A culture of violence; How political and social turmoil gave rise to Rome's radical ultras', The Gentleman Ultra, 1 May 2018

[29] Jones. T, 2016, 'Inside Italy's ultras', The Guardian, 1 December 2016

[30] Hodges-Ramon. L, Girard. W and Morris. N, 2018, 'A culture of violence; How political and social turmoil gave rise to Rome's radical ultras', The Gentleman Ultra, 1 May 2018

led to its first fatality when during the Rome derby a Lazio supporter, Vincenzo Paparelli, was hit in the head by a shipping flare rocket fired from the south curve by a Roma *Fedayn* supporter, dying within a few minutes.[31] Paparelli's death at the football was bookended with political violence. A year before Paparelli was killed, former Italian Prime Minister Aldo Moro was kidnapped and assassinated by the communist *Red Brigades*. Then a year after Paparelli's death 85 people were killed in the bombing of the Central Train station at Bologna, an attack allegedly perpetrated by the neo-fascist organisation *Nuclei Armati Rivoluzionari*.[32] A similar incident to the one that killed Vincenzo Paparelli was sadly repeated in Britain in 1993 when a marine distress flare was let off at the end of a World Cup qualifier between Wales and Romania, killing 67-year old John Hill.[33]

Trouble continued to blight Italian football through the 1980s and 1990s, despite a crackdown and stadium redesigns prior to the 1990 World Cup finals held in the country which removed all standing from grounds.[34] By the turn of the century the ultras were still going strong and retained a key role in Italian footballing life. In 2004 a group of Roma ultras caused their derby against Lazio to be stopped just after half-time after a false rumour, which claimed a police car had killed a boy, spread through the stadium. Fans from both sides staged a furious protest, ignoring repeated reassurances that nothing had happened over the stadium public address system.

Photographs of Roma's ultras surrounding their team's captain, Francesco Totti, became symbolic of the power of the firms. As Totti made his way back from his discussion with the ultras, he was said to have told his teammates: "If we play on, they're going to kill us".[35] Three years later a policeman, named Filippo Raciti, was killed during violent clashes between police and Catania's ultras. Raciti's death at the age of 40 led to Italian politicians renewing their efforts to quell the

[31]   Ed, 2011, 'History of Ultra movement in Italy', Libcom.org, 20 February 2011

[32]   Hodges-Ramon. L, Girard. W and Morris. N, 2018, 'A culture of violence; How political and social turmoil gave rise to Rome's radical ultras', The Gentleman Ultra, 1 May 2018

[33]   BBC, 2013, 'Football flare death lessons not learnt says victims son', BBC, 13 November 2013

[34]   Lord Justice Taylor, 1990, 'The Hillsborough Stadium Disaster', Home Office, London, p13

[35]   Hodges-Ramon. L, Girard. W and Morris. N, 2018, 'A culture of violence; How political and social turmoil gave rise to Rome's radical ultras', The Gentleman Ultra, 1 May 2018

ultras' violent tendencies. All Italian league matches were suspended for a week and strict new measures were brought in including demands that all banners brought into stadiums be pre-approved by clubs and bans on flares, megaphones and drums. Armoured vehicles became a fixture at games, and security cameras were installed at grounds around the country.

As is the case in Germany and despite its inherent violence, Italian ultra-culture can also feature a strong sense of camaraderie between fans of different clubs. For example, Napoli fans were so incensed that in 2013 the Italian football authorities saw fit to punish AC Milan with a suspended stadium closure for chants about Mount Vesuvius destroying the city or *"Terremotati"*, translating as 'the place for an earthquake', alongside, banners which labelled Napoli's supporters '*Cholerati (Cholera sufferers)*' after a deadly outbreak that swept through the city [forty years ago] in 1973,[36] that they ridiculed themselves, in support of their rivals. The Italian FA described AC Milan's initial chants as "territorial discrimination" and threatened similar punishments for any club whose supporters besmirched another. Napoli's ultras were the opposite of grateful for the intervention. In solidarity with their rivals they displayed a banner of their own: '*Naples cholera sufferers! Now close our curva*', while running through Milan's anti-Napoli songbook, in what Daniel Taylor called a "choreographed show of support for their belief that, in football, just about anything should be fair game, no matter who was hurt or insulted [...] they did not want the sport to be sanitised any more. They were, to quote one headline of the time, 'standing up for their right to be abused'".[37]

Threatened stadium closures notwithstanding, it is hoped the new security measures will reduce the darker aspects of Italy's ultras scene, while retaining the colour and drama they bring to Italian terraces, but, as *The Gentleman Ultra* points out, it is unlikely to ever be eradicated entirely: "Violence, is one of the key aspects that set the ultras apart from normal fans, being an ultra means being prepared for physical confrontation with opposition ultras. But despite

[36] Taylor. D, 2019, '*Football has become conditioned to chants about poverty. It's time to revise the songbook*', The Athletic, 21 December 2019

[37] Taylor. D, 2019, '*Football has become conditioned to chants about poverty. It's time to revise the songbook*', The Athletic, 21 December 2019

the deep-seated nature of these tendencies, the number who act in a violent way remains relatively small. For most ultras, the priority is to support their team in the most positive way, and the theatre they create contributes massively to the overall spectacle of *calcio*".[38] Former England goalkeeper Joe Hart expressed similar sentiments about Torino's ultras after spending a season on loan at the club:

"A big part I really loved about the culture of Italian football, especially Torino, was their ultras had a big say in the club—in a good way. One time we conceded five away to Napoli. It is a long way from Torino, but 300 fans went, partied the whole game, they were there for us, and a few of the guys didn't go over and clap the fans at the end, because they were a bit disheartened. The fans contacted the powers that be at the club and said: 'we want to meet with the players'. The fans were waiting for us in the car park [at training] and took over our team meeting. They didn't storm it, they just addressed the captain and said: 'We're not having that'. We all had to stand and listen, and we apologised, because they were right".[39]

In terms of the spectacle they create, Italian fans are famed for their elaborate choreographies. That said, chanting still plays a big role in their support and it was fans of Serie D side L'Aquilla Calcio, based in the small Italian city in the country's Abruzzo region, who originated a chant which has gone global: 'Allez, Allez, Allez', taken from the song. 'L'Estate Sta Finendo' ('The Summer Is Ending') which was originally a 1985 number one hit for the Italian disco duo Righeira. They were prolific composers and another of their songs 'No Tengo Dinero' was picked up by Roma as a serenade to their Brazillian midfielder Toninho Cerezo.[40]

After 'Allez, Allez, Allez' became the soundtrack to Liverpool's run to the Champions League final in 2018, *The New York Times* reporter Rory Smith attempted to work out how an Italian disco song had made its way onto the Kop 33 years after it was initially

[38] Winter. H, 2018, 'Joe Hart; Now I'm not looking over my shoulder I'm free', The Times, 27 October 2018

[39] Hodges-Ramon. L, Girard. W and Morris. N, 2018, 'A culture of violence; How political and social turmoil gave rise to Rome's radical ultras', The Gentleman Ultra, 1 May 2018

[40] Smith. R, 2018, 'How an Italian Disco Hit Became Liverpool's Champions League Anthem', New York Times, 23 May 2018

written. Smith believes L'Aquila's ultras picked up the song when one of the band, Stefano Righi, better known by his stage name, Johnson Righeira performed in the city.[41]

Back in April 2009, L'Aquila was the site of a major disaster when a magnitude 6.3 earthquake struck the town, killing 309 people.[42] With memories of the tragedy fresh, Righi reported that after he performed 'L'Estate Sta Finendo' in the town, friends began sending him clips of people from the town singing a version of it, having changed the opening line to; *"Un giorno all'improvviso* (One sudden day"). However, when Smith approached a leader of L'Aquila's ultras to confirm the story, he was told "the ultra code prevented him from speaking to the news media on or off the record".[43]

The Italian version differs from Liverpool's in that it is more generic and can be transplanted from one club to another easily with only minor tweaks, but it speaks of a never-ending love and loyalty and finishes with an implied threat of violence, ideally suited to the culture of Italian ultras. For example, Napoli's fans sing:

> *"One sudden day,*
> *I fell in love with you,*
> *My heart was beating,*
> *Don't ask me why,*
> *Time has passed,*
> *But I'm still here,*
> *And now as then,*
> *I defend this city,*
> *Allez, Allez, Allez"*

In March 2020, with the Coronavirus pandemic sweeping across the world, residents of Naples and Napoli players including Lorenzo Insigne, were recorded singing 'Allez, Allez, Allez' from their balconies,

[41] Smith. R, 2018, 'How an Italian Disco Hit Became Liverpool's Champions League Anthem', New York Times, 23 May 2018

[42] Jackson. P, 2016, 'Italy earthquake; Life after L'Aquila's heart was ripped out', BBC, 10 October 2016

[43] Smith. R, 2018, 'How an Italian Disco Hit Became Liverpool's Champions League Anthem', New York Times, 23 May 2018

in a display of solidarity with their community which continued the chant's powerful association with coming together to survive tragedy.[44]

Smith, with the help of Righi, who proudly continues to follow where 'Allez, Allez, Allez' pops up, was able to track the chant's rise from Serie D to the Champions League final, via Italy, Spain, Scotland, Portugal and Liverpool through YouTube clips and interviews with the key players:

"From L'Aquila, the song spread quickly through Italy; Genoa had a version, and so did Juventus. It was Napoli, though, that took to it most keenly. Each new group changed the lyrics, though each one started with the same three words; *'un giorno all'improvviso'*. From there, the song took flight. Atlético Madrid adopted it and so did Rangers in Scotland. The Super Dragons, FC Porto's ultra group, noticed it [and their] leader, Fernando Madureira, confirmed by text message that his cohort had seen a YouTube clip of Napoli's ultras in action and decided to borrow the tune. By February 2016, when Porto visited Borussia Dortmund in the Europa League, it had become one of their standard [chants]. During that visit to Germany, a group of Super Dragons was filmed singing it at a subway station.

"As far as Madureira is concerned, Liverpool lifted it directly from Porto: The teams played in the Champions League's round of 16 that season, and Madureira said he believed Liverpool's fans took the song up spontaneously in the stadium. The reality, though, is a little more convoluted. A few weeks after Porto played Dortmund in 2016, Phil Howard, a Liverpool fan from Wavertree, watched the video of the Super Dragons in the subway station. He had been in Dortmund for Liverpool's game there, and was searching for clips on YouTube, 'trying to see if I was in any of the videos'. Disappearing down a YouTube rabbit hole, he came upon the Porto video. 'I wanted to do a version of it straightaway,' he said. 'As stupid as it sounds, I didn't want Manchester United or Chelsea to get hold of it.' Howard texted a friend, Liam Malone, to alert him to the song. 'I told him this could be the next "Ring of Fire",' he said, referring to the Johnny Cash song that provided the soundtrack to Liverpool's 2005 Champions League win.

---

44 *The Guardian, 2020, 'Napoli fans in coronavirus quarantine sing 'Un Giorno All'Improvviso'*
   from balconies', The Guardian, 16 March 2020

"It took the two of them some time to come up with acceptable lyrics: It was not until December 2017, a full 18 months later, that Malone had a flash of inspiration. For the next few weeks, he and Howard tried to spread the word and popularise their creation. They were both at the game in Porto—three months later—where groups of Liverpool fans started singing it on the concourses and in the stands. Jamie Webster, an electrician and acoustic guitarist, was there, too. 'I'd heard murmurs of it at Anfield before,' he said. 'But in Porto there was a group of lads singing it. People did not know the words, but they were trying to follow them.' Like Malone, Webster saw the potential in the chant, too and sought out the song online, deciphering the lyrics, and setting it to music. 'I wanted to get it out there,' he said. Webster had the perfect stage. He performs regular sets at two venues that have become cornerstones of Liverpool's matchday scene: at the Halfway House pub near Anfield and at the BOSS Night events, run by a local music magazine.

"When he gave his version of 'Allez, Allez, Allez' its debut a few days after the Porto game, the reception was rapturous. 'It took four or five times, and the whole pub was up,' he said. 'I'm talking women in their 50s on tables, that sort of thing.' Film from that night was uploaded to YouTube, shared on Facebook and Twitter, and viewed hundreds of thousands of times. 'It just spiralled and spiralled,' Webster said. Now Webster is asked for his autograph by those who have seen clips of his shows and earlier this season, a group of fans from France came to Anfield determined to meet him. The song, though, is bigger still. By the time Liverpool beat Manchester City in the Champions League quarter-finals in April, all of Anfield was singing it. That moment—in Webster's mind—sealed the song's place in the Liverpool canon. 'These songs breed through success,' he said. 'If we had lost against City, maybe the whole thing would have died off.' Liverpool did not lose."[45]

Liverpool fans sang the song with gusto in both legs of the semi-final against Roma and it was then heard constantly around Kiev in the build-up to the final and then in the stadium during the game. Twelve

[45] Smith. R, 2018, 'How an Italian Disco Hit Became Liverpool's Champions League Anthem', New York Times

months on 'Allez, Allez, Allez' remained a staple in the Kop songbook and was taken on another European tour, as Liverpool reached a second successive Champions League final, this time completing the job by beating Tottenham Hotspur in Madrid.

"Every version gives the song a new life," Righi told Rory Smith. "It is very emotional for me. It makes me very happy. I always think that songs are like children: When they become big, they leave home, and they go their own way."[46]

The story of 'Allez, Allez, Allez' highlights another key moment in the history of chanting, the reach and power of social media to spread tunes, allowing them to be taken up and adapted elsewhere. However, the spread of chants across continents didn't start with 'Allez, Allez, Allez' and the internet's effect was evident over a decade before L'Aquila's chant went viral. On that occasion, back in 2003, another tune made the opposite journey and swept across Europe, before finally settling in Italy: The White Stripes hit, 'Seven Nation Army'.

The song's immediately recognisable seven-note riff popped into existence accidently, when during a sound check for a 2001 gig in Melbourne, White Stripes guitarist Jack White "stumbled across" it.[47] Two years later it became the foundation of the single which reached number one in the USA and Canada, but peaked at number seven in the UK singles charts.[48] Almost immediately its catchy nature inspired fans of Belgium's Club Brugge. After hearing it prior to their Champions League clash with Inter Milan, they took it into the San Siro where it provided the soundtrack to an improbable 1-0 win. As with the on-field success which aided the rise of 'Allez, Allez, Allez', Club Brugge linked the win with the chant and took it home with them to the Jan Breydel Stadium, where it became a staple and proved so popular that it eventually replaced the club's official goal music.

A year after their win in Milan, Brugge hosted Roma, whose fans were sufficiently impressed with Brugge's version, that they took it back to Italy with them. Continuing his links with his club's ultras,

---

[46] Smith. R, 2018, 'How an Italian Disco Hit Became Liverpool's Champions League Anthem', New York Times

[47] Doyle, P, and Glendenning. B, 2016, 'The Joy of Six: Football Chants', 6 May 2016

[48] Official Charts, 2018, '7 Nation Army; Chart Results', Official Charts.com, Retrieved 16 October 2018

Roma captain Francesco Totti announced he was a big fan, telling Dutch newspaper *Het Nieuwsblad*: "I had never heard the song before we stepped on the field in Brussels. It sounded fantastic and the crowd was totally into it. I quickly went out and bought one of the band's albums".[49] Known in Italy as the 'Po Po Po song',[50] Roma took it back to the Italian capital and the tune swiftly made its way from there across Serie A terraces, culminating in the Italian national side adopting it as their unofficial anthem for their successful 2006 World Cup campaign in Germany. On their triumphant return, Alessandro del Piero and Marco Materazzi were invited on stage at a Rolling Stones gig back where it all began in Milan, to lead an audience sing-a-long. Never one to miss a moment, a mere six years later UEFA adopted it as the official song of Euro 2012. Jack White for his part was delighted that his riff had become a football chant staple: "Nothing is more beautiful than when people embrace a melody and allow it to enter the pantheon of folk music".[51]

North of the Italy, beyond Austria and Switzerland, sits Germany, another European footballing powerhouse, both on and off the pitch. Whereas English footballing traditions were well set before the Second World War, the story in Germany is very different, in part because the country had no national professional league until around the time Liverpool's Kop was finding its singing voice. Up until the inaugural Bundesliga season in 1963/64, German football had been divided geographically and played in five regional *Oberligen*.

The lack of a national league in Germany was due to the very different foundation of German football clubs from their English equivalents. In both countries the sport was increasingly popular in the late 19th century, but whereas football was seen as a way to develop the morals and physical attributes of young men in Victorian Britain, the perception was the exact opposite in Germany, where it was dubbed 'the English disease' and treated with contempt by the establishment.[52]

[49] *FourFourTwo, 2016, '50 best football chants', FourFourTwo, 22 March 2016*

[50] *FourFourTwo, 2016, '50 best football chants', FourFourTwo, 22 March 2016*

[51] *Doyle, P, and Glendenning. B, 2016, 'The Joy of Six: Football Chants', 6 May 2016*

[52] *Davidson. N, 2014, 'Pirates, Punks and Politics', Sports Books Ltd, York, p54*

The root of this contempt for football could be traced back to two embarrassing military defeats almost a century earlier, when in 1806 Napoleon had rolled over the Prussians in the twin battles of Jena and Auerstadt, which had cost Prussia dearly in terms of land and influence. To try and prevent future defeats on the battlefield the Prussian Army was reformed and placed a renewed emphasis on physical education. Five years after the defeats to Napoleon, German staunch nationalist, Friedrich Ludwig Jahn, organised the first gymnastic event. Jahn was not a fan of sport, or the English, and felt gymnastics was the perfect preparation for young men to succeed in life, and war, while also promoting the type of unity that would be essential on the battlefield. Not everyone agreed with Jahn's evangelical promotion of gymnastics, however, and in 1819 he was arrested for his views, which the authorities felt were too revolutionary, but by then his pro-gymnast message was out.[53]

With the gymnastics movement up and running, gymnastic clubs began to spring up around Germany, and in turn other sports coalesced, making them multi-sports clubs, including football. To this day most German football clubs remain multi-sport clubs, for example Germany's most successful football team, Bayern Munich, retain teams competing in basketball, bowling, handball, table tennis and even chess, although their gymnastics team was dissolved in 2014.[54] The 'T' in the name of their cross-city rivals TSV München 1860 stands for 'Turen' or 'gymnastics', which was the club's principal sport when they were founded in 1860. The club's football team didn't arrive until as late as 1899.[55]

Once football had its grip, however, it began to supplant the other sports and ultimately became Germany's national game. Such is football's popularity in Germany that the Bundesliga now boasts the largest average attendance of any league in Europe, while Borussia Dortmund and their envied Yellow Wall, play host to the highest average crowd

[53] Curran. A, 2015, 'The origins of football in Germany', Bundesliga Fanatic, 26 February 2015

[54] Bundesliga, 2017, 'Fan friendly Bundesliga the best attended league in Europe' Bundesliga.com, 14 November 2017

[55] Curran. A, 2015, 'The origins of football in Germany', Bundesliga Fanatic, 26 February 2015

of any club on the continent.[56] It was not a straightforward climb to the top, however, and, as with English and Italian football, the 1980s were dark days and saw low attendances. In the 1985-86 Bundesliga campaign the average attendance was a mere 17,600, compared to 26,100 just shy of a decade earlier and a whopping 43,302 from between 2013-18.[57] As with the game in England and Italy, racism was a major problem and the impact of that can still be felt today.

Broadly, as we have seen with their comments around Dietmar Hopp, Germany's ultra-scene is predominantly left-wing, and examples of inclusive messages are common place on German terraces. German football journalist Felix Tamsut documents some of them on his Twitter feed. In one weekend in March 2020 he tweeted anti-racism examples from Bayern Munich, Red Bull Leipzig and Fortuna Dusseldorf fans, alongside St Pauli fans publicly opposing sexist comments from former German international Mario Basler, Werder Bremen fans announcing "A woman's place is in the stands" and FC Kaiserslautern fans calling for improved women's rights and people to come together to "smash the old men's structures".[58] Tamsut also documented the protests of SC Freiburg's ultras, when a prominent right-wing politician, Dubravko Mandic purchased a season ticket despite announcing "I hate football, but as a populist I understand that football moves the masses, so I bought season tickets to SC Freiburg".[59] The club's ultras responded immediately and marked their opening home game with a series of banners, including *"Piss off, Nazi"*, *"Freiburg is diverse"*, *"AfD are disgusting"* and *"Deport Mandic"*.[60] Mandic responded by threatening to sue for libel, but fans of other clubs followed suite in attacking him, with Mainz fans marking their game between the two clubs in January with a simple, but effective banner of their own; *"Mandic, you Nazi, piss off"*.[61]

[56] Curran. A, 2015, 'The origins of football in Germany', Bundesliga Fanatic, 26 February 2015

[57] Kidd. R, 2018, 'German Bundesliga is world's best supported league by attendance, says report', Forbes, 11 April 2018

[58] Tamsut. F, 2020, @ftamsut, Twitter, 8-10 March 2020

[59] Tamsut. F, 2020, @ftamsut, Twitter, 9 January 2020

[60] Tamsut. F, 2020, @ftamsut, Twitter, 9 January 2020

[61] Tamsut. F, 2020, @ftamsut, Twitter, 19 January 2020

The attitude to racism on the terraces has historically varied across Germany and, due to a rise of right-wing sympathies in the former East, still does. One such example is BFC Dynamo, known as the club of the hated Stasi police force before the fall of the Berlin Wall, who attracted a predominantly right-wing fan base. Robert Claus, the author and German football right-wing extremism expert, told German news agency DW:

"There is a long history of right-wing, racist assaults and other incidents around BFC games. Even prior to reunification, the power within the BFC fan scene lay with right-wing extremists. The authorities didn't really know how to deal with them because they couldn't comprehend how an extreme-right sub-culture could even exist in an anti-fascist socialist state like the GDR. BFC is very much a club which belongs to its milieu and lives from what it has. In contrast to other clubs, BFC have never really managed to open themselves up to new generations or different types of fans. Of course, there are also people at BFC who aren't hooligans or Nazis, but otherwise it's an incredibly homogeneous support."[62]

This was highlighted in August 2018 when BFC fans joined with a right-wing ultra group from FC Magdeburg to mark the funeral of a well-known neo-Nazi activist from the eastern city of Chemnitz, itself the scene of large-scale far-right demos in September 2018, with a wreath and accompanying message; "*In memory of our friend Tommy Haller. The group united. Fists clenched. We have sworn solidarity. MD/BFC hooligans*".[63] During his lifetime, Haller had founded the hooligan group 'HooNaRa', short for "*Hooligans Nazis Racists*", while simultaneously heading up the club's security.[64] Chemnitz fans marked Haller's death with a minute's silence during their next match, which also saw former captain Daniel Frahn celebrate a goal by holding up a t-shirt that read "*Support your local hools*", which initially saw him

[62]   Ford. M, 2019, 'Stasi club' BFC Dynamo: What happened to the record East German champions?', DW, 7 November 2019

[63]   Ford. M, 2019, 'Stasi club' BFC Dynamo: What happened to the record East German champions?', DW, 7 November 2019

[64]   Knight. B, 2019, 'Chemnitz football club condemns racism among own fans', DW, 25 August 2019

banned for four matches and fined €3,000 by the league.[65] For their part Chemtizer FC sacked Frahn for socialising with known hooligans and threatened their own fans with legal action.[66]

The starkest example of where the left and right extremes of the political spectrums meet in German football can be found in the central northern port city of Hamburg. Hamburg is home to one of German football's biggest and most successful clubs, Hamburger SV, or HSV. The "SV" in their name is short for 'Sport-Verein', which translates as 'Sports Club' highlighting their multi-sport roots. Meanwhile, across the city, you will find the home of FC St Pauli, a club who have over the last three decades built a global following without, unlike their neighbours, ever achieving any notable on-field success. Instead FC St Pauli is famed for their staunchly left-wing political stance, which dates back to the racism of the 1980s. English author Nick Davidson's book *Pirates, Punk and Politics* delves into how a club was radicalised over a period of years and occurred in a similar way to the osmosis of fans into Dulwich Hamlet, described earlier by Tom Lamont. Included within his account of how St Pauli's lurch to the left took place, Davidson includes this description of how the rise of the far-right, alongside an increasing squatter movement within the St Pauli district, forever altered Germany's fan scene:

"The game [in Germany] had long been treated with a suspicion bordering on contempt by many members of the left-wing intelligentsia (as in England). Indeed, the politicisation of fans on the terraces had a distinctly right-wing flavour about it during the 1980s. The far-right had started to infiltrate stadiums and took hold in the politics of many fan groups. This mirrored the problems British fans experienced with the National Front.

German football was developing a particular problem with neo-Nazi groups. The leader of the neo-Nazi *Aktionsfront Nationaler Sozialisten* (ANS) Micheal Kühnen ordered his followers to recruit new members from the terraces. A Hertha Berlin fan group was named 'Zyklon B' after the gas used in Nazi death camps and in

---

[65] Knight. B, 2019, 'Chemnitz football club condemns racism among own fans', DW, 25 August 2019

[66] Knight. B, 2019, 'Chemnitz football club condemns racism among own fans', DW, 25 August 2019

December 1984 fans of HSV and Borussia Dortmund were actively involved in far-right Molotov cocktail attacks on the squats of [Hamburg residential street the] Hafenstraße. The empty houses of the Hafenstraße were first squatted in the autumn of 1981. West Germany, like much of Western Europe had been gripped by recession since the late 1970s and the district of St Pauli had been hit particularly hard. However, in Germany the strength of the unions had minimised the effect of the economic downturn on the country's blue-collar workers; instead it was those leaving school and university who were particularly badly affected. Young people were finding it impossible to find work and to afford their own place to live. This stagnation and lack of opportunities for the young, coupled with urban decline [in the district], provided fertile conditions for those looking for an alternative way of life. Empty buildings in areas like St Pauli provided somewhere for this mixture of disaffected youth—the unemployed, punks and anarchists—to create viable social spaces in which to live, socialise and establish community projects like soup kitchens, meeting rooms and bookshops.

There was no orchestrated plan for the residents of the Hafenstraße [and] the punks to take over the terraces at [St Pauli's home ground] the Millerntor. In hindsight, you could argue that it had been a deliberate, pre-meditated decision to attend, infiltrate and radicalise a football club. It would have been a thing of genius; after all, the terraces of a football club provide a highly visible platform to express your viewpoint in great numbers. Their appearance was gradual and organic. The process took time, and although these new fans took their politics with them into the stadium, this wasn't their *raison d'être*. In the first instance the fans from the Hafenstraße started visiting St Pauli because it was fun and, crucially, it was local. Plenty of Hamburger SV supporters were dismayed at the change in atmosphere in the Voksparkstadion and despite HSV going through something of a golden age, some of these fans started to attend games at the Millerntor too. Unlike at HSV, there was no hooligan element shouting fascist slogans or intimidating fellow fans. For English fans steeped in decades of city rivalry, crossing the line and changing team is unthinkable, yet in Hamburg at that time the intense rivalry that exists today, simply wasn't there".[67]

Chants from around the time, highlight the divide. For example, sections of the HSV fanbase were known to chant:

> **"Adolf Hitler knows exactly,**
> **German Champions HSV"**

In which is an implied praise of Hitler, alongside the idea of HSV (and by implication Hitler too) as being Champions of Germany.

Another HSV chant from the late 1980s singled out St Pauli's Brazilian forward Leonardo Manzi, while labelling the rest of the St Pauli team as homosexual:

> **"Ten gay men and a nigger,**
> **That's St Pauli's kicker"**

With "kicker" here translating as 'team'.

In response, St Pauli's Millerntor home became the place where you went to watch professional football in Hamburg without what German football author Raphael Honigstein described as "a fairly prominent right-wing faction" that was present at HSV's stadium.[68] As this anti-fascist identity began to become established, St Pauli's fans began to use chanting to display their fiercely left-wing identity, such as this chant borrowed from left-wing Italian ultras and now sung by the St Pauli ultras group USP:

> **"Siamo tutti antifascisti,**
> **(Clap, clap, clap, clap, clap, clap, clap, clap, clap),**
> **Siamo tutti antifascisti,**
> **(Clap, clap, clap, clap, clap, clap, clap, clap, clap)"**

Which translates as: *"We are all anti-fascists"* and is also sung by left-leaning clubs across the world.

---

[67] Davidson. N, 2014, ' Pirates, Punks and Politics', Sports Books Ltd, York, p76-80

[68] Mengem. E, 2018, 'They beat up our goalkeeper; Derby Days Hamburg – St Pauli', Copa90, 14 October 2018

That's not to say it is, or ever was, a clear-cut division of right and left-leaning fans, split between the clubs and today HSV fans no longer chant *en masse* about Hitler and the fanbase at the Volksparkstadion is no longer overtly racist. There has also been a rise of left-wing fan groups who now call the Volkspark home.

Copa90 covered the rivalry with St Pauli in 2018 and one interview with an HSV fan highlights this and suggest St Pauli fans overplayed HSV's racist elements, in order to help foster their own anti-fascist identity: "Football has never been that political at Hamburg SV. [The rivalry] started when St Pauli brought into football all the politics. They told everybody we are a right-wing club. Of course, there were big problems, but they were not just at Hamburg's ground, it was everywhere in Germany. We are not right, we are not left, we are in the middle. St Pauli is too far on the left-wing. Why do you have to support St Pauli if you are against fascism? To be against fascism is what normal people are. You don't need a football club to express that".[69]

St Pauli's left-wing identity was set however and in response their fans were frequently on the receiving end of a derogatory chant by fans of other clubs which labelled them as "ticks", a term used against left-wing people generally as it associates them with an animal regarded as surviving off the blood and sweat of others. The chant is sung to the tune of Bonnie Tyler's 1977 single 'It's a Heartache', a German version of which, *'Lass mein Knie, Joe'*, was released the following year by Wenche Myhre and reached number five in the charts. 'You are ticks' references a number of left-wing and squatting stereotypes:

> *"You are ticks,*
> *Anti-social ticks,*
> *You're sleeping under bridges,*
> *Or at the Banhhofsmission"*

'Bahnhofsmission' refers to a German aid agency which dates back to 1894 and provides food, clothing and a bed to people in need.[70]

---

[69] Mengem. E, 2018, 'They beat up our goalkeeper; Derby Days Hamburg – St Pauli', Copa90, 14 October 2018

[70] Bahnhofsmission, 2020, 'About the Bahnhofsmission', Bahnhofsmission website, 22 April 2020

As with the 'Yids' chant at Spurs, the St Pauli fans took a negative and subverted it, reclaiming the chant as a badge of honour by simply replacing "You" with "We", immediately turning a perceived negative into something celebratory:

"We are ticks,
Anti-social ticks,
We're sleeping under bridges,
Or at the Bahnhofsmission"

Another St Pauli political chant was invented during a match in Stuttgart, which didn't involve St Pauli but a club their fans have a long-standing friendship with, Celtic. The chant, which has yet to make it into the Millerntor, arose during Celtic's Europa League tie at VfB Stuttgart. It celebrated St Pauli's promotion back to Bundesliga 2 and was set to the tune of the old East German national anthem:

"Shit on the fatherland,
Beat the Nazis and beat the fascists,
Beat them where you just meet them,
Risen [to the] 2nd League,
This is our St Pauli"

In being so overtly political, St Pauli remain an exception rather than the rule among football clubs, although they are not alone in Germany in expressing political ideals. Joining St Pauli on the left of the political spectrum are Eintract Frankfurt, who have proactively banned fans who are members of the far-right political party Alternative for Deutschland (AfD), a move also being considered by HSV,[71] while Dynamo Dresden, Chemnitz, Locomotiv Leipzig and Hansa Rostok all contain significant right-wing elements within their fanbases.[72]

The less political German clubs, are famous for having anthem-style chants that are similar to English football's early parochial chants like

[71] *The Local Germany, 2018, 'Eintracht Frankfurt hope to start movement by banning AfD members from club', The Local Germany, 29 January 2018*

[72] *Falk. A, 2017, 'Right-wing extremism in Eastern German Ultras', Bundesliga Fanatics, 15 November 2017*

'On the Ball City' and 'Blaydon Races', featuring multiple verses and a chorus. Bayern Munich, for example, has 'Stern des Sudens' ('The Star of the South') written by German actor, musician and composer Willy Astor and since translated into 12 other languages by Canadian singer Cindy Gomez.[73] The English version goes:

"Which football team of Munich do they know all over the world?
What's that club's name that holds the records hereabout?
Who has already won, whatever there was to win?
Who has been chasing up the Premier League for decades?

FC Bavaria, Star of the South, you'll never go down,
Because we stand by each other in good and in bad times,
FC Bavaria, German Champion Club, that's the name of my club,
Yes, that was it, that is it, and that will always be.

Where do they attack while listening, where do they spy daily?
Where is the press, where is the turmoil, where do they
always discuss?
Who plays in front of a sold out stadium everywhere?
Who always faces the big pressure of the rivals anew?

FC Bavaria, Star of the South, you'll never go down,
Because we stand by each other in good and in bad times,
FC Bavaria, German Champion Club, that's the name of my club
Yes, that was it, that is it, and that will always be.

No matter if it's the Premier League, a Cup or Champions League,
What can be more wonderful than a Bavarian victory?
There's life here, there's love here, there's fire here
And it remains Bavaria Munich, Germany's best from
eternity to eternity

FC Bavaria, Star of the South, you'll never go down,
Because we stand by each other in good and in bad times,

73   Bild, 2016, 'Bavaria's cult song in 12 languages', Bild, 27 September 2016

FC Bavaria, German Champion Club, that's the name of my club
Yes, that was it, that is it, and that will always be"

'Star of the South' is a chant dripping with Bayern's proud history. In parts it borders on the nauseatingly smug, asserting that as a club they're known throughout the world, hold the most records and have won everything there is to win. Then it gets oddly paranoid, lamenting eavesdropping attacks and daily spying, before reverting back to boastful claims about sold out stadiums and repeated dismissals of would-be challengers, before rhetorically asking: "what can be more wonderful than a Bavarian victory?". Journalist Nick Miller described hearing a rendition at Bayern's Allianz Arena as sounding like "the plodding soft theme to a children's cartoon" but sung at a volume that gave it "real clout".[74]

But these efforts pale into insignificance alongside those of FC Köln fans who according to *FourFourTwo* journalist Huw Davies "transform a dire song into a good one" with their anthem 'Mer Stonn Zo Dir' ('We stand by you, FC Köln').[75] The song takes the tune of Scottish folk song 'The Bonnie Banks o' Loch Lomond',[76] first published in 1841,[77] which was then covered by local pop group Höhner and sung in the local Kölsch dialect:

"Ehrenfeld, Raderthal, Nippes, Poll, Esch, Pesch, and Kalk,
Everywhere, there are fans of FC Köln,
In Rio, in Rome, (Bergisch, definitely not München) Gladbach, Prüm,
and Habbelrath,
Everywhere, there are fans of FC Köln

Joy or sorrow, future and past,
A feeling that unites—FC Köln,
Whether forward, whether back—a new match means a new chance,

[74] Miller. N, 2016, '50 best football chants', FourFourTwo, 22 March 2016

[75] Davies. H, 2016, '50 best football chants', FourFourTwo, 22 March 2016

[76] Hazra. I, 2015, 'A country called FC Köln', The Economic Times, 7 September 2015

[77] Fuld. J, 2000, 'The book of world-famous music; classical popular and folk', Courier Corporations, Massachusetts, p336

A feeling that unites—FC Köln,

We pledge to you here our loyalty and honour,
We stand by you, FC Köln,
And we walk with you, through fire if it must be,
Remaining always by your side,

(Whether) Young or old—poor or rich,
Together, we are strong, FC Köln,
Through thick and through thin—no matter where,
Only together are we strong, FC Köln,

We pledge to you here our loyalty and honour,
We stand by you, FC Köln,
And we walk with you, through fire if it must be,
Remaining always by your side" [78]

'Mer Stonn Zo Dir' is another anthem which features numerous verses and a chorus in the tradition 'On the Ball City'. Also like 'Star of the South', it delights in the national, and even global reach of the club it salutes. The predominant theme of 'Mer Stonn Zo Dir', however, is of togetherness, loyalty and uniting regardless of background. Or, as editor and journalist Indrajit Hazra puts it: "At the RheinEnergieStadion, the nation state withers away. In its place stands this massive glob of belonging. The glue holding it together is not nationality, religion, language or even region. Yes, much of it is about belonging to a city, Cologne, and the city belonging to you. But that's not all there's to it. As the line in the Kölsch dialect from the stadium roar explained: 'In Rio, in Rome, Gladbach, Prüm and Habbelrath/Everywhere, there are fans of FC Köln.' The glue is its own glue, and it's the football club of Cologne". [79]

Over in Spain, unity, regardless of background, coupled with boasts of worldwide fame, are also the principal themes of Barcelona's anthem 'El Cant del Barça' ('The hymn of Barcelona'. Written for the club in 1974 by two Catalonians, Jaume Picas and Josep Maria Espinàs, it was

[78]   Haulk. R, 2014, 'Mer stonn zo dir, our hymn in English', *AmericanGeissbock*, 2 July 2014

[79]   Hazra. I, 2015, 'A country called FC Köln', *Economic Times*, 7 September 2015

then set to a bespoke composition by fellow Catalan, composer Manuel Valls, to celebrate the club's 75th anniversary:

"The whole stadium,
Loudly cheers,
We're the blue and claret supporters,
It matters not where we hail from,
Whether it's the south or the north,
Now we all agree, we all agree,
One flag unites us in brotherhood,
Blue and claret blowing in the wind,
One valiant cry,
We've got a name that everyone knows,
Barça, Barça, Baaarça

Players, Supporters,
United we are strong.
We've achieved much over the years,
We've shouted many goals,
And we have shown, we have shown,
That no one can ever break us,
Blue and claret blowing in the wind,
One valiant cry,
We've got a name that everyone knows,
Barça, Barça, Baaarça". [80]

La Liga rivals Real Madrid wanted in on the bespoke anthem act, so in 2014 they asked a local journalist, Manuel Jabois, to pen some lyrics celebrating their historic tenth Champions League title which were then set to a tune by record producer Nadir Khayat. The result—'Hala Madrid y Nada Más'—contains none of the unity of Barcelona's offering, but does contain a reference to stars coming from near and far to old Chamartin, the district in Madrid in which the club has their Santiago Bernabeu stadium, which neatly ties the song into their famous global Galatico recruitment policy:

[80] *Barcelona, 2018, 'The FC Barcelona anthem', Barcelona.com, Retrieved 17 October 2018*

"The history you've made,
The history you'll make,
Because no one can resist
Our willingness to win,

The stars are now coming out,
My old Chamartín,
From far away and from nearby,
You gather us all here

I wear your shirt,
Right next to my heart,
The days you play,
Are everything I am,

The Arrow is running, the arrow is running,
My Madrid is attacking,

I am struggle, I am beauty,
The cry I learned,
Madrid, Madrid, Madrid,
Hala Madrid, Hala Madrid, Hala Madrid,
And nothing more, And nothing more,
Hala Madrid"

Carlo Ancelotti, the manager at the time, and his squad were all enlisted to sing on the original and it initially proved popular. Within just 24 hours it leapt to the top of the iTunes download charts in Spain, as well as Hungary, Costa Rica, Guatemala and El Salvador,,[81] although it's popularity on the terraces appears to have faded since.

Before there was 'Hala Madrid y Nada Más' Real Madrid fans would frequently sing a song, which contains no actual words and was made famous in South America: 'Dale Boca', frequently now known as 'Dale Cavesse', the story of which is a whole other chapter.

---

[81] *Real Madrid, 2014, 'The song 'Hala Madrid y Nada Mas", Real Madrid.com, 26 May 2014*

13. FURTHER AFIELD

'DALE BOCA'

If one chant highlights the power of social media, and in particular YouTube, where modern-day chanting is concerned, it is 'Dale Cavese'. Beginning life as 'Dale Boca', this chant travelled from Venezuela to Buenos Aires and from there has gone global. Frequently, although not exclusively, lyric-less, 'Dale Cavese' is based on the toe-tapping melody of the song 'Moliendo Café', originally composed in Venezuela during the 1950s by either Hugo Blanco, or his uncle Jose Manzo Perroni, depending who you believe.[1]

In 1958 the song was recorded for the first time by Venezuelan folk singer Mario Suárez before being covered three years later by Blanco himself. Blanco's cover proved hugely popular and shot to number one in both Argentina and, oddly, Japan.[2] A number of artists followed Blanco's lead in covering 'Moliendo Café', but it wasn't until Julio Iglesias released a version on his 1976 album 'America' that the tune really took off. Shortly after Iglesias re-popularised it, fans at Boca Juniors began to sing it in their stadium widely known as 'La Bombonera' ('The Chocolate Box'). There it remained for three decades, becoming known as 'Dale Boca' ("Come on Boca") until it suddenly emerged on the Amalfi coast in 2006, having arrived in Italy on a CD of Boca's favourite chants brought back from a trip to La Bombonera by a friend of a prominent member of SS Cavese 1919's ultras. Track 4, 'Dale Boca', stuck in the mind of an unnamed Cavese ultras' leader. Shortly afterwards he began singing the chant in a bar and, aided by the catchy repetitive tune, was quickly joined by four mates. The group then repeated the song a few nights later when SS Cavese entertained Ancona in Italy's Serie D. With SS Cavese 3-2 ahead, the ultras' Curva Sud erupted with their newly adopted song.[3]

[1] Billboard, 1961, 'Hits of the World', Billboard Issue 73 (27), Nielsen Business Media, 7 October 1961

[2] Billboard, 1961, 'Hits of the World', Billboard Issue 73 (4), Nielsen Business Media, 13 November 1961

[3] Copa90, 2016, 'Dale Cavese; the football chant that took over the internet and the world', 12 June 2013

"La la la la la la la la,
La la la la la la la la la laaaa,
La la la la la la la la,
La la la la la la la la la laaaa,
Oooooohhhh oooohhh ooooohhhh ohhhhh ohhhhh,
Oh oooohhh oooohhh ooooh oh ohhhh,
Oooooohhhh oooohhh ooooohhhh ohhhhh ohhhhh,
Oh oooohhh oooohhh ooooh oh ohhhh"

The moment was captured on film and when the footage of a celebratory bouncing terrace, moodily lit by flares and framed by numerous flags, was uploaded to YouTube by Cavese fan Attilio Rufolo, it quickly went viral. A decade on, the footage has been watched almost five million times.

As the catchy tune went global supporters of clubs around the world adopted it for themselves. In 2018, as well as being heard at Boca and SS Cavese, documentary makers *Copa90* recorded versions at clubs in Brazil, Austria, Japan, Indonesia, USA, Ukraine, England, Scotland, Wales, Belgium, Australia, Germany, Uruguay, the Netherlands, Egypt, Sweden, Chile, Romania, Poland, Colombia and Kosovo. Real Madrid fans took it to their hearts, seemingly more so than they did the manufactured 'Hala Madrid y Nada Más'. In Greece Aris Thessaloniki fans, whose filmed vocal support during a basketball fixture against Panathinaikos went viral, have added words, as have Montpellier fans in France. While Turkish side Besiktas, whose fans once held the world record for the loudest decibel level recorded at a sports match when they hit 132db,[4] have created their own call-and-response version. The current holders for the loudest noise at a sporting event are the NFL team the Kansas City Chiefs, whose fans were recorded at 142.2db during a victory over the New England Patriots in 2014,[5] which is loud enough to potentially rupture eardrums.[6]

[4] *FourFourTwo, 2016, '50 best football chants', FourFourTwo, 22 March 2016*

[5] *Guinness World Records, 2020, 'Loudest crowd roar at a sports stadium', Guinness World Records, Accessed 11 March 2020*

[6] *Purdue University 2020, 'Noise Comparisons', Purdue Unitversity, Accessed 14 March 2020*

The carnivalesque sound of 'Dale Boca/Dale Cavese', like the ticker-tape which became synonymous with the 1978 World Cup Finals hosted in Argentina, may have emerged from the terraces of Argentina, but neither chant nor rainstorms of paper are reflective of the fan scene they came from. The history of passionate support in the country pre-dates a similar scene in Italy, Germany and Spain. In Argentina, ultras groups, known as the Barra Bravas, began to gather on the terraces as early as the 1920s. Almost immediately the Barra Bravas brought violence with them and quickly established a reputation for creating an intimidating atmosphere for away teams, their fans and the match officials. According to Argentine journalist Amílcar Romero, their ability to influence through fear led to a natural escalation of violence, because if you are travelling away from home and being threatened, or "squeezed" as Romero terms it, the only response was to counter-act that with an intimidating group of your own, in turn creating a "dirty war".[7]

Problems with violence escalated following Argentina's poor showing at the 1958 World Cup finals in Sweden. Despite high expectations, Argentina flopped in Scandinavia and finished bottom of their group behind West Germany, Northern Ireland and Czechoslovakia, conceding ten goals in just three games, including six in their crucial final game against the Czechs. Inspired by a desire to not repeat such a failure on the international stage, all aspects of Argentinian football were reviewed with an aim to improve each area and garner every possible advantage. The Barra Bravas, due to their ability to create such a hostile environment for the opposition, were considered an essential part of that process, as Romero explains: "It is necessary to try to control as much as possible everything that happens within the field; control chance, limit it as much as possible. The Barra Bravas begin to be fundamental; they took on more and more importance. It is the breath, the psychological service over the rival, the player number 12".[8]

To this day, the effect the fans have on the outcome of the game remains revered in Argentina. Non-stop feverish singing for 90 minutes

[7]   Martinez. F, 2003, 'The Barras appear with the industrialisation of football', Pagina12.com, 13 July 2003

[8]   Martinez. F, 2003, 'The Barras appear with the industrialisation of football', Pagina12.com, 13 July 2003

at the football has its own word; "Aguante", which one fan described as a mindset unique to Argentina: "football in Europe is fun—a recreation—here it is passion".[9] The reverence given to vocal backing is reflected in the most boisterous section in Boca Juniors' La Bombonera stadium. A vast concrete terrace which vibrates as fans rhythmically bounce up and down, accompanied by a frenzy of drums, chants, fireworks and blatant intimidation of visiting players and officials is still called 'La Doce' ('Number 12'), the fabled '12th man'.[10]

One way in which the Barra Bravas create that intimidating atmosphere is through the liberal use of violence. In 1994, when River won a Superclásico derby 2-0 away at Boca, fans of both clubs clashed and two River fans were murdered, leading to one Boca fan going on television and boasting among laughing friends: "The game finished 2-2. River scored twice, but we killed two of them", after which "2-2" was spray-painted around Buenos Aires.[11] Clashes between rival groups of fans were so serious that in 2014, a fan of Lanus, Javier Gerez, 42, was reportedly struck by a rubber bullet fired into a group of brawling fans by police and killed during an away game in Estudiantes' La Plata stadium. He was the 17th fan to be killed since 2000. In response, the Argentine Football Association (AFA) immediately implemented a ban on all away fans with Regional Security Minister Ricardo Casal insisting; "The measure will remain in place until the football authorities take action to curb violence in football".[12]

At the time of writing almost five years later, the ban has not been completely lifted, though there are trials to allow away fans to return to grounds taking place at some Superliga clubs, but notably none of the big-five; Boca Juniors, Independiente, Racing Club, River Plate and San Lorenzo.[13] Not that a lack of away fans has removed violence from Argentinian stadiums. The second leg of the 2018 Copa Libertadores

[9] *Mengem. E, 2018, 'The Biggest Game of All Time; Derby Days Superclassico', Copa90, 15 December 2018*

[10] *Burns. J, 2016, 'Argentine football controversies mirror the country's politics', Financial Times, 19 September 2016*

[11] *Mengem. E, 2018, 'The Biggest Game of All Time; Derby Days Superclassico', Copa90, 15 December 2018*

[12] *BBC, 2013, 'Argentina bans football away supporters after fan death', BBC, 12 June 2013*

[13] *Buenos Aires Times, 2018, 'Away fans will be able to attend Superliga matches this season, official confirms', Buenos Aires Times, 17 July 2018*

between Boca and their fierce Buenos Aires rivals River Plate was postponed twice after the Boca Juniors team bus was attacked en route to River's El Monumental stadium. With the game in jeopardy, home fans clashed with police who resorted to firing tear gas and rubber bullets.[14] Ultimately the game was moved across the Atlantic Ocean to Real Madrid's Santiago Bernabeu and the competition, named after the people who liberated South America from Spain,[15] was won by River who triumphed 3-1 after extra-time.

With the violence also comes additional crime. The scale of corruption in Argentinian football, explicitly linked to the Barra Bravas at each club, causes it to feature on the pages of the financial newspapers as much as it does the back pages. In recent years the Argentine government has adopted a "zero-tolerance" policy towards football violence, alongside tougher sentences aimed at "civilising" the national sport.[16] But having turned a blind eye to the problem since the 1960s, along with the Argentine Football Association, they had allowed each club's Barra Bravas to deeply embed themselves in organised crime.

An investigation by The Economist described the Barra Bravas as "violent mini-mafias", listing their criminal activities as money-laundering, drug-dealing and gun crime, often with the complicity of police, politicians and club officials from presidents down to matchday security guards.[17] One member of Boca's Barra Bravas boasted to The Guardian in 2011: "In England you think your fans, 'los hooligans', were powerful but they were nothing compared to us. All you did there was drink and fight. We drink, we fight, and we also do business. We're not just monkeys singing for the clubs in the stadiums and then killing each other in the streets. They could learn a thing or two from us".[18]

Following Gerez's death at Lanus' game at Estudiantes in 2014,

---

[14] Wilson. J, 2018, 'Copa Libertadores: second leg of final called off again hours before kick-off', The Guardian, 25 November 2018

[15] Mengem. E, 2018, 'The Biggest Game of All Time; Derby Days Superclassico', Copa90, 15 December 2018

[16] Burns. J, 2016, 'Argentine football controversies mirror the country's politics', Financial Times, 19 September 2016

[17] D.S, 2018, 'Game Theory; Foul Play', The Economist, 18 February 2018

[18] Kelly. A, 2011, 'The barra bravas; the violent Argentinian gangs controlling football', The Guardian, 21 August 2011

the manager of Estudiantes at the time, Mauricio Pellegrino, told the press that football violence was "a social problem, [which] reflects the violence in society".[19] *The Economist* agreed saying: "football, with its visceral extremes often mirroring political upheavals, exercises a powerful grip on Argentine culture". The magazine pointed out that Argentina's President Mauricio Macri had also been president at Boca Juniors from 1995 until 2007,[20] where alongside 'Dale Boca', fans are known to bounce en masse, while chanting: *"El que no salta es un inglés" ("If you don't jump you're an Englishman")*.[21] Macri's attempts to temper the violence and political influence of the Barras Bravas, which he began back in 1995 with mixed results, has a new urgency after Argentina was taken to task by the Financial Action Task Force (FATF), an international body set-up to fight money launder-ing, who placed the country on a "grey list" of countries who aren't deemed to be doing enough to combat corruption. An appearance on the grey list acts as a warning that unless more is done the country will be moved onto a "black list", from which countries struggle to do business with any of the 37 FATF member nations,[22] including the economic powerhouses of the United States, France, Mexico, China, Japan and Germany.[23] As a result, in February 2018, the government forced the AFA to adopt a new financial-disclosure requirement for the Superliga and its clubs. *The Economist* called it a "step in the right direction" before adding: "having shown scant regard for existing laws and regulations, the Barra Bravas seem unlikely to pay much heed to new rules on financial disclosure. If Argentina's government is serious about ending the corruption, it will need to confront the gangs on the terraces and in the streets. That is an altogether tougher prospect. [This is] a long-overdue effort to clean up the game, but pales in comparison with the scale of the problem".[24]

[19] BBC, 2013, 'Argentina bans football away supporters after fan death', BBC, 12 June 2013

[20] D.S, 2018, 'Game Theory; Foul Play', The Economist, 18 February 2018

[21] Burns. J, 2016, 'Argentine football controversies mirror the country's politics', Financial Times, 19 September 2016

[22] D.S, 2018, 'Game Theory; Foul Play', The Economist, 18 February 2018

[23] FATF, 'FATF Member Nations and Observers', fatf-gafi.com, Retrieved 19 October 2018

[24] D.S, 2018, 'Game Theory; Foul Play', The Economist, 18 February 2018

As with the hooligan problem in Britain under Thatcher, the issue runs deeper than tribal terrace loyalties. In a country where almost a third of people live below the poverty line, the Barra Bravas, like England's hooligan firms, are a symptom of wider issues. For example, take this exchange between a member of Boca's Barra Bravas and *The Guardian's* Annie Kelly in 2011:

"What 'else do we have to be proud of if it isn't our team or the club shirt on our backs?' he asks. He gestures angrily around his house, at the crumbling walls, the damp mattresses where his six children sleep, the curling football posters and flickering light bulbs. He takes me outside and points to two teenagers sitting under a faded mural of Villa Fiorito's most famous son—Diego Maradona. For a few pesos, locals take tourists to see the pitch where he honed his skills, now nothing more than a patch of cracked, weed-clogged concrete, or to look at the rubbish-strewn front yard of the Maradona family house. The two boys lean back against the cracked paint and smoke paco, a cheap, toxic mix of cocaine base paste. The drug has become endemic in Argentina's poorest barrios, claiming countless young lives every year. 'Those two boys, they used to play football with my sons,' says Mendez. He points to one of them: what was once a leg is now a stump wrapped in dirty bandages. 'That kid, he was so high on that stuff he lay on the railway tracks and was hit by a train. In a year they'll both be dead'".[25]

Diego Murzi, a member of Salvemos al Futbol, an advocacy group dedicated to modernising Argentine soccer, spoke to Rory Smith of *The New York Times* about the situation after the clashes outside El Monumental before the 2018 Copa Liberatores Final second-leg that was postponed and moved to Spain:

"I have written a Master's thesis and I am finishing a Ph.D. on how to solve the problems in Argentine football and even I find it difficult to define. It is a combination of factors: the climate of suspicion that pervades our game; the policies of prevention and control of violence that have always failed; and the culture around our football, which is violent, macho, forgetful and thinks only of success. It means defeat is

[25] Kelly. A, 2011, 'The barra bravas; the violent Argentinian gangs controlling football', The Guardian, 21 August 2011

unthinkable, a fate to be avoided at all costs. For players, that might mean a little casual brutality toward an opponent or some deliberate theatricality. In a country where many see their soccer team as the principle source of their identity, where far too many feel they have little else to live for, and where the economy is struggling and inflation rampant, it can have much more serious consequences for fans. For some, it creates an environment where any measures in support of their team, or to the detriment of a rival, can be considered. That may be why River fans targeted the Boca Juniors bus: because this was a game they could not lose. When defeat does come—and defeat always comes—it is met with rage that defies control".[26]

In 2011 River Plate were relegated to the Second Division for the first time in their history. After the game which sealed their fate, against Belgrano, fans rioted, trashing El Monumental and setting parts of it alight. It is estimated that around 100 people were seriously injured in the riots, with at least two fatalities, including that of a 23-year-old fan who jumped in front of a train and took his own life.[27]

On the other side of Buenos Aires, Boca fans greeted the relegation of their rival with glee. They had referred to River Plate as "Gallinas" meaning "chicken" ever since River led, then lost a Copa Libertadores final to Penarol in 1966 and they celebrated their relegation with a new chant, which is still sung to this day:

"Gallinas,
It's a stain that you will never erase,
You were relegated to the B,
Burning El Monumental"

The Independent's football writer Miguel Delaney visited the country for the 2018 Copa Liberatores final and found the same problems and the same resultant conflict between feverish, passionate support and violence:

"There are many profound sociological reasons for this negative

[26] *Smith. R, 2018, 'For Copa Libertadores at a Crossroads, a Weekend to Forget', New York Times, 26 November 2018*

[27] *Mengem. E, 2018, 'The Biggest Game of All Time; Derby Days Superclassico', Copa90, 15 December 2018*

relationship, from the lack of identity upon which an immigrant state was founded to the extremes of economics [that] have endured, but the effects are multifarious. Argentine football just feels like it is in a perpetual state of unsustainable frenzy. That creates the spectacle so many of us came to the Libertadores final for, but it also creates a lot of huge problems even beyond the violence, and thereby further feeding that violence. The entire football culture is a logical end point of the way support seems to be going on social media in the UK, where tribalism rules, where saying anything mildly critical of a team makes you the enemy. Argentina is the extreme illustration of all that, if not a result of it. The country's situation is the result of so many interwoven sociological issues, although it's difficult not to simplistically think that people's extreme identification with their club is the result of extreme economic disparity. It's what they cling to, what gives a sense of self in a society with so many breaking points. In the hours after the Libertadores final second leg had been postponed for a second time, on a metro train back down from the El Monumental stadium on the Sunday, River fans began to sing some of the songs that make their matches such occasions. All of the chants to the tune of 1960s rock hit came out, until there was a new one. Its subject? The attack on the Boca bus and how their rivals had "shit themselves". Never mind the other effects, the other problems. It was a result, of sorts".[28]

Just as in 1994, off the pitch actions mattered as much as what happened on it.

While undoubtedly a problem outside the ground, on the terraces at least, the Barra Bravas are much admired for their vibrant support of their clubs. The fans' devotion to their team's colours, coupled with the rivalry makes Boca's La Bombonera the only stadium in the world where Coca-Cola have changed their logo's colours, making it black and white, rather than the traditional red and white, which is associated with River Plate.[29] Their loud vocal backing, coupled with colourful visual displays of banners, streamers, flags and ticker tape have been much admired around the world, inspiring fan groups

[28] Delaney. M, 2018, 'Welcome to Argentina, the country that loves football too much', The Independent, 26 November 2018

[29] Mengem. E, 2018, 'The Biggest Game of All Time; Derby Days Superclassico', Copa90, 15 December 2018

across South America and recently, the United States. Delaney, like many others, describes the violence explicitly as "the flip side to the much-shared and much-admired footage of over 60,000 Boca fans cramming into the Bombonera on Thursday for what was supposed to be their last training session ahead of the second leg. It was hard not to be entirely enamoured by that, such passion".[30]

As Major League Soccer begins to gain a foothold in the States, fan groups are beginning to emerge, and they are bringing with them a mix of cultural influences, including English, European ultra and South American Barra Bravas. As such, chants formerly associated with US sports in the marching band style one-liners such as:

"U. S. A,

U. S. A"

Or:

"Let's go,

Defence,

Let's go"

... have been abandoned and left to fans of the NFL and NBA. These simple, ubiquitous chants have instead been replaced with more complex and bespoke offerings. However, due to the relatively young age of the fan groups across the MLS, coupled with the lower levels of away support, their chants remain more parochial than confrontational, mimicking the development of chanting in England up until the mid-1960s.

That is not to say that MLS games are lacking in atmosphere, because the fan scene that has developed in the country is a veritable pick-n-mix of football culture and has adopted the best bits of the different terrace cultures of more established footballing nations. DC United, for example, have a Barra Bravas group founded by Bolivian fan Oscar Zambrana and co-lead by American Jay Igiel, who told

[30] Delaney. M, 2018, 'Welcome to Argentina, the country that loves football too much', The Independent, 26 November 2018

the BBC: "We have South American roots and that's the basis of our culture in terms of the songs that we do, the chants that we sing. Some of the other groups are more European, or English-based, but we're different in that respect. We're a little less organised, but we're a little louder, crazier, more passionate. We have members from 40 different nationalities among our members. The passion we bring. The energy that we bring, makes a big difference to the players. One of the things I love about the Barra, especially coming from [Washington] DC, where political affiliation and status mean so much, [is that] in the Barra no-one cares. It doesn't matter if you're from Bolivia, or Mexico, or the United States or Eastern Europe. It doesn't matter if you're a Democrat or a Republican, or how much you make or what you do for a living, it's just all about the passion for the game. We embody what America is all about, it's a melting pot of cultures and it is everyone coming together, making a contribution so the whole is better than the sum of the parts".[31]

Zambrano goes on to explain why he helped establish a fan group in a country with no history of fan culture: "I always liked football and I was part of a Barra group in Bolivia, so I created a supporter group using the traditional name we have in South America, the Barra Bravas, to teach Americans about football culture. We get to the ground four hours before the match starts, we enjoy ourselves and we socialise with all our other members. We come together as a family. Then, 40 minutes before the game begins, we get our drums and our flags and march together into the stands, where we do our main job: support the team. You'll hear American fans chanting in Spanish and English. You'll hear Hispanic fans chanting in English and Spanish and lastly, those who don't speak the languages, just jump, that's the only thing we ask of them".[32]

The mix of the two languages and cultures can be seen in 'Vamos United'. The chant originated as 'Vamos Peruanos' among the Barra Bravas at Peruvian top-flight club Universiatrio de Deportes, popularly

[31] Sparrow. T, McKenna. B, Barr. F, 2014, 'La Barra Bravas; Why US football fans chant in Spanish', BBC, 4 June 2014

[32] Sparrow. T, McKenna. B, Barr. F, 2014, 'La Barra Bravas; Why US football fans chant in Spanish', BBC, 4 June 2014

known as 'La U',[33] before making its way to Washington and becoming so synonymous with DC that they sewed the lyrics into their 2015 away shirt:[34]

"Vamos,
Vamos United,
Esta Noche Tenemos Que Ganar"

Which links back to more traditional US sporting chants, referencing the *'Let's go'* motif, favoured there and almost nowhere else, translating as:

"Let's go,
Let's go United,
Tonight we've got to win"

DC also boasts splinter groups from the Barra Bravas, including the 'District Ultras' set-up in 2010 by Srdan Bastaic, who wanted to introduce a more European feeling. The District Ultras are now famed for impressive European-style tifos[35] and match the Barra Bravas with their vocal backing, including encouraging anyone not singing to join in with this, to the tune of Bob Marley's 1980s hit 'Get up, Stand up':

"Get up,
Stand up,
Get up off your ass"

It's not just in DC that this has happened. Orlando City recently created a purpose-built but poorly-named ground, the Orlando City Stadium. It was designed in consultation with their ultra-groups The Ruckus and The Iron Lions, who have separate areas in 'The Wall'. The result is a stadium that maximises atmosphere, but in a

---

[33] *Vergara. C, 2017, 'The story behind the cry 'Vamos Chilenos'', Latercera, 2 December 2017*

[34] *MLS, 2015, 'DC United unveil new secondary jersey', MLS.com, 8 February 2015*

[35] *Whiting. A, Weber. G, Cartagena. R, 2017, 'How to be a DC United fan', Washingtonian.com, 6 March 2017*

safe environment. Each group of ultras has their own bespoke end. These feature safe-standing terraces, inspired by those in Germany, decked out with all manner of flags and banners, and platforms for 'capos', similar to those seen in Morocco, who stand at the front of ultra-sections leading the chanting through a megaphone. These are supplemented by safety-checked smoke bomb operators who, when the situation demands it, release clouds of purple-and-white sulphur into the air in co-ordinated displays the Italian ultras would be proud of.

Like their DC equivalents, Orlando's fan groups have also adopted the English phenomenon of chanting. However, their practice of disseminating fan song books ahead of each game would look oddly pre-prepared viewed through the prism of the more off-the-cuff, context-inspired chanting synonymous with English fans. One reason for doing that however is the bi-lingual nature of the chanting at Orlando City. Without a football culture steeped in centuries of island isolation Orlando's footballing history is one in which English and Spanish speaking fans are inextricably linked and as such, their chants are too. To take but one example, Orlando have their own version of 'Allez, Allez, Allez', named in Spanish, 'Ahora y Por Siempre' and featuring English and Spanish lines, with fans slipping seamlessly from one to the other:

> *"Suddenly one day,*
> *I fell in love with you,*
> *The pounding of my heart,*
> *Revealed to me the truth,*
> *The years will carry on, no matter what we do,*
> *Ahora y por siempre (now and forever),*
> *The Wall will shoulder you,*
> *Allez, Allez, Allez,*
> *Allez, Allez, Allez"*

Orlando's version features a final flourish. On completion of the song, the fans launch any drinks they are been holding into the sky, in scenes mimicking those at many English pubs when England scored in the 2018 World Cup. The fans do the same when the team scores. Writer Adam Hurrey described this new trend by noting: "If one man throws his beer, it's weird and uncalled for. If 2,000 people in a converted Croydon warehouse do it in unison, it becomes something of a spectacle".[36] At DC United you're pre-warned this beer chucking will happen with the optimistic: "You will get showered with beer when we score".[37]

Multiculturalism is also a big facet of the football fan scene in North Africa and Morocco. In 2014, Raja Casablanca's ultras the Green Boys claimed third place in the 'Ultras World' End of Year awards thanks in large part to clips of them which went viral as the year drew to a close. (Eastern Europe claimed the top two spots courtesy of Legia Warsaw and Red Star Belgrade.[38]) Football is an institution in Morocco and Raja Casablanca are one of the country's biggest clubs, with 12 top-flight titles, tied with FAR Rabat. Only one club have more Wydad Casablanca, who have 15 and against whom Raja have a fierce, tribal, rivalry.

Established in March 1949, Raja are 12 years younger than their city-rivals, but immediately the neighbours were not keen on one another. "From day one, Raja Casablanca prided itself on being the club of the people and has become the beating heartbeat of the city," explained journalist Liam Newman in his profile of the club for *These Football Times*. He went on: "[It] was established as an outlet for the city's working-class youth to show their displeasure at the nation's political structure of the time and also as direct opposition to Wydad, who tend to represent the middle classes. These sentiments are high-lighted by the eagle emblem, which signals ideologies of strength and resistance, while the club's choice of green colours symbolises hope".[39]

The chant that went viral celebrates Raja's run to the World Club Cup Championship in 2013 where, having beaten Auckland City, Mexico's Monterrey and Atlético Mineiro of Brazil, they lost 2-0 to German Champions Bayern Munich:

---

[36] Hurrey. A, 2018, 'It came, it flew, it soaked', The Independent, 13 July 2018

[37] Whiting. A, Weber. G, Cartagena. R, 2017, 'How to be a DC United fan', Washingtonian.com, 6 March 2017

[38] World of Ultras, 2014, 'Top 10 ultras of 2014', YouTube.com, 29 December 2014

[39] Newman. L, 2014, 'A world of ultras; Raja Casablanca', These Football Times, 3 December 2014

> *"Oh, Oh Oh, Oh, Oh Oh,*
> *Oh, Oh Oh, Oh, Oh Oh,*
> *Dalé dalé dalé ohhh,*
> *Dalé ohh dalé ohh,*
> *You get out all Moroccans in the streets in all cities,*
> *You make the Moroccan migrants happy and you surprise forty*
> *million people,*
> *Courteous of people young and old,*
> *And the greens play the role of the nation,*
> *I choke when I remember Agidir and the past,*
> *Monterey and Auckland City and I cry because of happiness,*
> *Mineiro can't forget Moutaoualii and the generation,*
> *And on the name of Raja they create a street in Brazil,*
> *Oh, Oh Oh, Oh, Oh Oh,*
> *Oh, Oh Oh, Oh, Oh Oh,*
> *Dalé dalé dalé ohhh,*
> *Dalé ohh dalé ohh"*

Just as football reflects the social lives, hopes and frustrations of its fans in England, Italy, Argentina and elsewhere, Morocco is no different. Social scientist and photo-journalist Abderrahim Bourkia visited Casablanca and reported: "In Casablanca and Morocco football is a huge part of the popular culture. It is more than a game for the masses. People live and breathe football and it forms a big part of Moroccan identity. Signs and artworks [by each club's ultras] appear in every neighbourhood. They show the inter-group dynamics and social identity articulated by the supporters. The two teams on the pitch are always in confrontation and so are the fans".[40]

This loyalty, no matter what happens on the pitch, coupled with a sense of being the working-class underdogs is highlighted in another popular Raja chant called 'La Grande Storia' ('The Great Story'):

> *"Give him my love,*
> *Come on, come on please give him Champion,*

[40] Bourkia. A, 2018, Casablanca; ultra culture and beach football', Goal-Click.com, Retrieved 19 October 2018

Give him my love,
Come on let's go please my heart

Ohhh wheeeey or we or the great story,
Ohhh wheeeey or we or, we are,
Or we or we or the beautiful glory,
Or we or we or,
You win for us,

Come on guys come on,
My curve my house,
The government go, go,
Tear down the ruthless government

Come on guys come on,
My curve my house,
The government go, go,
Tear down the ruthless government"

A clip of Raja's Green Boys singing 'La Grande Storia' on loop for almost four minutes and only briefly stopping to celebrate a Raja goal, before returning to chant as if nothing happened, has been viewed over one million times on YouTube. Among those who viewed the video were fans who stood on Orlando City's The Wall. The group's leaders, Rodrigo Guillen and Jake Beard, wanted a new chant but didn't want just another version of 'Vamos Chilenos'. In a move that highlights the new global inter-connectedness of the ultra groups, they turned to the internet for inspiration where they came across the clip of the Green Boys singing 'La Grande Storia'. "The song is about love," said Guillen. "It's really an epic love ballad".[41] Together Guillen and Beard adapted the song and made it their own, renaming it 'La Grand Victoria' and changing the lyrics into a mix of Spanish and English:

41 *Guillen. R, 2015, 'A Supporters Anthem – 'La Grande Victoria", OrlandoCity.com, 27 August*
  205

"Dale mi amor
Vamo vamo por favour,
Dale Campeón,
Dale mi amor,
Vamo vamo por favour de corazón,

Ohh eh oh e ohhh return victorious,
Ohh eh oh e ahh and stay true,
Orrlandoo City a team so glorious,
Ohh eh oh e ahh we follow you,

Passion pours out from the heart,
So we have been here from the start (and),
Rain or shine we do our part,
'Cos that's how we made our name,

And now that the story grows,
Other teams are sure to know (that),
Orlando City will take the throne,
And that's why we follow you"

"It was important for us to make it clean, and make it for everyone, but also it was important to make it our own, to make it about how we feel about the club," Guillen explained. "The bit about staying true, that was important for us, because we all, players, supporters and club, need to remember who we are and where we came from," he added.[42] At the next home game, the two ultra-groups got together, Beard brought his guitar and together they sat around drinking beer and learning the words, before taking it into the stadium where it has since been sung before every game.

---

[42] Guillen. R, 2015, 'A Supporters Anthem – 'La Grande Victoria", OrlandoCity.com, 27 August 205

14. IT'S THE HOPE THAT GETS YOU

'I HAD A WHEELBARROW'

While the chants filled with swearwords and citing incidents with intrinsic shock value—death, abuse or taboo subjects—make the headlines and give football chanting a bad name, this doesn't tell the full story. There is one final aspect of chanting, which has helped sustain it through its evolution from music hall to show-tune, through hate-fuelled abuse and good-natured ridicule and cement its place as a social phenomenon, helping to bind fans to their clubs and each other: chanting purely for the sake of chanting.

As we have seen, chanting is a way of expressing pride or worshipping something you are proud to identify with in a very public, vocal and visual way, just as the Aboriginal clans who came together to worship their totems have done for millennia. Within these ritualistic celebrations, Aborigines experience the social existence of their clan viscerally. The emotions of the community are focused on the physical representation of themselves, and by extension the Aborigines are worshipping their own society, just as a football team is a physical embodiment of an area, whose fans come together to sing and chant in celebration of that area.

Chanting not only allows us an opportunity to publicly celebrate the identities we are proud of, it also makes us feel good. Remember the findings of the study by the Sidney De Haan Research Centre for Arts and Health on singing, which detailed how coming together with a large number of like-minded people, even those from a wide variety of ethnographic and economic groups, improves our immediate mood and long-term sense of wellbeing. Simply by gathering in one location as a group and indulging in some vocal backing of our team, we are better as individuals at dealing with anxiety, we feel more connected to each other, and by extension less lonely. Crucially we also feel happier when we make our way home after the game, even if our team lost.[1]

As one fan told the Social Issues Research Centre: "The joy in the stadium is a lot greater than at home in front of your TV. A goal is scored and you are in tears of joy, hugging other people, everyone is celebrating. You are hugging complete strangers and know they feel

[1] McLean. T, 2008, 'Choral singing makes you happy', *Sydney Morning Herald*, 10 July 2008

the same. Everyone is celebrating together, regardless of class. Millionaires and those on welfare, everyone partying together".[2] In this way, chanting provides the antithesis to the 'pain as entertainment' model of fandom described by Nick Hornby, or what journalist Jim White describes as "widespread enslavement to self-harm [as] the only explanation of why thousands upon thousands of us continue to follow clubs whose principal business strategy seems to be to extract cash from our pockets in exchange for the inflicting of pain".[3] As early as 1981 Desmond Morris was recording Oxford United fans airing a number of chants, whose only purpose was distraction from the dull football on view, including the simple:

> **"We are bored,**
> **We are bored"**[4]

Chanting is the way fans put the fun back into our increasingly corporate and sterile game. As Pete Miles writes: "be it with friends, acquaintances or even on your own, these [are the] lasting evocations of people having fun at football. And we can all remember when football was fun can't we?"[5]

This aspect of messing about with your mates in the crowd is not a new one, and as early as 1898, four years before Norwich City would be formed and adopt 'On the Ball City', match reports were citing the efforts of fans to entertain themselves and enliven dull games:

"The spectators wanted their money's worth and such remarks as 'play the game', 'come off the field', 'time', 'chuck it', and others which will scarcely bear repeating were hurled at the players." Soon after the second half got under way the ball was kicked into the crowd, and the spectators refused to give it back. The match report continued:

"several attempts had been made by the spectators to keep the ball when it went out of play, and a certain section now succeeded in

---

[2] Social Issues Research Centre, 2008, 'Football Passions', Social Research Centre, London, p7

[3] White. J, 2007, 'County fans top of stress league', The Telegraph, 6 January 2007

[4] Morris. D, 1981, 'The Soccer Tribe', Jonathon Cape Publishing, London, p310

[5] Miles. P, 2016, 'Beyond the Turnstiles', Ockley Book, Huddersfield, Yorkshire, p23

doing so, the referee leaving the field and requisitioning a new one. The struggle for the old one continued for some time, but at last it was thrown into the arena again. Immediately afterwards, from a long return by McLintock, another mighty tussle ensued. Several policemen joined in the melee but were overpowered, and there was every indication of a right royal row until somebody stronger than the rest got hold and punted the ball up on the roof of the stand. All would have been quiet had not some meddlesome person climbed on to the roof, and from there thrown down the ball into the struggling mass below. Again, attention was entirely diverted from the game, which went on unwatched, unnoticed, play being of an uneventful character. Then the ball bounced high on to the cycle track, and from thence into the crowd, and the disorderly scenes were resumed. The ball was kept by the crowd, and immediately afterwards, someone rushing along the track to keep another ball in play ran plump into a leviathan policeman, and knocked him sprawling under the rails, amongst the feet of the crowd. These incidents proved more funny than the play, which settled down into a steady, uninteresting scramble again".[6]

Chanting is far from being irrelevant, but in being fun, it frequently is irreverent. Take Notts County's anthem: 'I had a Wheelbarrow', a perfect example of chanting, that on the face of it is seemingly pointless, and as a result sums up all that is good about chanting. Sung to the tune of 'On Top of Old Smoky', an early 20th century American folk song which made its way into popular consciousness in 1951 when Pete Seeger's folk group the Weavers released a version which sold over a million copies, the chant is simply:

"I had a wheelbarrow,
The wheel fell off,
I had a wheelbarrow,
The wheel fell off,
County, County, County."

---

[6] Burnton. S, 2018, 'The forgotten story of evil Football League test matches', The Guardian, 28 November 2018

In its simplicity and its complete disregard for anything remotely to do with football, 'I Had a Wheelbarrow' has all the ingredients for a perfect football chant.

As with other chants, its origins are disputed and, depending on who you believe, either rooted in folklore and the memories of famous comebacks or misfortune. As many of the chants discussed have shown, folklore and legend are a crucial ingredient in the fan experience. These tales provide a shared history and common thread that runs through the generations, tying you to your peers in a unifying bond no matter their age, sex or background. One fan, in describing how they had been introduced to the game explained: "Every generation has their heroes and stories with good and bad moments just like the fairy tales. Older people always tell the stories to the younger ones, so the stories get passed down through the generations. Those story-telling moments are really important for the club as they form tomorrow's generation of supporters who go on to tell the same stories to their children. Often in the stories the truth is not 100%, things may be exaggerated [and] the way the older ones remember the stories changes as time goes on [that isn't important, what is important is that] the story passes down through generations".[7]

Or put another way, as author Tim Marshall concludes: "The terraces are among the last places in the country where our old folk songs and music hall ditties are handed down to the next generation, [even] nursery rhymes, for example 'The Farmer in his Dell' becomes *"We're gonna win the league"*, albeit in radically altered form".[8] This sense of passing down apocryphal tales is certainly at play with 'I had a Wheelbarrow', about which there are numerous theories as to how it originally came to be a fixture at Meadow Lane.

One version of the origins of 'I had a Wheelbarrow', promoted by the club's official website, is that the chant came into existence on 16 April 1990 during an away game against Shrewsbury Town. In this version County fell 2-0 behind leading to joyous chanting from the home fans whose repertoire included their own sadly long forgotten chant to the tune of 'On top of Old Smokey'. County fans, not used

[7] Social Issues Research Centre, 2008, 'Football Passions', Social Research Centre, London, p16

[8] Marshall. T, 2014, 'Where do chants come from', The Telegraph, 1 August 2014

to the Shropshire burr of their rivals' singing, are believed to have misheard the Shrewsbury version and repeated it back as *"I had a wheelbarrow, the wheel fell off"*. As audio confusion reigned, County staged a remarkable comeback and scored twice in quick succession to level the game. As noted with other chants, such as 'Allez, Allez, Allez', the chant was immediately associated to success in supporters' minds and as such earned further airings as the season wore on. More success was to come and County, who remained unbeaten from that point on, clinched promotion at Wembley, with 'I had a Wheelbarrow' continuing to provide the soundtrack to promotion.[9]

Mick Chappell, County's honorary club historian, suggests that: "Most Notts fans favour the 'Shrewsbury theory', so folklore prevails",[10] however it is not the only theory. Another popular version as to the origins of 'I Had a Wheelbarrow' concerns Neil Warnock's appointment as manager in 1989. Warnock is alleged to have later told a local interviewer: "When I first came to Notts County all I had was a wheelbarrow... and the wheel fell off that",[11] prompting the fans to adopt it as their anthem. A final version is more literal and concerns the groundsman suffering a wheel-losing mishap with his barrow that was immediately and verbally immortalised as he made his way around the pitch in front of County's vocal Kop.[12]

'I Had a Wheelbarrow' is simple, annoyingly catchy and inclusive—it has a repetition of two short, easy-to-understand and easy-to-remember sentences, contains no offensive language and contains nothing controversial or potentially divisive. On top of all that the chant is capped off with a rousing rendition of *"County, County, County"*, bringing a community together as one. Furthermore, 'I Had a Wheelbarrow' is an example of a chant that is self-deprecating. In direct contrast to, for example, Bayern's long-winded self-congratulation 'Star of the South', the entirety of 'I Had a Wheelbarrow' is the inference that as a club they are so hopelessly mismanaged and poor that even

[9]   *Notts County FC, 2015, '25 years since wheelbarrow song first sung', NottsCountyFC.co.uk, 16 April 2015*

[10] *Mick Chappell, 2018, Email interview, 15 November 2018*

[11] *Punk Football, 2018, 'The wheelbarrow song', PunkFootball.com, Retrieved 22 October 2018*

[12] *Miller. N, 2016, '50 best football chants', FourFourTwo, 22 March 2016*

their wheelbarrow is broken. There are no world records or spying allegations to be found here.

Finally, it is completely irrelevant to football. 'I Had a Wheelbarrow' expresses no particular support, derision, masculinity or geographical relevance and yet it perfectly encapsulates what it is to be a football fan: you get a new wheelbarrow and bundled up in it are abstract ideas of potential, excitement and things you can achieve. Then just as everything looks good, the wheel falls off, the promise remains unfilled and the excitement you felt turns to abject disappointment. Yet, despite all that, you still love the wheelbarrow. You'll get a new wheel for it and it'll be as good as new. You believe again. That is the life of a football fan and is particularly apt for fans of Notts County as in 2007 the club was declared to be the most stressful team you could support. This accolade was bestowed upon them based on how often they narrowly missed out on promotion, or got relegated, their regular failure to win at home, their ability to lose matches from winning positions, their consistency in first reaching but then losing in the play-offs, their ongoing financial problems leading to uncertainty over the club's future, and their frequent changes in ownership and of manager.[13]

Since the calculation was announced in 2007, County have seemingly attempted to cement their place at the top of that particular table. In the intervening 13 years, at the time of writing County have made their way through 16 different managers and been both promoted and relegated, before finally surrendered their tag as the 'oldest Football League club' with relegation to the Conference in 2019; more rollercoaster than wheelbarrow. Off the pitch has been no better, with County having had two winding up orders issued against them and been taken over four times, including a disastrous period as the plaything of shadowy group Munto Finance, in which they appointed former-England manager Sven-Goran Eriksson as Director of Football and signed Sol Campbell. Eriksson lasted seven months, Campbell lasted just 29 days and one game. Nor is there an end in sight as at the time of writing, ahead of their first season outside the Football League in their 157-year history, County are again up for sale, by an

---

[13]   White. J, 2007, 'County fans top of stress league', *The Telegraph*, 6 January 2007

owner, who while responding to fan criticism of his running of the club accidently posted a photograph of his penis on social media.[14]

Through all this turmoil, 'I Had a Wheelbarrow' has survived, in part because the sole point of the song is to simply sing it.

Notts County aren't the only club to have an anthem that appears to have very little to do with football. Another is Stoke City whose fans are famed for singing the 1968 Tom Jones single, 'Delilah'. The original, which despite being the sixth highest selling single of 1968, only reached number two in the UK charts,[15] talks about a spurned lover enacting violent revenge, and is far from being an obvious football song:

"I saw the light on the night that I passed by her window,
I saw the flickering shadow of love on her blind,
She was my woman,
As she deceived me I watched and went out of my mind,

My, my, my, Delilah,
Why, why, why, Delilah,
I could see, that girl was no good for me,
But I was lost like a slave that no man could free,

At break of day when that man drove away I was waiting,
I crossed the street to her house and she opened the door,
She stood there laughing,
I felt the knife in my hand and she laughed no more,

My, my, my, Delilah,
Why, why, why, Delilah,
So before they come to break down the door,
Forgive me Delilah I just couldn't take any more,

She stood there laughing,

14 Reid. B, 2019, 'Notts County's Alan Hardy quits Twitter after accidentally posting intimate picture', Nottingham Post, 27 January 2019

15 EveryHit, 2018, 'Top selling singles of 1968', EveryHit.com, Retrieved 23 October 2018

I felt the knife in my hand and she laughed no more,

My, my, my, Delilah,
Why, why, why, Delilah,
So before they come to break down the door,
Forgive me Delilah I just couldn't take any more,

Forgive me Delilah I just couldn't take any more"

As with 'I Had a Wheelbarrow', credit for how 'Delilah' came to be adopted by Stoke City fans as their song is folkloric. The most frequently repeated version is that prior to an away game against Derby County in April 1987 Derbyshire police requested that the Stoke fans gathered in a local pub and refrained from singing songs full of offensive language. Stoke fan Anton Booth is said to have accepted that challenge and clambered onto a table to belt out a rendition of 'Delilah'.[16] The song caught on and evolved into a shortened, cruder version in which the knife becomes a penis. Booth and his mates took it from the pub and on to the Baseball Ground terraces, where they adopted the additional tradition of hoisting Booth aloft to sing their version's opening line;[17]

"At break of day when that man drove away I was waiting,
Ooooo oooo oooo,
I crossed the street to her house and she opened the door,
Ooooo oooo oooo,
She stood there laughing,
Ha ha ha ha,
I put my dick in her hand and she laughed no more,
Ooooo oooo oooo,

My, my, my, Delilah,
Why, why, why, Delilah,
So before you come to break down the door,

[16] *Brown. P, 2016, 'Why Stoke fans sing Delilah', FourFourTwo, 25 March 2016*

[17] *BBC, 2011, 'Stoke City fans back Tom Jones' Delilah to top charts', BBC, 5 May 2011*

Forgive me Delilah I just couldn't take anymore

My, my, my, Delilah,
Why, why, why, Delilah,
(Clap, clap, clap)"

While this version of how the club came to adopt the song is popular, football journalist Paul Brown uncovered another theory after speaking to some older Stoke fans. The fans Brown spoke to claimed the emergence of *'Delilah'* on the terraces in the Potteries began during a concert at Stoke's old Victoria Ground in 1975, 13 years before Booth hauled himself towards a Derbyshire pub ceiling. The concert was apparently headlined by Prog Rock band Yes, but also featured the Sensational Alex Harvey band who had enjoyed a top ten hit with a cover of 'Delilah' earlier that year. Brown quotes fans who were at the gig recalling the crowd raucously singing along to the song and continuing to sing it when they returned to the ground for football.[18]

As well as Stoke's version, 'Delilah' is also sung by Welsh rugby fans. Loud and increasingly frequent renditions at Wales' Millennium Stadium during the 2014 Autumn Internationals led to former Plaid Cymru president Dafydd Iwan requesting the fans sing something else saying: "it is a song about murder [which] tends to trivialise the idea of murdering a woman and it's a pity these words now have been elevated to the status of a secondary national anthem. I think we should rummage around for another song instead of 'Delilah'".[19]

Iwan's request made national news before being dismissed by Stoke fans, with Bryan Shaw, a spokesman for the Stoke City Supporters Club, telling ESPN: "It's just a song we sing to encourage the team. I don't think anybody among the fans would ever even think it has anything to do with domestic violence. It's all tongue-in-cheek and I'm sure it's just an issue of today's society where 99% of the country just get on with it but someone looks for a hidden meaning".[20] Shaw's comment ignores the obvious, rather than hidden, meaning of the lyrics but does

[18] Brown. P, 2016, 'Why Stoke fans sing Delilah', FourFourTwo, 25 March 2016

[19] ESPN, 2014, 'Stoke fans defend right to sing Tom Jones song', ESPN, 11 December 2014

[20] ESPN, 2014, 'Stoke fans defend right to sing Tom Jones song', ESPN, 11 December 2014

highlight that the song is irrelevant to football lyrically. Instead the chant's worth is being measured by basis of the noise levels it helped generate alone. In effect, Shaw's defence for the chant is: 'the words of the chant aren't important, what is important is that it's ours and in singing it we come together'.

Another example of a club's fans taking a pop song and making it their own for no obvious logical or lyrical reason comes from the Derbyshire town of Chesterfield. Despite being nowhere near the sea, Chesterfield's fans sing the first verse of the nautically themed song 'Sailing', which was originally written in the 1970s by the Sutherland Brothers but made famous in 1978 by Rod Stewart:

> *"I am sailing,*
> *I am sailing,*
> *Home again,*
> *'Cross the sea,*
> *I am sailing,*
> *Stormy waters,*
> *To be near you,*
> *To be free"*

Why the Spireites fans sing it is not known, but the club did win the Fourth Division title in 1984-85, just after the BBC re-aired their popular documentary *Sailor* about HMS Ark Royal and which featured 'Sailing', still Stewart's biggest selling UK hit,[21] as the theme song. Nick Miller interviewed Chesterfield fans for *FourFourTwo* and offers another theory: "Stormy waters' reflects life in the lower leagues".[22]

While the origins of 'I Had a Wheelbarrow', 'Delilah' and 'Sailing' are hard to definitively trace decades after their appearance on the terraces, some irreverent chants have roots that are easy to pinpoint and the inspiration for them can come from anywhere. Take this example from Bradford City fans who for no discernible reason, other than one of their number had purchased a half-time snack, during their 3-0 League One demolition of Doncaster Rovers began singing:

---

[21] *Sedghi. A, 2012, 'UK's million selling singles; the full list', The Guardian, 4 November 2012*

[22] *FourFourTwo, 2016, '50 best football chants', FourFourTwo, 22 March 2016*

"He's eating a pie,
He's eating a pie,
He's eating a pie,
He's eating a pie,
He's eating a pie"

This first verse started quietly, but quickly grew louder as more and more people in the packed away end picked it up. Meanwhile the chant's subject grinned along looking only slightly embarrassed. As the first verse drew to a close, a second verse quickly started up:

"Does he want some sauce?
Does he want some sauce?
Does he want some sauce?
Does he want some sauce?
Does he want some sauce?"

As verse two rumbled along, the pie-eating man began to nod along and before the verse was over a quick-thinking fellow fan stepped in, and to large cheers, handed him a sachet. The pie-fan held his gifted sachet aloft in celebration in the manner of a cup-final winning captain, prompting a final joyous concluding verse:

"He's got some brown,
He's got some brown,
He's got some brown,
He's got some brown,
He's got some brown"

The chant, since christened 'The Ballad of the Pie', was picked up by national newspapers and even prompted *The Daily Mirror* to run a poll asking: "Is this the best chant of all time?" and offering two voting options; "Yes" and "Without doubt".[23]

Later that year League One would produce another similar chant

[23]   *Thomas-Mason. L, 2015, 'Bradford fans produce the greatest chant of all time', Daily Mirror, 5 April 2015*

when a plant pot emerged among Barnsley fans in the away end during their 3-0 defeat at Rochdale's Spotland. With the game rapidly slipping away from the Tykes their fans took to entertaining themselves by passing around the pot and wearing it as a hat. Each time a fresh head received its new plastic green adornment the away end cheered, following up with a chant to the tune of American Gospel hymn 'He's Got the Whole World in His Hands':

> *"He's got a plant pot on his head,*
> *He's got a plant pot on his head,*
> *He's got a plant pot on his head,*
> *He's got a plant pot on his head"*

As the chant caught on, the pot was thrown from person to person, at one point being placed on the head of a hi-viz vested steward. To his credit, the steward merrily jigged along with the pot on his head accompanied by the loudest rendition of the verse all afternoon.

Unlike the decades-old anthems of Notts County, Chesterfield and Stoke City, chants like 'The Ballad of the Pie' and 'He's Got a Plant Pot on His Head' burn brightly but briefly, perfectly capturing a single moment-in-time.

Seemingly pointless chanting is not limited to English football and food is a popular subject for chants around Europe. St Pauli fans have one of their own that has endured since a group of fans following the club's amateur team away from home stopped at a motorway service station, which specialised in Greek food such as Gyros (similar to a kebab), tzatziki and salad. Enjoying the simplicity, the fans began chanting the menu and to this day in the Millerntor you can still hear;

> *"Gyros,*
> *Tzatziki,*
> *And salad"*

It's not just food that inspires irreverent chanting. During a friendly against Ajax Amsterdam, Bradford City fans borrowed the tune of Welsh hymn 'Cwm Rhondda', better known as 'Guide Me O Thou Great Redeemer' and indulged in a chorus of;

"Did you bring us,
Did you bring us,
Did you bring us any drugs?" [24]

Leeds United fans were inspired to sing another of these brief moment-in-time chants, when ahead of their League One game at Peterborough United in 2008, their fans were met with two mobile chlamydia testing vans distributing sexual health leaflets and offering free testing. With the game not going Leeds' way, their fans took the highbrow melody 'La donna è mobile' from Giuseppe Verdi's '*Rigoletto*' and chimed up with:

"We've got McAllister,
You've got chlamydia"

While in Spain, fans of Deportivo de La Coruña celebrated their 2002 Copa Del Rey final victory over Real Madrid in their Santiago Bernabéu home, held in their ground to mark Real's centenary year, by serenading their hosts with a rousing rendition of *"Happy birthday to you"*.[25]

What these chants highlight is the inventiveness and humour which exists among football fans, despite them still being widely associated with hooliganism to such an extent that ahead of the 2018/19 season Chorley Town Council banned all football fans from the town centre citing their belief that "many residents" found the presence of fans "intimidating".[26] In justifying their ban Chorley Council cited a video of around 200 Wolves fans celebrating in the town following their promotion to the Premier League in May 2018. When the Football Supporters' Federation asked Lancashire Police about the events that day, they reported it had been a good-natured day in which the only issue had been a broken glass in one pub.[27]

[24] *Marshall. T, 2014, 'Where do chants come from', The Telegraph, 1 August 2014*

[25] *Mengem. E, 2018, 'Derby Days Galicia, Copa 90, 4 March 2018*

[26] *Watson. J, 2018, 'Chorley Council criticised for telling 'intimidating' football fans they are not welcome in town centre', The Independent, 16 August 2018*

[27] *Watson. J, 2018, 'Chorley Council criticised for telling 'intimidating' football fans they are not welcome in town centre', The Independent, 16 August 2018*

This skewed perception of football fans is a problem unlikely to abate any time soon, largely because unruly fans make good copy for the press. In 1974 *The Daily Mirror* published a 'League of Violence' and quickly reversed the first version to put the club with the most arrests for hooliganism, Manchester United, at the top, thus implying their hooligans were the most successful, implicitly challenging other firms to up their game.[28] But, as the Social Issues Research Centre concluded: "In the past, we have studied football hooliganism in some depth. Even then, however, we were struck by the fact that although problems do occur at football matches from time to time—sometimes tragically so—the vast majority of fans we met were witty, intelligent, passionate about their team and, well, just nice people. Rarely, however, do they feature in [the] commentary".[29] In *Soccernomincs* Simon Kuper and Stefan Szymanski quoted an estimate from 1995 that suggested that of all the academic research done on sports fans, 96% of it concerned hooligans.[30] Writer Pete Miles agrees and notes how the actions of football fans have gone way beyond football in improving their local communities: "One only has to look at the popularity of the ultras groups attached to clubs like St Pauli, Union Berlin, and goddamn it, even little Clapton, erstwhile whipping boys of the Essex Senior League. For years Clapton were followed by critically low numbers but an ultras insurgence in recent years has seen the club reborn, with positive impacts not only on the club but also the locality. Local charities and food banks have felt the impact of the ultras, and on the field the club hasn't looked back. What [this represents] are parables of a modern religion".[31]

By their nature chants are designed to drown out dissenting opinion, presenting one united front—'we, the amorphous mass, thinks *this*'—and offering an enveloping volume as proof. Thus, the powerful, unifying effect of chanting is not just limited to football fans but is increasingly becoming a way to express 'us' and 'them' identities in

[28] *Domeneghetti. R, 2017, 'From the Back Page to the Front Room', Ockley Books, Huddersfield, p183*

[29] *Social Issues Research Centre, 2008, 'Football Passions', Social Research Centre, London, p7*

[30] *Kuper. S, Szymanski.S, 2012, 'Soccernomins', Harper Sport, London, p242*

[31] *Miles. P, 2016, 'Beyond the Turnstiles', Ockley Book, Huddersfield, Yorkshire, p23*

other areas of life, such as politics. This move from terrace to ballot box was first seen in May 2017 when Labour's Jeremy Corbyn, the leader of the opposition, took the stage at the Wirral Live music festival, incidentally hosted in a football ground, Tranmere Rover's Prenton Park. When Corbyn appeared, the crowd, taking inspiration from Club Brugge, adapted the White Stripes tune 'Seven Nation Army' to become the simple *"Ohhh Jeremy Corbyn"*. Videos of the chant quickly went viral and versions followed Corbyn wherever he went during the course of his 2017 General Election campaign, culminating in a raucous rendition that welcomed him to the main stage at Glastonbury.

Alongside 'Oh Jeremy Corbyn' another, more complex pro-Corbyn chant emerged to the tune of 'September' originally released in 1978 by Earth Wind and Fire, which had also gone viral as a football chant tune earlier that year:

> *"1, 2, 3, 4,*
> *Ohhh wheeey ohhhh,*
> *Jeremy Corbyn,*
> *Ohhh wheeey ohhhh,*
> *He's dancing round the Tories,*
> *Ohhh wheeey ohhhh,*
> *He'll never take your dole away"*

Guardian journalist Andrew Harrison commented that the chant's popularity marked a key moment in politics, stating: *"'Oh, Jeremy Corbyn'.* For some people this adaptation of the football chant based on the White Stripes' 'Seven Nation Army' is nothing less than an anthem for a political watershed. Ubiquitous and inescapable, it's a shared celebration of the moment when a no-hoper led an unprecedented popular movement and knocked established wisdom back on its heels. For others, it's symbolic of the empty hero-worship that constitutes the new left, of vapid communal feel-good moments and a cult of personality masking politics that shade from the inept into the disturbing. Either way, it is the earworm to beat all earworms".[32]

On the other side of the political spectrum sit the Football Lads Alliance, who claim to be a broad coalition of football fans who have come together under the umbrella of "anti-extremism".[33] One member told *The Independent*: "It's about making the government understand that people are fed up. Terrorism is being ignored by the government... Lads [from rival clubs] who've been opposed for years are coming together to say that it should be addressed".[34] To convey this, the Football Lads Alliance frequently use chanting on their marches, with one favourite being:

> **"Eng-ger-land,**
> **Eng-ger-land,**
> **Eng-ger-land"**

Frequently followed with:

> **"We want our country back,**
> **We want our country back"**

Despite being unclear as to who or where they want 'their country' back from, these chants rather belie their claim to be anti-extremist and highlights the levels of distrust of multiculturalism that lurk just below the surface of a group, predominantly seemingly concerned with Islam. "Muslims aren't part of the country," said a 45-year old man from east London, quoted in *The Independent's* investigation into the group, adding; "They don't mingle. They send their kids to madrassas. We're being overrun and can't say nothing about it. If you say so you get called racist".[35]

Harrison goes on to caution that due to their ability to sweep people

[32] Harrison. A, 2017, 'Oh Jeremy Corbyn; how Seven Nation Army inspired the political chant of a generation', The Guardian, 8 October 2017

[33] Bryant. B and Frymorgen. T, 2018, 'Football Lads Alliance; we could have a civil war in this country', BBC, 9 May 2018

[34] Worley. W, 2017, 'Football Lads Alliance; inside the far-right group', The Independent, 7 October 2017

[35] Worley. W, 2017, 'Football Lads Alliance; inside the far-right group', The Independent, 7 October 2017

up in a moment, chants can be both a force for good, and problematic at the same time: "Chants can create unity—but they can also create the illusion of unity. Mass chanting can become coercive. Who wants to be the only person in the hall who's not singing along? Or worse the loser, the one who's not singing anymore? Humans are social. We want to belong. But if we've learned anything over the past three years it's that when you make political decisions based on the need to be part of something rather than the issues, it can lead you into dark places".[36]

That said, even with our fierce tribal loyalties increasingly on public display in politics as in football, for the most part we continue to co-exist, even when seemingly so diametrically opposed. Authors John Goddard and Stephen Dobson put this down to our ability to see chanting for what it is; a way to express our own identities and form transient bonds and communities of like-minded people, united in a common goal in a predominantly harmless way. As they conclude after studying one of the fiercest rivalries in British football: "As Celtic and Rangers supporters who have just spent 90 minutes hurling the most virulent abuse at one another return, for the most part quite amicably, to their normal lives alongside one another in their homes and workplaces, one is tempted to see Scottish football's present-day brand of sectarianism as perhaps just a shade stylised".[37]

In part this could be because our attachments to football clubs are not as strong as we might believe. This could be because we're not as tribal as we think we are, even within the football teams we support. In *Soccernomics*, Simon Kuper and Stefan Szymanski found that while football fans overwhelmingly self-identified as "loyal supporters", only around 50% of fans at any one game were likely to have been at the same game a season before. As our everyday lives lead to people adopting a looser attachment to clubs: "The object of their love might not have changed, but the intensity has. Many [fans] may once have been [week-in, week-out devotees] who fell for a team as an eight-year-old when their father took them to their first game.

[36] Harrison. A, 2017, 'Oh Jeremy Corbyn; how Seven Nation Army inspired the political chant of a generation', The Guardian, 8 October 2017

[37] Dobson. S, and Goddard. J, 2014, 'The Economics of Football', Edward Elgar Publishing, p342

However, by the time they are 28, or 88, they are no longer the same fan. For many people fandom is not a static condition but a process".[38] The implication is that as fans going to matches, we are increasingly performing expected modes of behaviour including the verbal abusing of the opposition, but outside the stadium we ultimately recognise that for most of us, it is just a game.

Football chanting defies its perception as a hideous exhibition of the worst of human behaviour. Instead it is predominantly inclusive and brings people together, making us laugh, boosting our mood and lowering our levels of anxiety. As we have seen, when efforts are made to control or eradicate the noise and passion, football quickly becomes a pale imitation of the game we love.

That is not to say that football chanting and those who engage in it should be given carte blanche to sing whatever they want, and the continued crackdown of abuse that draws on prejudice should be wholeheartedly supported. Chanting is by no means all bad, however, and any group of people who can sing publicly, loudly and proudly about their broken wheelbarrow are worth applauding. We are funny, loyal, passionate and social animals, keen to share our experiences and stories with the generations that follow our own. Chanting displays the best of us, more frequently than it displays the worst of us.

One popular chant asks: *"Who are ya?"*. Everything else we chant provides the answer.

[38] *Kuper. S, Szymanski. S, 2012, 'Soccernomics', Harper Sport, London, p255*

ACKNOWLEDGEMENTS

'WHO ARE YA?'

It may be my name on the front, but this book is the result of many people's efforts, encouragement, research and patience. Transferring it from my brain to these pages has been both the best and hardest thing I have ever done and without the help and guidance of these people, I probably would have given up 200 words in and flounced off to play *Football Manager* in my pants.

First, I want to thank David Hartrick and Ockley Books for taking a chance on it and believing that a book on football chanting really should begin in Victorian Britain with a pair of classical composers and their pianos.

Also, Paul Whitty from Sound Diaries, whose invitation for me to speak at his *Sounding Cultures of Football* conference at Oxford Brookes University in June 2018 really kickstarted this whole thing.

Then there are all the people who provided practical help, principal among them my fellow *AlongComeNorwich*-sters Jon Punt and Tom Parsley, for reading and making sense of the messy first drafts. The efforts of those two, both on this book and on our little Nodge fanzine, have substantially improved the quality of my words and my overall enjoyment of football. When I offered them a copy as a thank you, Jon memorably replied: "What's the point? I've already read it," which is fair but does mean this is all he's getting. Also to our graphics-extraordinaire Ben Stokes for his work on potential covers. Thanks, buhs.

I am indebted to many other people for picking the bones out of areas in which they have far more expertise than me. In no particular order I am hugely grateful to Proud Canaries Co-Founder Di Cunningham, *World Football Index's* Adam Brandon, music-library James Chaplin, legal whizz Nick Cartwright, finance-literate Josh Cadwallader, exiled Liverpudlian Adrian Galvin and Notts County's Honorary Club Historian Mike Chappell. I'm also thankful to Sven Sakowitz for his patience at explaining the context and subtleties of both the German language and their sense of humour. Despite having to ask four or five times "Why do you keep saying 'German Master' when you mean 'Champion'?" Sako never once sounded anything other than bemused. *Danke mein freund*. I'm also grateful to Felix

Tamsut for taking the time to ensure that the complicated and, at the time of writing, still evolving protests against Dietmar Hopp were covered accurately. Then there is the wonderful Ffion Thomas and Andy Lyons from *When Saturday Comes*, author Nick Davidson and Jim Dolan from *Pride of Irons* for letting me reproduce so many of their words. Also thank you to Roger Domeneghetti for his thorough proof-reading efforts. Finally, Shaun Waller, who has been no help whatsoever but really wanted to see his name in print.

I'm also extremely grateful to my parents, first of all for conceiving and birthing me, but then bringing me up in such a way that I could enjoy and appreciate crude, borderline offensive humour, while retaining a sense of self-awareness and moral compass, however skewed that may be. They then sensibly decided to find new partners, doubling both the number of adults looking out for me, and the number of gifts we received at Christmas and birthdays. A special mention should go to my Dad, Mark, for taking my offhand query about chants from his youth and escalating that into an unending number of suggestions, dredged through the fog of a mind addled by night shifts at the Post Office, and most of which added immeasurably to the story. You can stop sending me fistfuls of newspaper cut-outs paper-clipped to week-old *Private Eye's* now though, cheers.

Finally, my wife Jo without whom this simply wouldn't exist as anything more than a long-held pipe dream, that I had neither the drive, energy nor confidence to pursue. An indefatigable and inspirational human, Jo is one of those people who, leading by example, make you want to be the very best version of yourself you can be and without her, my life would look very different and be infinitely poorer.

Thank you and never mind the danger.

THE HISTORY OF
FOOTBALL CHANTING

ANDREW LAWN